POSTCARD HISTORY SERIES

Philadelphia's 1926 Sesqui-Centennial International Exposition

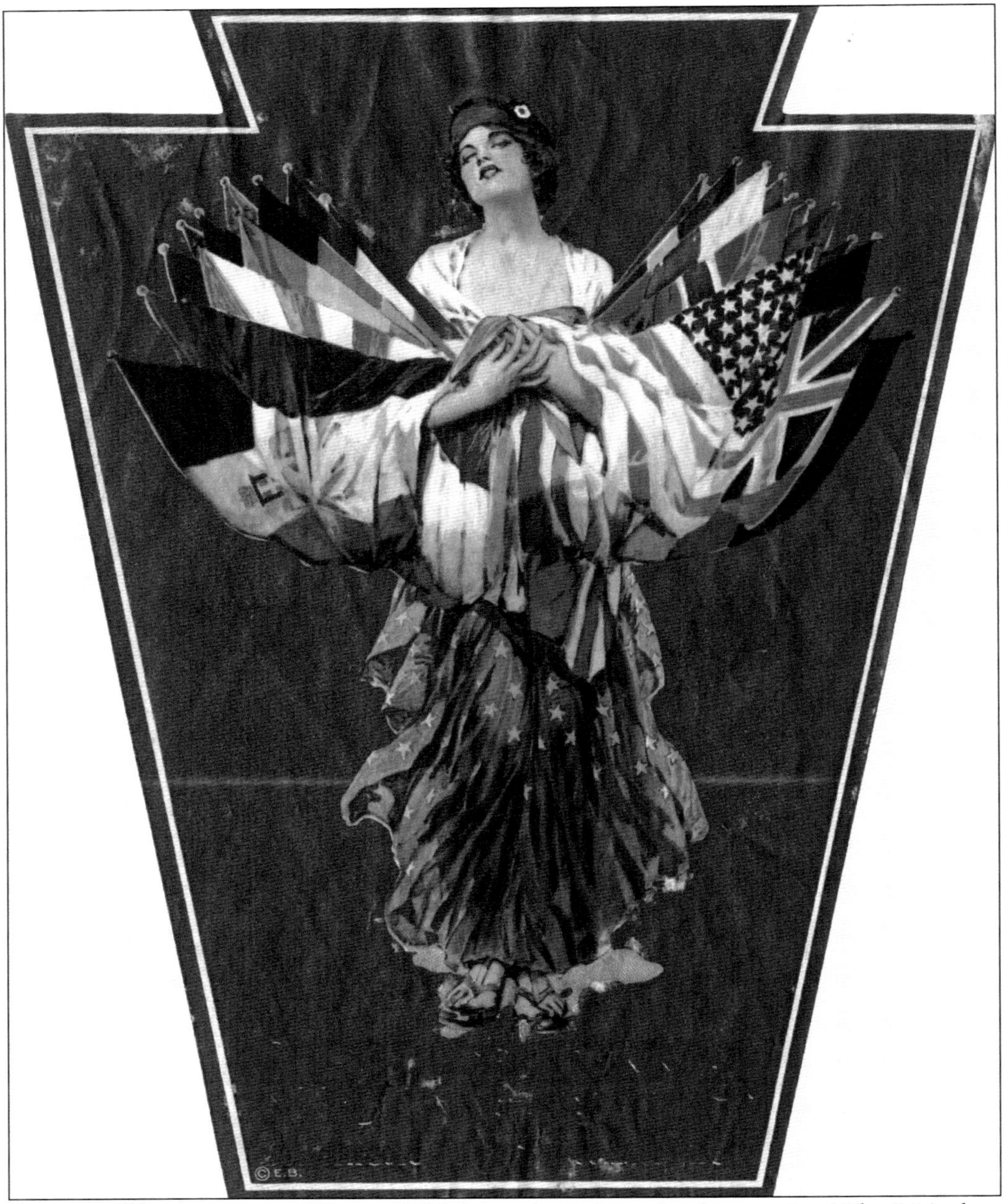

America Welcomes the World. This image is of a large decal measuring 12 by 9.5 inches. The design was taken from the official exposition poster titled "America Welcomes the World," which was the work of artist Dan Smith. Shown is Lady Liberty, with the flags of many nations held in her arms. It was hoped that such illustrations would help promote the Sesqui-Centennial International Exposition. The woman who posed as Lady Liberty was actress Lois Wilson (1894–1988). (Elliot Brewer.)

On the front cover: Please see page 25. (Author's collection.)
On the back cover: Please see page 31. (Author's collection.)

POSTCARD HISTORY SERIES

Philadelphia's 1926 Sesqui-Centennial International Exposition

James D. Ristine

ARCADIA
PUBLISHING

ISBN 978-0-7385-6544-6

Published by Arcadia Publishing
Charleston SC, Chicago IL, Portsmouth NH, San Francisco CA

Printed in the United States of America

Library of Congress Control Number: 2008941563

For all general information contact Arcadia Publishing at:
Telephone 843-853-2070
Fax 843-853-0044
E-mail sales@arcadiapublishing.com
For customer service and orders:
Toll-Free 1-888-313-2665

Visit us on the Internet at www.arcadiapublishing.com

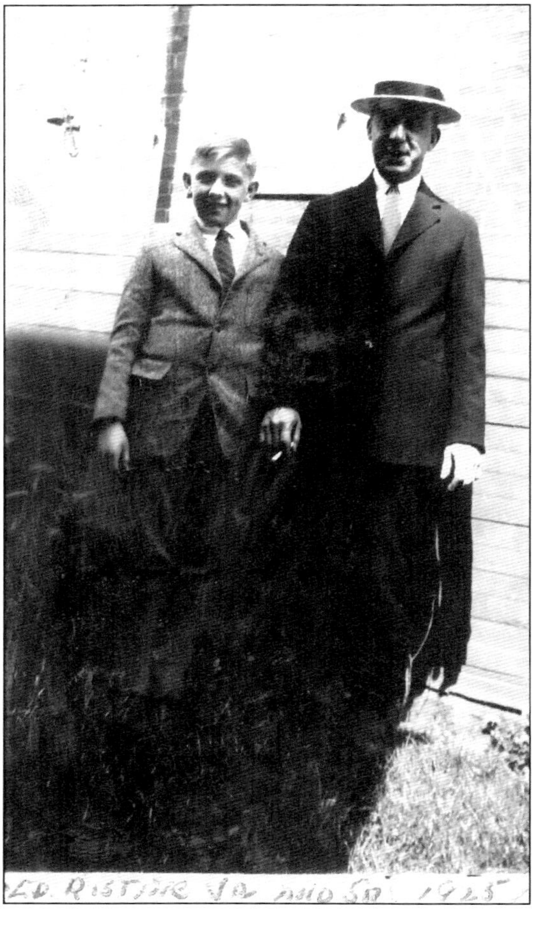

I dedicate this book to my grandfather Edward J. Ristine Sr. (1882–1946). This 1925 photograph shows him standing next to my father. According to family history, the company that he owned, Ristine Wire Goods Manufacturing, located at 628 Filbert Street in Philadelphia, was involved in the construction of the framework for the giant Liberty Bell that stood at the entrance to the exposition.

Contents

ACKNOWLEDGMENTS

I would like to begin by giving recognition to the work of John D. Cardinell, the official photographer of this Sesqui-Centennial International Exposition. Not only did he leave behind an extensive photographic record documenting the exposition, but he also was responsible for publishing a multitude of postcards utilizing some of these images. The majority of the postcard views found in this book were created by him. It is even likely that some of the postcards in this book that are attributed to unknown publishers are in fact his as well. If it were not for John D. Cardinell and others who published postcards related to this exposition, the visual history of this great event would be incomplete.

Appreciation is also given to Vince Kowalski, a friend and now retired librarian, who was very helpful in assisting me in tracking down some of the reference materials that I utilized in the writing of this book. Finally, as always, I am extremely grateful to my wife, Debbie, for proofreading my work and providing support for me in this project.

All the postcard images that appear in this book are from the author's personal collection. When known, the publisher is indicated at the end of each caption.

Introduction

In 1926, Philadelphia honored the 150th anniversary of American independence by holding the Sesqui-Centennial International Exposition. Only 50 years earlier, the city had hosted the highly successful Centennial Exposition of 1876. On May 9, 1921, the official Sesqui-Centennial Exhibition Association was established to plan, organize, and administer this major international event. It was eventually decided that the Philadelphia Sesqui-Centennial International Exposition would be held in South Philadelphia at the southern end of Broad Street. It was to include the area between Eleventh and Twentieth Streets and from Packer Avenue to the League Island Navy Yard. At the time, much of this area was swampland. An immense building project, involving the filling in of the land and the construction of buildings, was begun. On March 19, 1925, Pres. Calvin Coolidge issued a proclamation inviting the nations of the world to come and participate in the Sesqui-Centennial International Exposition.

The official opening ceremonies were held on May 31 with the exposition running until December 1, 1926. Greeting visitors as they neared the entrance was a colossal 80-foot-tall replica of the Liberty Bell. Illuminated at night with 26,000 lights, the glow from this symbol of the Sesqui-Centennial International Exposition was visible throughout the city. There were five major exhibit halls: the Palaces of Agriculture, Fine Arts, Liberal Arts, Education, and Machinery and Transportation. These buildings housed exhibits of every type. There were technological innovations, locomotives and agricultural equipment, artwork, historical artifacts, and much more to be seen. Many states and foreign nations sponsored displays in these "palaces," while a small number erected their own exhibit buildings as well.

Among the major attractions was a living history exhibit named High Street, a reconstruction of a 1776 street complete with replicas of 20 famous structures. There was a section known as the Gladway, which featured theaters, restaurants, amusements, and private exhibit buildings. Nearby were man-made lagoons where visitors could take rides on authentic Italian gondolas. Other bodies of water provided for recreation and boat rides as well. A replica of a Viking ship, specially sailed from Norway, was displayed. Then there was Treasure Island, an amusement and entertainment area, featuring rides and diversions for young and old. Everything from a miniature railroad to roller coasters provided thrills and delights on the exposition grounds.

Broad boulevards allowed visitors easy access to all the major structures. Transportation could be had on special electric-powered buses called "party cars." Major events such as plays, pageants, concerts, and even some sporting events were held in the 10,000-seat auditorium built especially for the exposition. A major construction achievement was the stadium capable of holding over 100,000 people. Here spectacular pageants, rodeos, and sporting events were held. One highlight was the famous Jack Dempsey versus Gene Tunney heavyweight boxing championship fight, which was attended by over 120,000 spectators. This was to be one of the greatest sporting events of all time. Intended to be a permanent structure, this stadium was to go on to serve Philadelphia's sports teams until the 1980s.

Adding to the extent of the exposition grounds was the entire League Island Navy Yard, which was opened to the public. Here vessels of all types were placed on display. Battleships, destroyers, submarines, and even the historic USS *Constellation* and USS *Olympia* were on hand for visitors to see. There were displays of military equipment and even a military camp with 1,000 soldiers, who performed drills and demonstrations. Four flying fields near the exposition provided hundreds of acres on which to display aircraft and to hold national air races. All these features, and many others, provided visitors to the Sesqui-Centennial International Exposition with an abundance of things to see and experience.

Despite all that it offered, the Sesqui-Centennial International Exposition proved to be financially unsuccessful and was ultimately forced into receivership in 1927. Problems seemed to plague the exposition from its start. Lack of proper funding and delays in construction resulted in initial plans having to be drastically scaled down. The original director of the exposition, Col. David C. Collier, resigned in protest over budget problems. His replacement, Capt. Asher C. Baker, had to step down due to illness only days before opening day and died a few weeks later. Left in charge was E. L. Austin. Unfortunately, even the weather did not cooperate; it rained 107 out of the 184 days the exposition ran. This resulted in diminished crowds. Only 6,408,289 visitors, much less than had been anticipated, attended. However, the exposition did leave its mark on the history of the city. The stadium went on to serve the city for decades, and the reclamation of the swampland used as the site made future development possible. The Benjamin Franklin Bridge, built to connect the city to New Jersey for the exposition, still remains a vital part of the local transportation system. Some of the roadways and a few of the smaller structures also linger on to this day. The great Philadelphia Sesqui-Centennial International Exposition is now part of history, a major cultural event that should not be forgotten.

One

Welcome to the Sesqui-Centennial

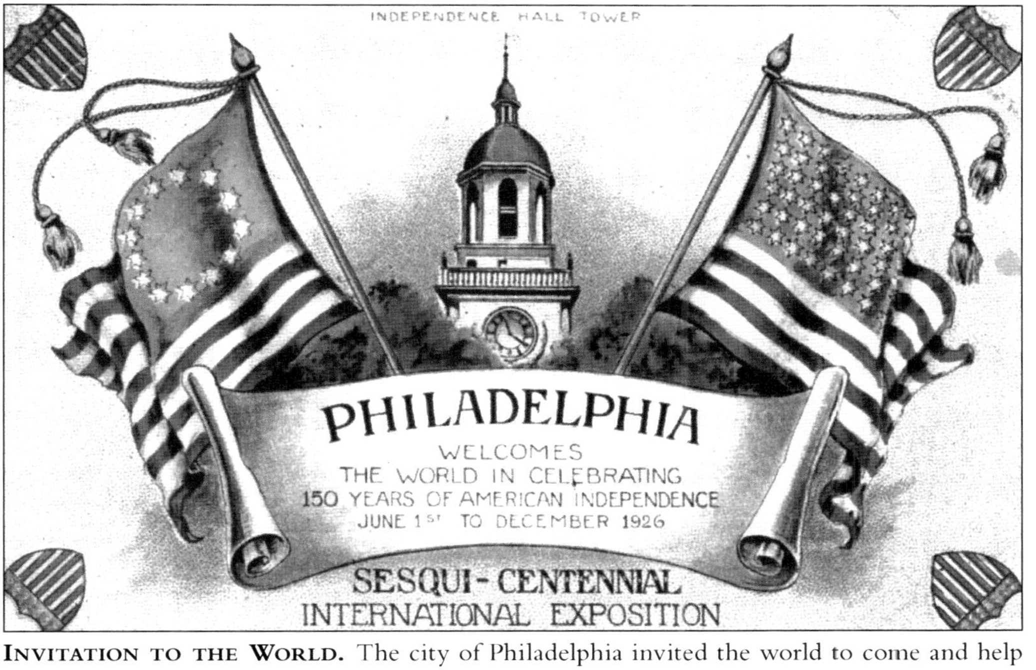

Invitation to the World. The city of Philadelphia invited the world to come and help celebrate the nation's 150th birthday by hosting the Sesqui-Centennial International Exposition. It was only fitting that Philadelphia, the home of Independence Hall, the birthplace of the signing of the Declaration of Independence, and the site where the Liberty Bell first rang out "liberty throughout our land," would host this momentous occasion. (John D. Cardinell.)

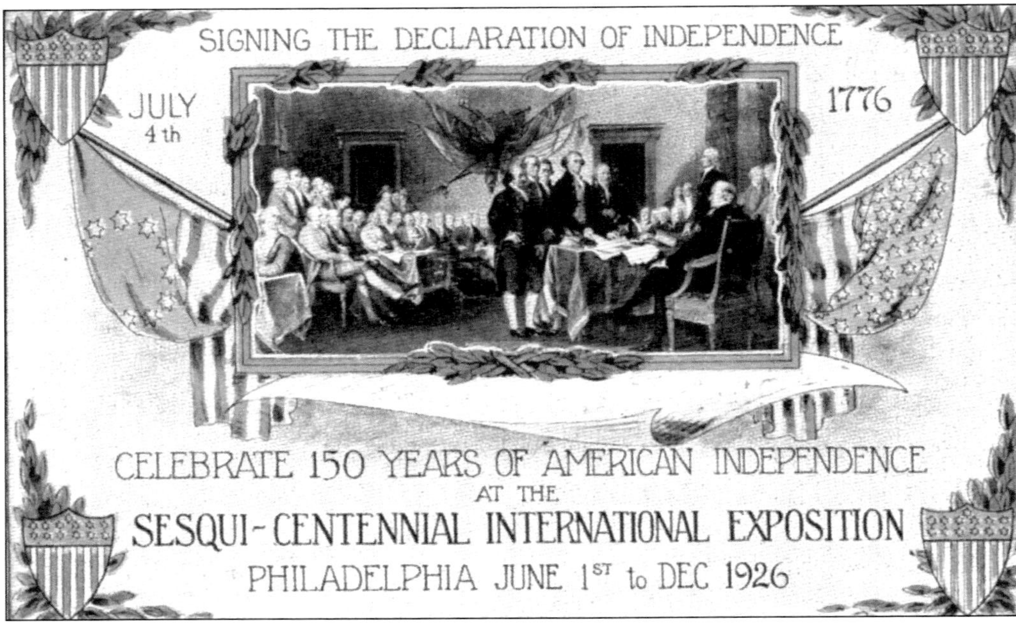

Celebrating American Independence. To help promote the event, numerous styles of postcards, many depicting historic images or symbols, were published. This particular example shows a famous scene depicting the signing of the Declaration of Independence. The exposition was scheduled to run from June 1 to December 1, 1926. (John D. Cardinell.)

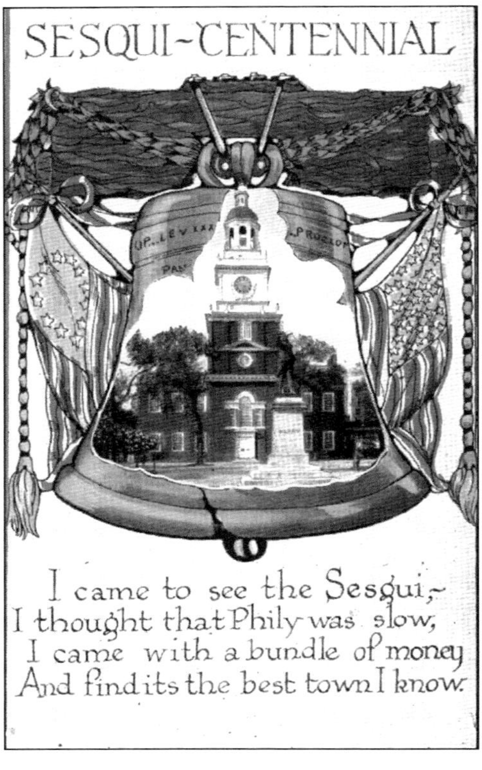

"I Came to See the Sesqui." Visitors who came from out of town to attend the Sesqui-Centennial International Exposition often took the opportunity to make side trips to see some of the city's numerous historic landmarks. Many would, as stated on this promotional postcard, "find it's the best town I know." (Tichnor.)

INDEPENDENCE HALL. One of the most recognizable landmarks in Philadelphia is Independence Hall. Construction of this historic building was completed in 1753. Located at 500 Chestnut Street, it originally served as the Pennsylvania State House. It is of course best known as the birthplace of the Declaration of Independence and the U.S. Constitution. During the duration of the Sesqui-Centennial International Exposition, more than 500,000 people visited the site. (John D. Cardinell.)

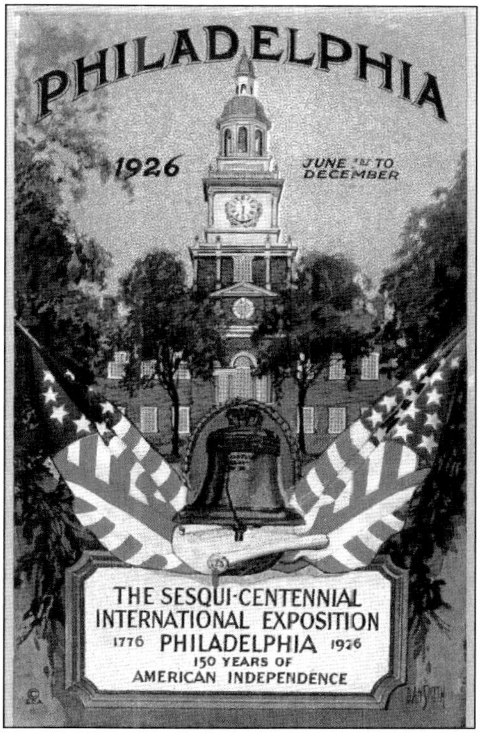

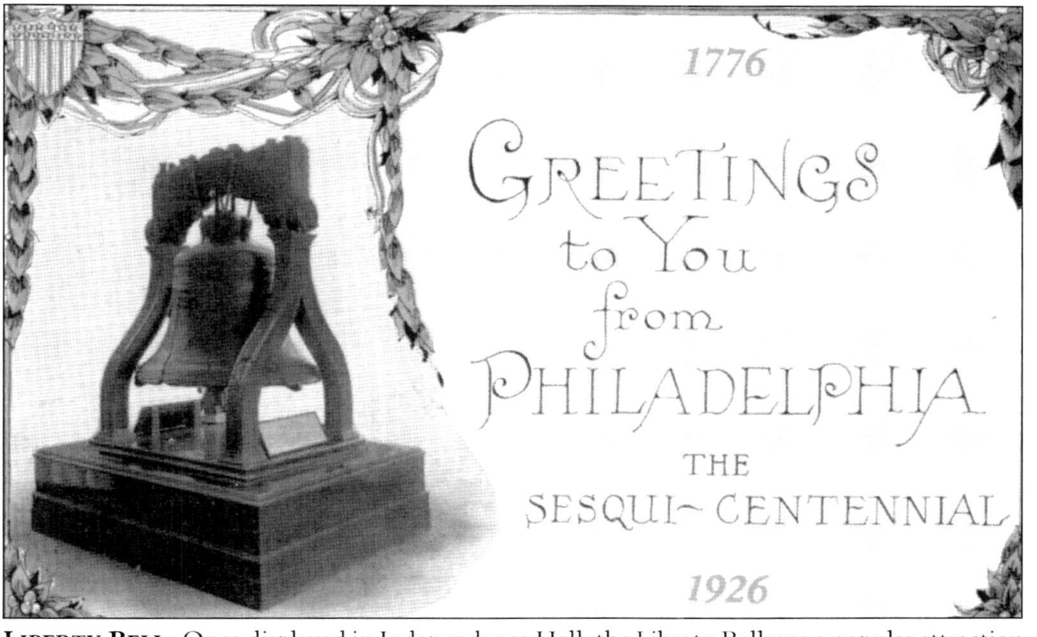

LIBERTY BELL. Once displayed in Independence Hall, the Liberty Bell was a popular attraction during the time of the exposition, just as it is today. The bronze bell, weighing 2,080 pounds, bears the inscription, "Proclaim Liberty Throughout All The Land" and is renowned as a symbol of freedom. At present this celebrated bell is on exhibit across the street from Independence Hall in the Liberty Bell Center. (Tichnor.)

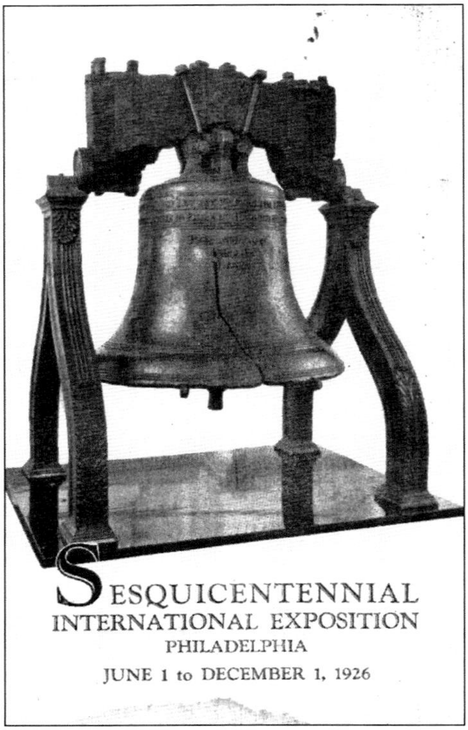

SYMBOL OF LIBERTY. This is how the Liberty Bell appeared when on exhibit in Independence Hall during the Sesqui-Centennial International Exposition. Originally ordered from England in 1752, the bell cracked upon its first tolling in this country. After it was repaired, it remained in use until cracked again in 1835 when rung for the funeral of Chief Justice John Marshall.

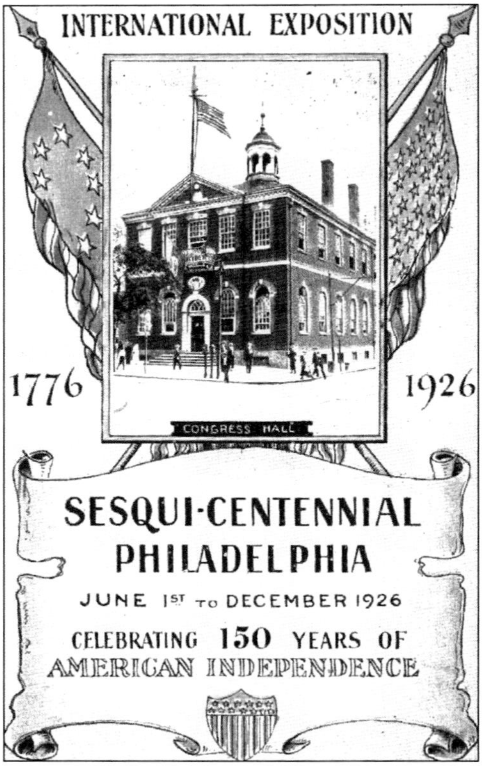

CONGRESS HALL. Just a short distance from Independence Hall, on the corner of Sixth and Chestnut Streets, is Congress Hall. Erected in 1789, it was here that the U.S. Congress met between the years 1790 and 1800. It was the site of George Washington's second inauguration, and in later years, it served as a city courthouse. (John D. Cardinell.)

CARPENTERS' HALL. Also standing not far from Independence Hall, at 320 Chestnut Street, is Carpenters' Hall, built in 1771 by the Carpenters' Company, the nation's oldest trade guild. It was here that the first Continental Congress met in 1774. During the Revolutionary War, the building served as a military hospital and later as the first Bank of the United States. It is open today to the public. (John D. Cardinell.)

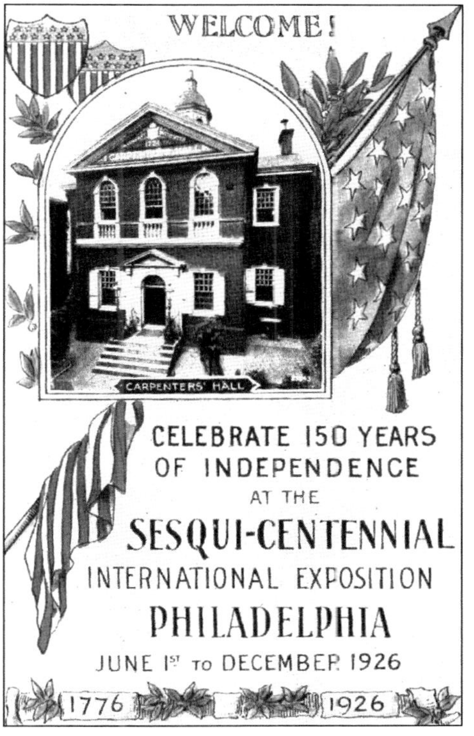

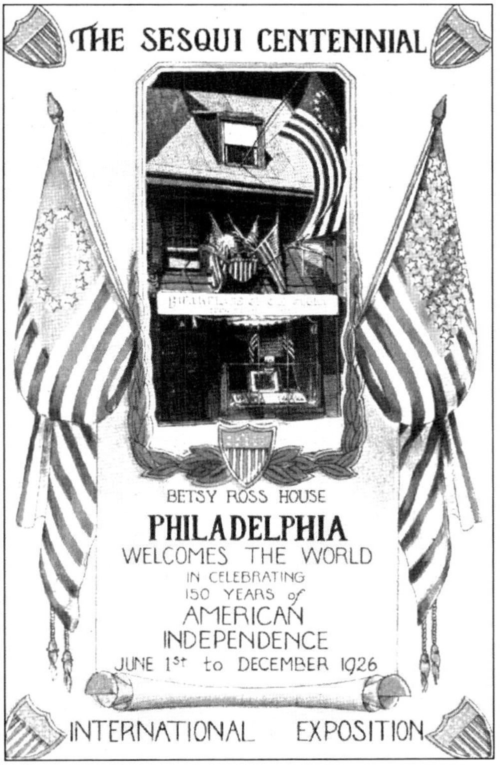

BETSY ROSS HOUSE. Found at 239 Arch Street is the reputed home of Betsy Ross, who is said to have lived here from 1773 until 1785. The Georgian-style house, built in 1740, is two and a half stories tall and has nine rooms. It is seen here decked out in flags and a banner proclaiming it to be the "Birthplace of Old Glory." (John D. Cardinell.)

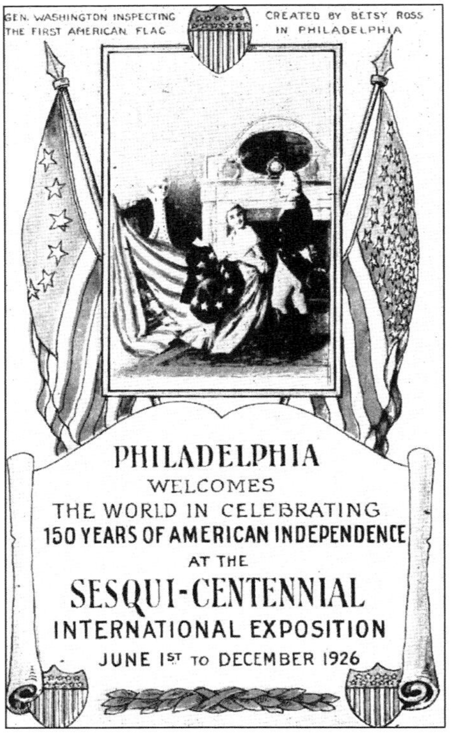

FIRST FLAG. This postcard, publicizing the Sesqui-Centennial International Exposition, shows Betsy Ross presenting a flag to George Washington. According to legend, Washington, along with Robert Morris and George Ross, went to Ross and asked her to make a flag based on their design. The result was the nation's first flag of "the stars and stripes." (John D. Cardinell.)

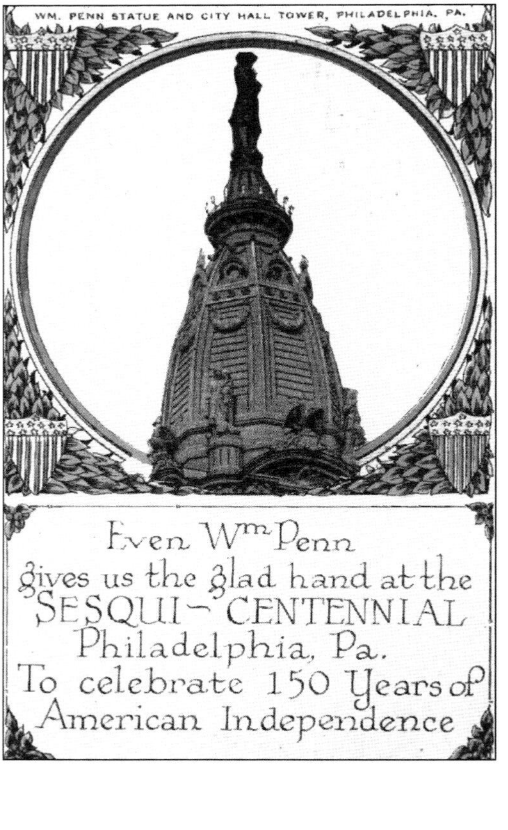

CITY HALL TOWER. Standing atop Philadelphia City Hall is a statue of William Penn. The bronze figure is the work of sculptor Alexander Milne Calder (1846–1923) and is 37 feet tall and weighs 27 tons. Placed on the building in 1894, it is still the largest sculpture to be found on top of any building in the world. This postcard states that even William Penn welcomes visitors to the Sesqui-Centennial International Exposition. (Tichnor.)

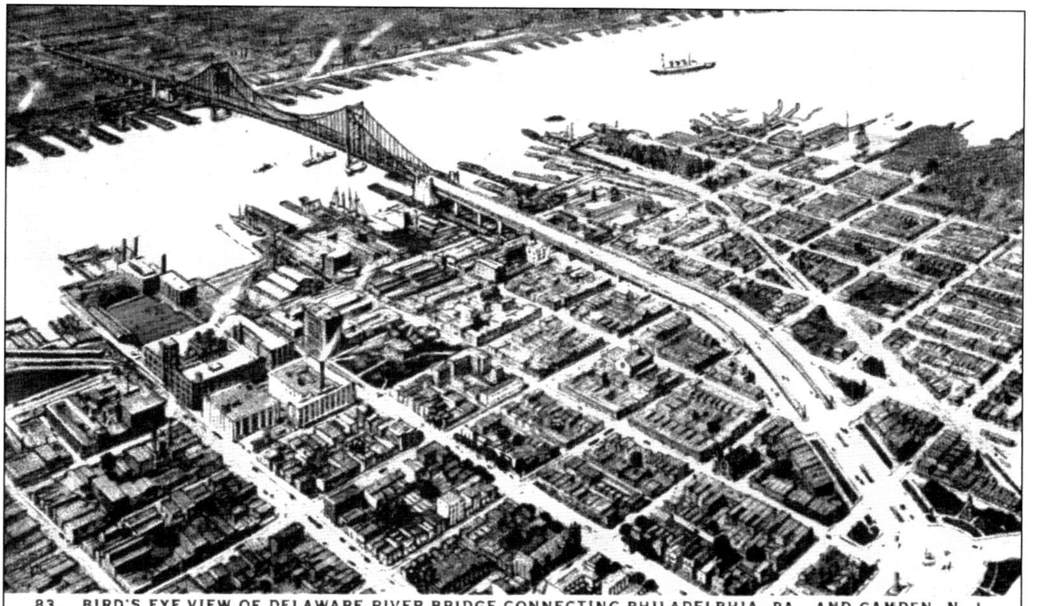

83. BIRD'S EYE VIEW OF DELAWARE RIVER BRIDGE CONNECTING PHILADELPHIA, PA., AND CAMDEN, N. J.

BIRD'S-EYE VIEW OF BRIDGE. It was planned that most visitors to the exposition would be coming by automobile. To allow for easy access from New Jersey, a new bridge was built to replace the ferry system that connected Philadelphia with Camden. The Delaware River Bridge, since renamed the Benjamin Franklin Bridge, opened to traffic at midnight on July 1, 1926, just in time for the Sesqui-Centennial International Exposition. (Sabold-Herb Company.)

270:—Delaware River Bridge, Philadelphia, Pa.

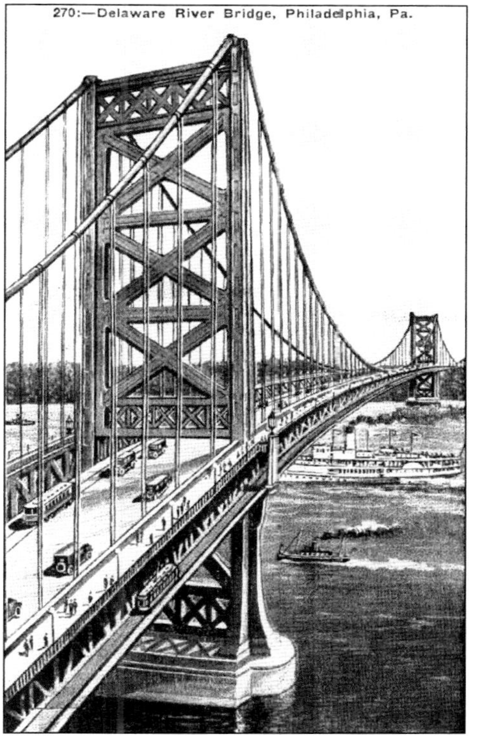

DELAWARE RIVER BRIDGE. With a main span stretching 1,750 feet and a distance of 3,536 feet from anchorage to anchorage, the Delaware River Bridge was the world's largest suspension bridge for three years. The original cost for this structure was \$45.2 million. In 1926, the toll for crossing was 25¢ per automobile. (P. Sander.)

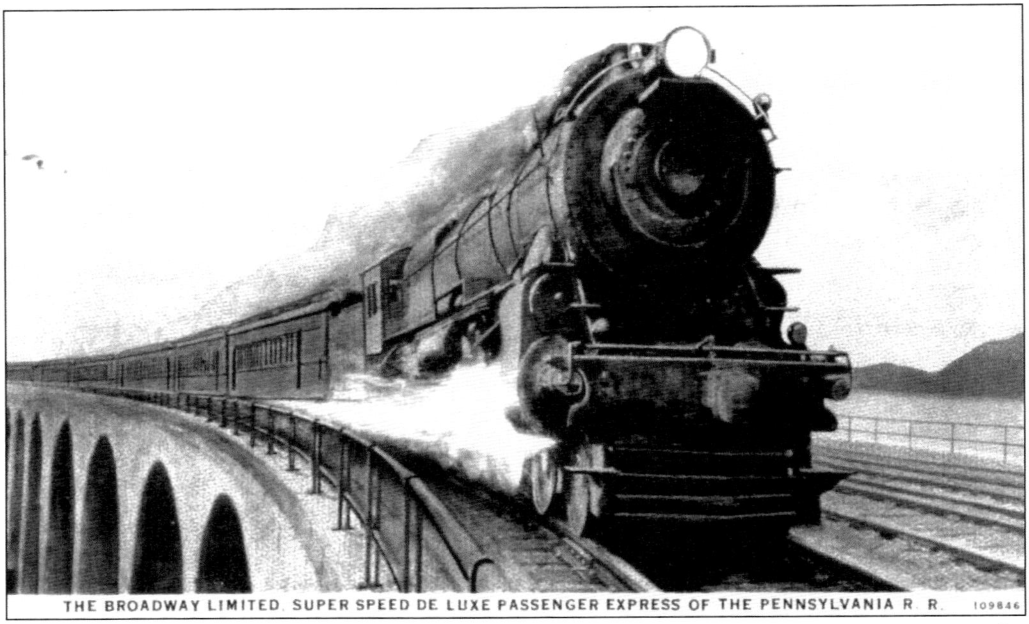

THE *BROADWAY LIMITED*. One means by which visitors arrived from great distances was by train. One of these trains was operated by the Pennsylvania Railroad and was named the *Broadway Limited*. During the Sesqui-Centennial International Exposition, this train made daily overnight runs from Chicago to Philadelphia in just over 18 hours and made a trip from New York City back to Chicago in 20 hours. (John D. Cardinell.)

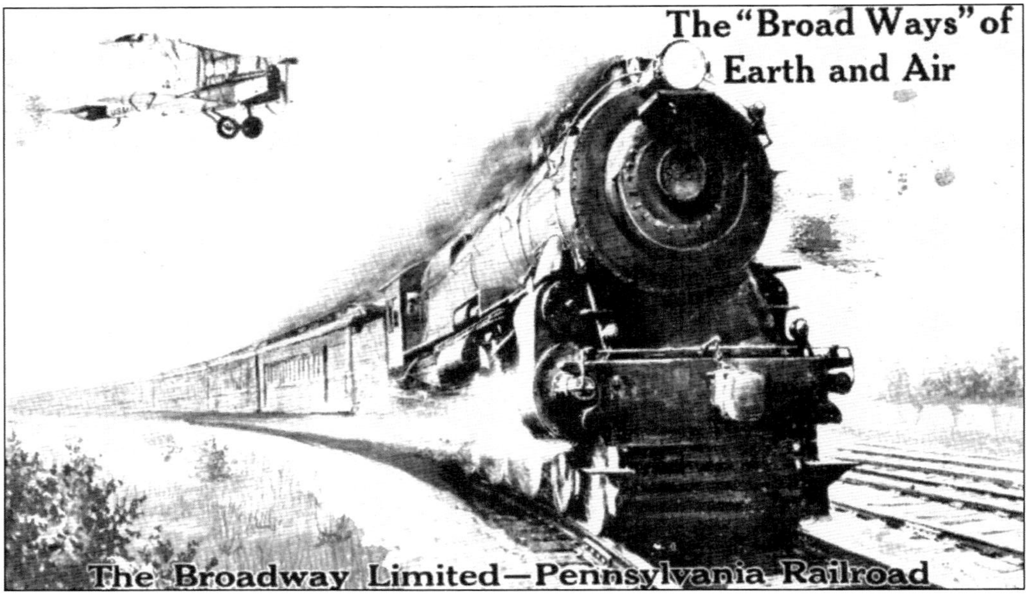

DELUXE RAIL SERVICE. The Pennsylvania Railroad was especially proud of its *Broadway Limited*. Deluxe long-distance service was its theme, offering passengers such amenities as a barber, valet service, baths, a stenographer, writing desks, stock quotations, daily newspapers and magazines, and the latest in baseball and football scores in season. Special excursion tickets to the Sesqui-Centennial International Exposition were sold daily.

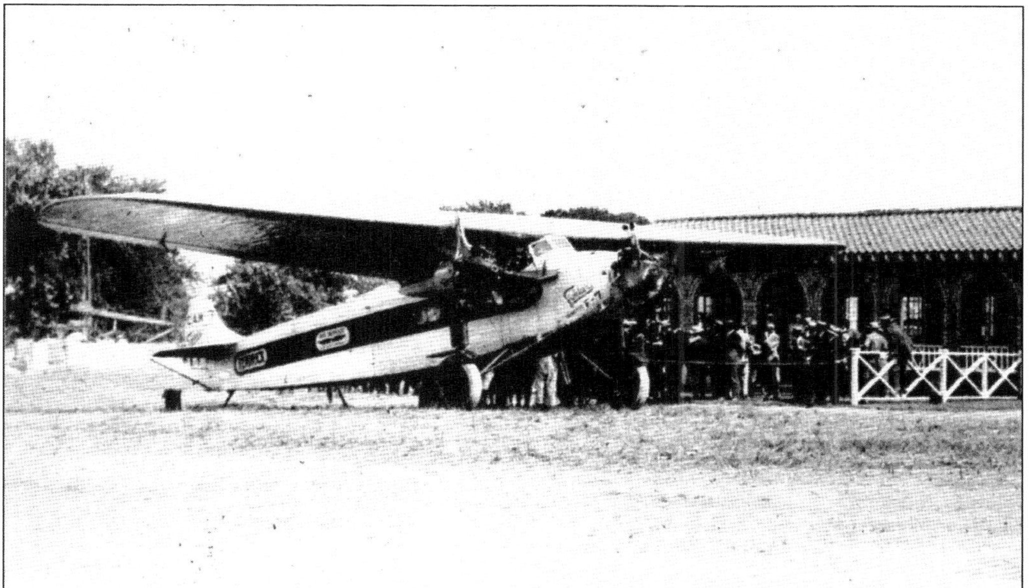

P. R. T. PASSENGER AIRPLANE "KENDRICK" TAKING OFF AT WASHINGTON FOR PHILADELPHIA.

AIR SERVICE. Special air service between Washington, D.C., and Philadelphia began officially on July 6, 1926. The Philadelphia Rapid Transit Air Service operated three aircraft, each of which carried eight passengers as well as mail and cargo. Some 489 flights were made with a total of 2,618 passengers transported at a round-trip cost of $25. Shown here is the airplane nicknamed the "Kendrick" in honor of Philadelphia's mayor. (PRT Air Service.)

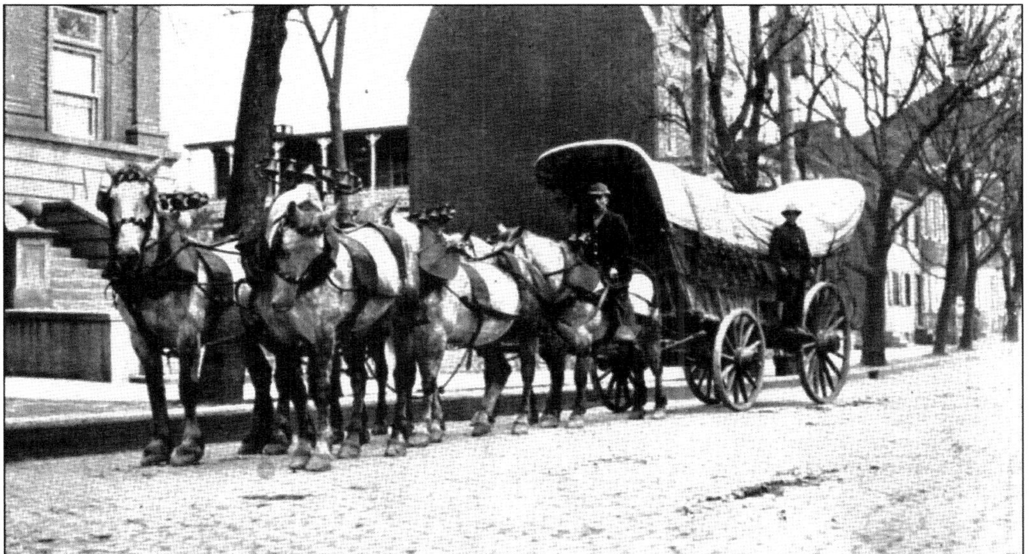

OLD CONESTOGA WAGON, EN ROUTE TO PHILADELPHIA SESQUI-CENTENNIAL
LEAVING LANCASTER OCT. 19, ARRIVING PHILADELPHIA, OCT. 20, 1926

CONESTOGA WAGON. Perhaps the most unusual means of transportation that was used to convey people to the exposition was this Conestoga wagon. At least 130 years old at the time, this wagon carried the mayor of the city of Lancaster as well as a number of other individuals from that city for a visit to the Sesqui-Centennial International Exposition in October 1926.

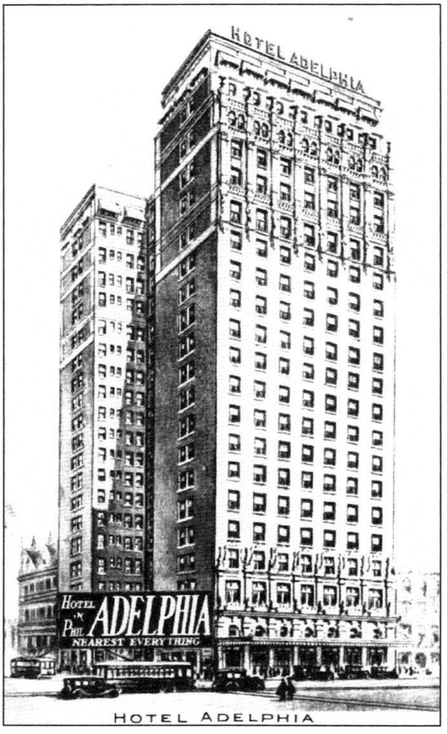

ADELPHIA HOTEL. In 1926, the city had some 350 hotels ready to accommodate those arriving to visit the Sesqui-Centennial International Exposition. Among these hotels were some of the most noted hotels in Philadelphia's history. This is an advertising postcard for the Adelphia Hotel located at Thirteenth and Chestnut Streets. Built in 1912, its slogan was "Nearest to everything in Philadelphia."

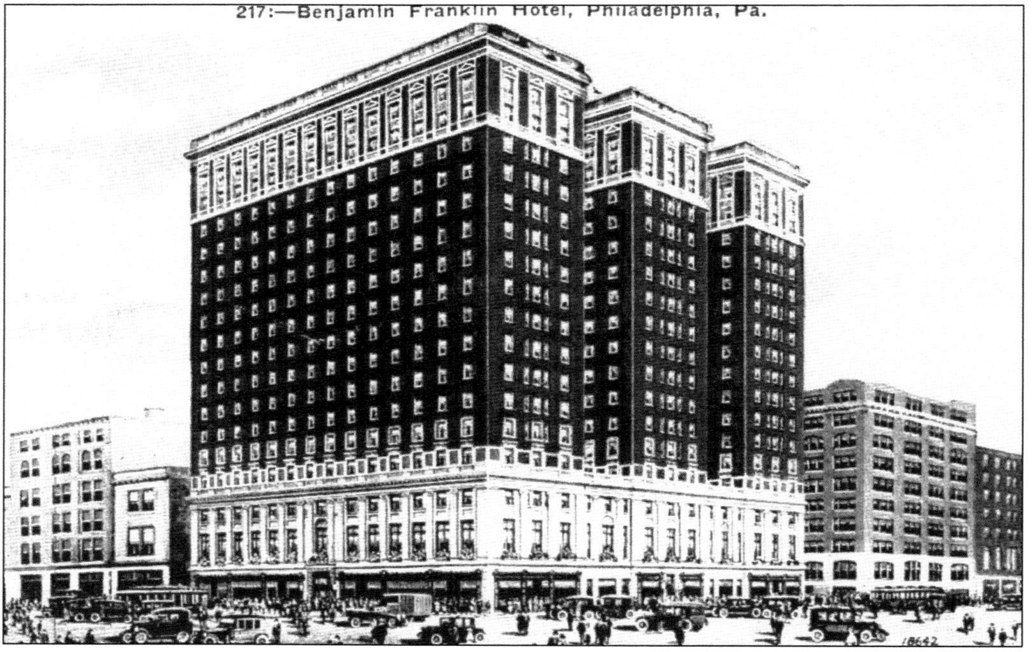

BENJAMIN FRANKLIN HOTEL. Opened in 1925 at the corner of Ninth and Chestnut Streets, this hotel was designed in the Georgian style by the architect Horace Trumbauer (1868–1938). Built of red brick and limestone, the hotel stood 18 stories high and had 1,220 guest rooms. The building, which still stands, was converted into offices and apartments in 1980. (P. Sander.)

THE BELLEVUE-STRATFORD. Located at 200 South Broad Street, this 19-story grand hotel first opened its doors in 1904. Costing over $8 million to build, it was considered the most luxurious hotel in the city. The hotel had over 1,000 rooms and was renowned for its magnificent ballroom. During the Sesqui-Centennial International Exposition, numerous official luncheons and formal receptions were held here.

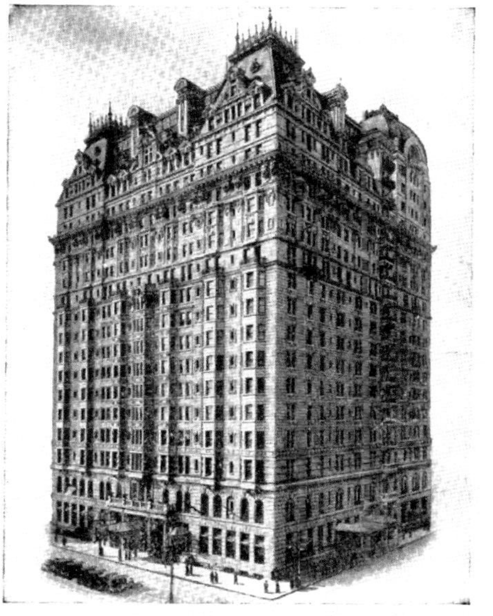

THE BELLEVUE-STRATFORD, Philadephia, Pa.

The Sesqui-Centennial City

Affiliated Hotels: The Waldorf-Astoria, New York
The Willard, Washington. D. C. The Windsor, Montreal, Canada

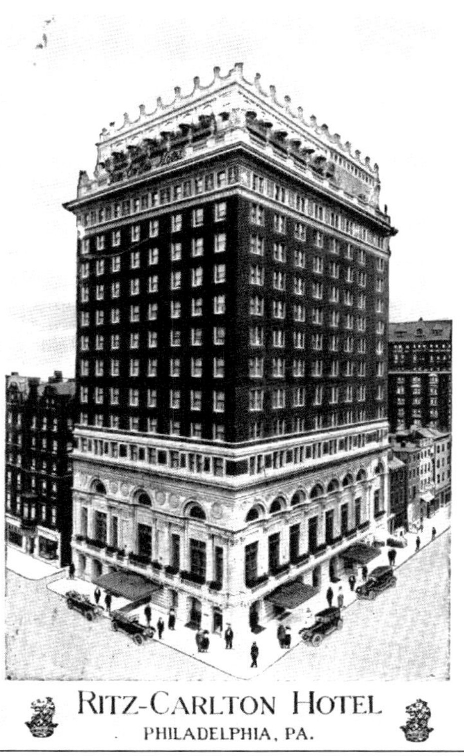

RITZ-CARLTON HOTEL
PHILADELPHIA, PA.

RITZ-CARLTON HOTEL. Opened in 1912 by the Widener family, the Ritz was designed by the well-known architect Horace Trumbauer (1868–1938). Found at Broad and Walnut Streets, it was near the center of the city's social and theater districts. With its rooftop garden restaurant, and featuring both large and small public meeting rooms, it was well suited to attract some of those coming to the exposition. (E. C. Kropp.)

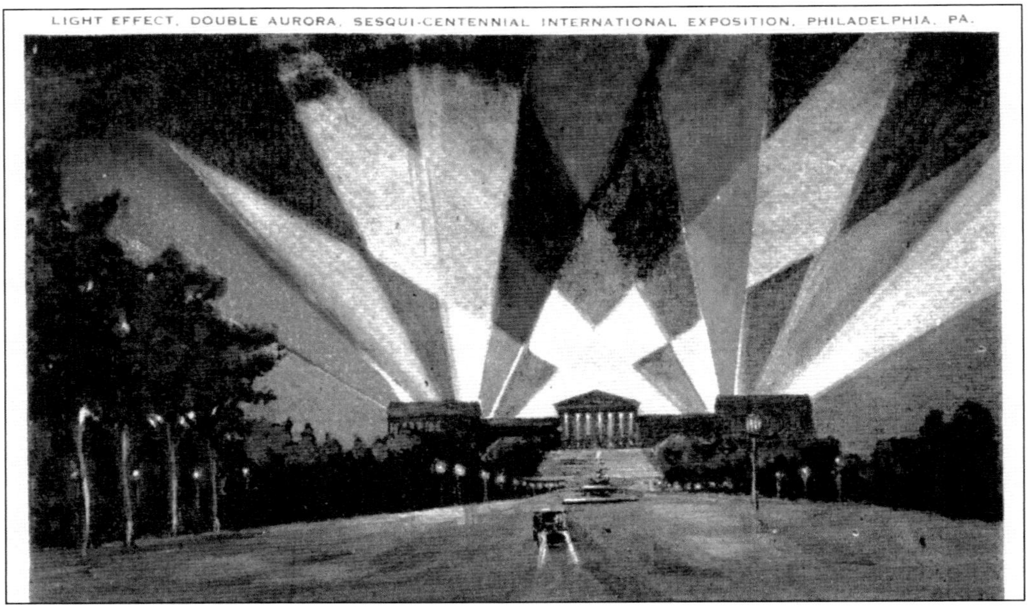

AURORA LIGHTING. Visible in the sky behind the Philadelphia Art Museum are some of the lighting effects projected skyward from the grounds of the Sesqui-Centennial International Exposition several miles to the south. Known as the "Auroral Display," these colored lights were produced by 14 high-intensity searchlights having a combined illumination of 6.3 million candlepower. Such dramatic lighting effects helped draw attention to the exposition. (John D. Cardinell.)

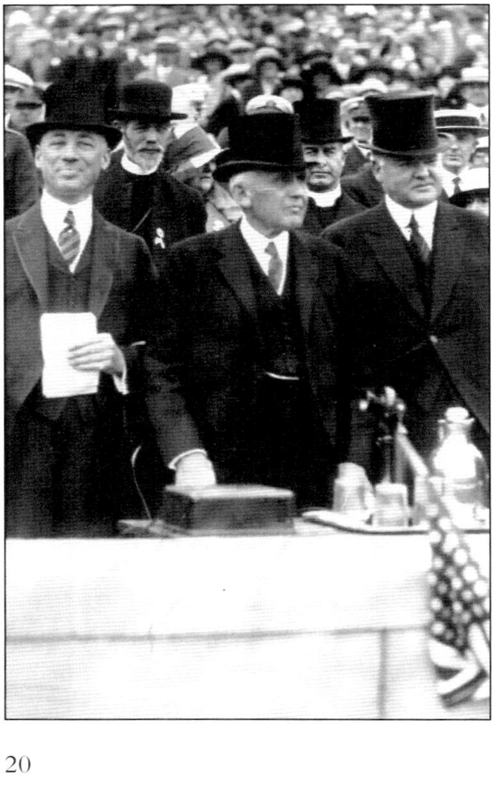

OPENING CEREMONIES. Opening day was held on May 31 with approximately 50,000 people witnessing the ceremonies that took place in the new stadium. Seen here at the gala event are Philadelphia's Mayor W. Freeland Kendrick, Secretary of State Frank B. Kellogg, and Secretary of Commerce Herbert Hoover. After a day filled with activities, followed by a huge fireworks display held at 10:00 p.m., the Sesqui-Centennial International Exposition was officially open to the public. (International Newsreel.)

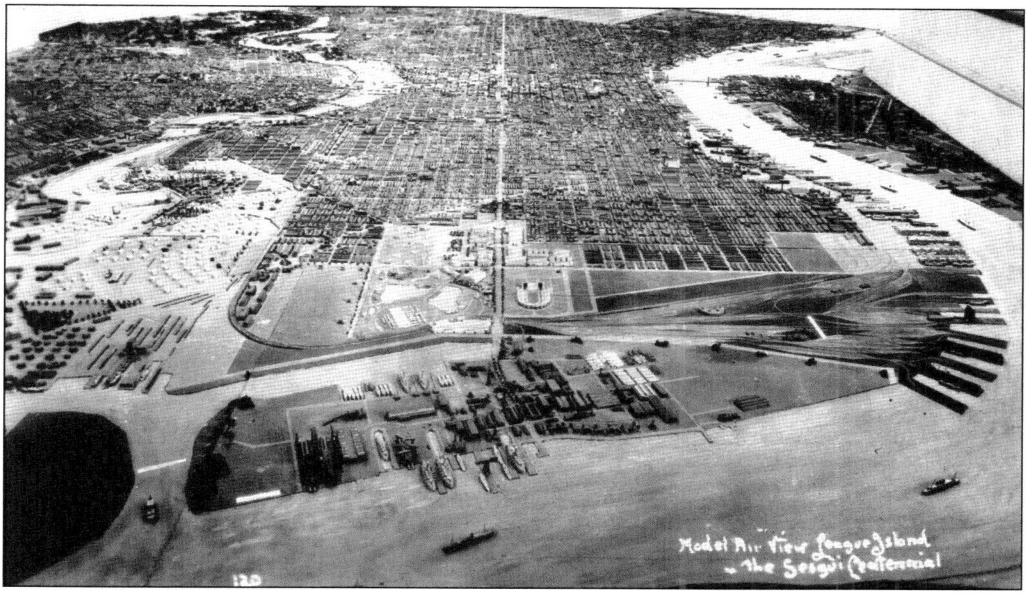

MODEL AERIAL VIEW. Seen here is a model that was created to display the general layout of the exposition. This particular view is looking north up Broad Street toward Center City, with the Delaware River and navy yard in the foreground. The location of the actual exposition was only about three miles from city hall.

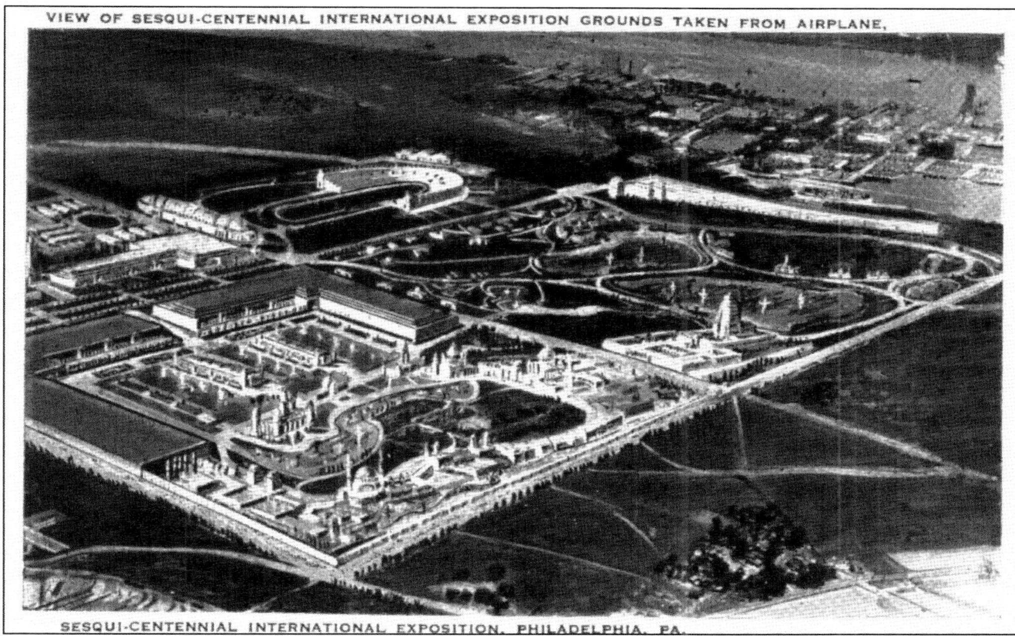

AIRPLANE VIEW. A panoramic view of the exposition grounds taken from an airplane shows the vast area of land utilized by this event. At the southern end of Broad Street, the Sesqui-Centennial International Exposition site covered about 1,000 acres adjoining the navy yard, which is visible in the upper right of this postcard image. Much of the land had been marsh and had to be filled in before construction could begin. (Tichnor.)

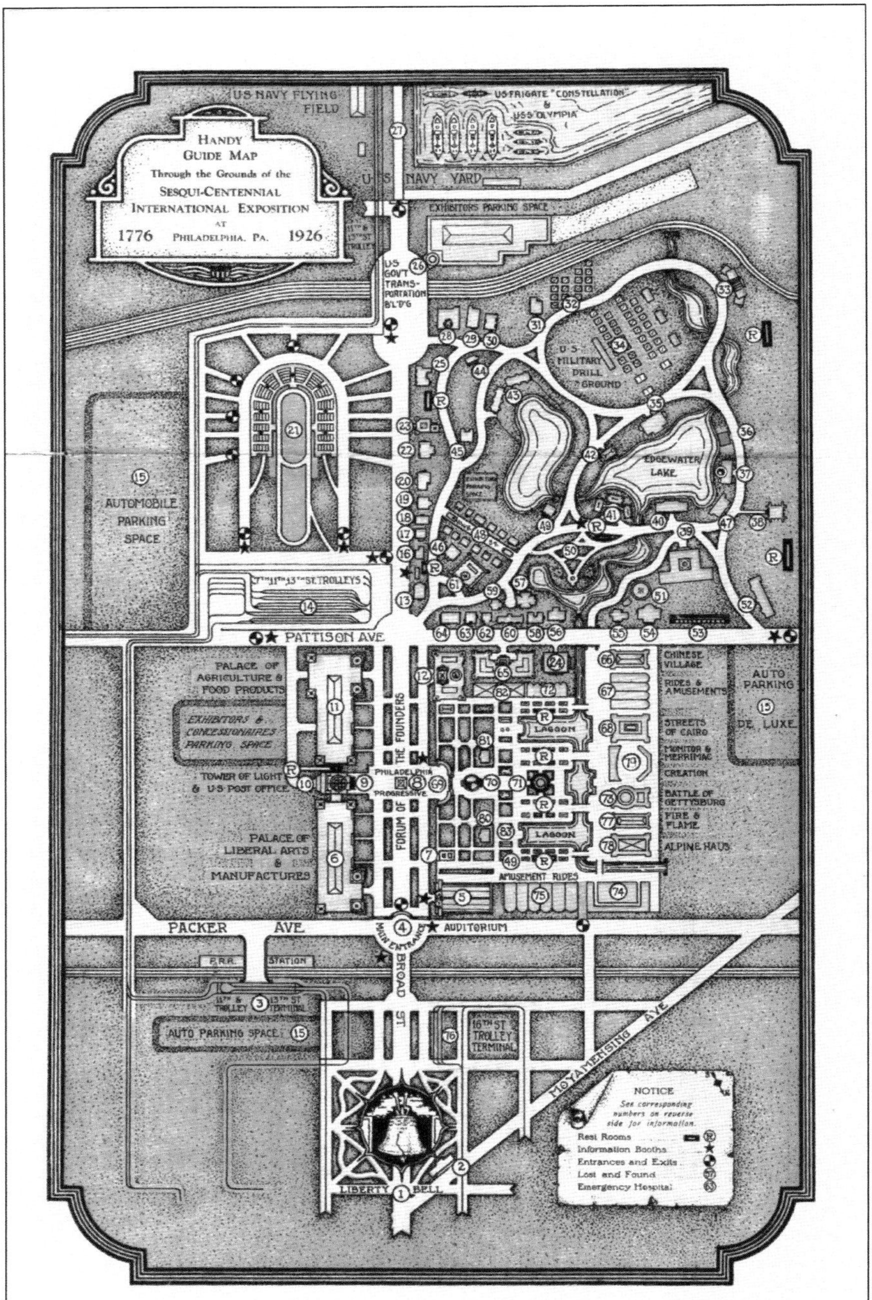

MAP OF THE SESQUI-CENTENNIAL. The "Complimentary Official Guide Map" seen here was provided to those visiting the Sesqui-Centennial International Exposition. It shows the general layout of the exposition grounds and pinpoints the location of all the major attractions. This should prove to be quite helpful to the reader of this book as well. At the top of the map is the navy yard, which is at the south end of Broad Street, while the giant replica of the Liberty Bell, located just north of the main entrance, is at the bottom of the diagram.

Two

The Main Entrance and Broad Street

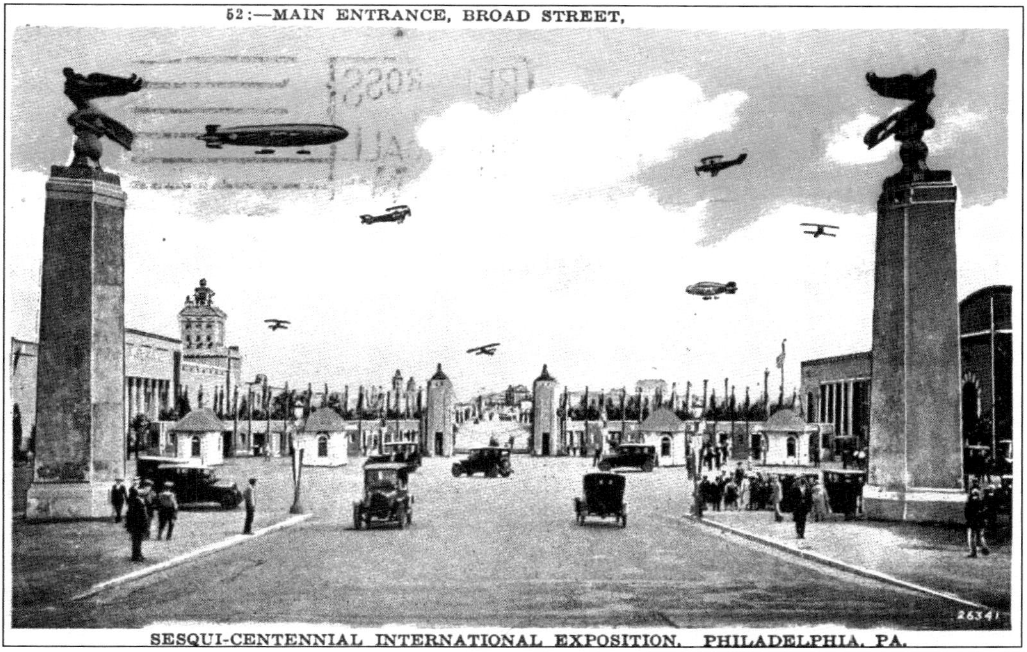

Main Entrance. The main entrance to the exposition was located at the intersection of Packer Avenue and Broad Street. On opening day, May 31, 1926, there were 55,509 paid admissions with another 26,975 entering free. During the course of the Sesqui-Centennial International Exposition, entrance fees were 50¢ for adults and 25¢ for children. (John D. Cardinell.)

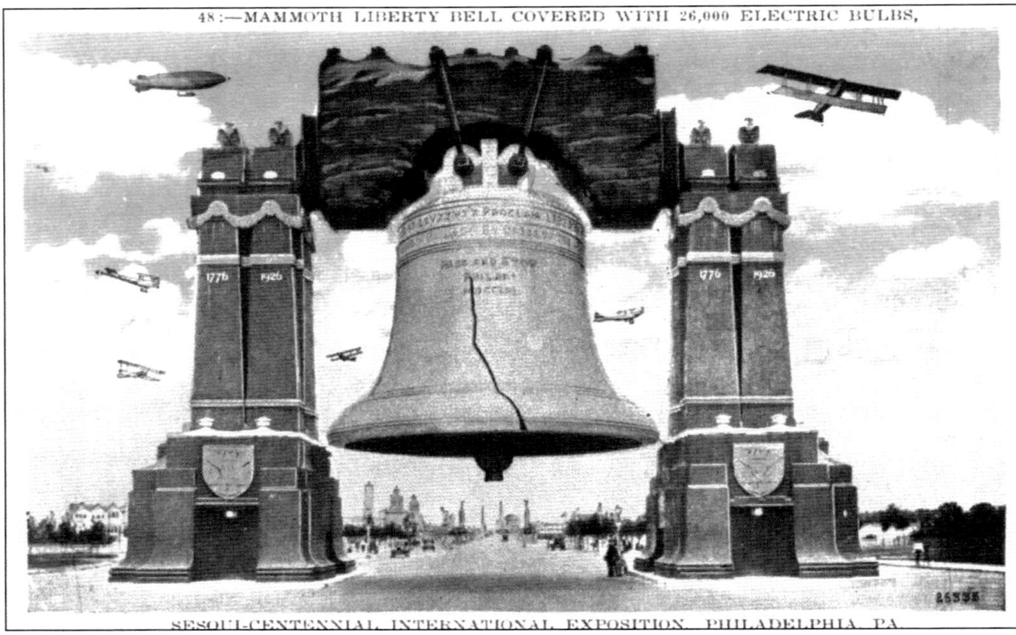

MAMMOTH LIBERTY BELL. Welcoming people as they approached the main entrance was a huge replica of the Liberty Bell, which cost approximately $100,000 to construct. Towering 80 feet high, this magnificent structure served as a symbol for the Sesqui-Centennial International Exposition. The bell itself weighed 42 tons and had a road clearance of 20 feet 7 inches, which made it possible for cars and trucks to drive underneath. (John D. Cardinell.)

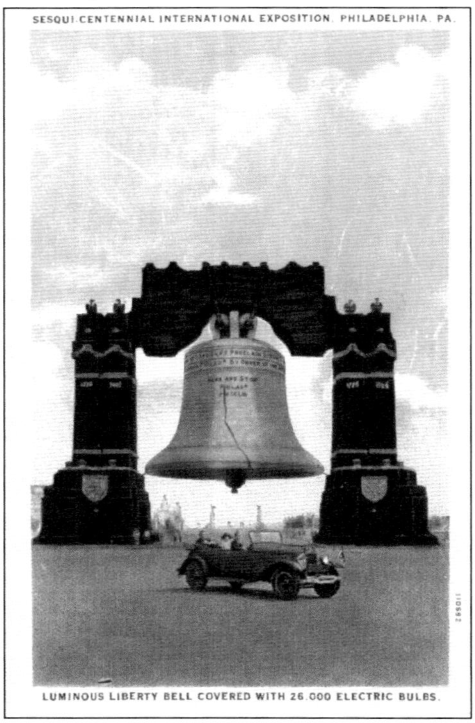

SYMBOL OF FREEDOM. This colossal re-creation of the original Liberty Bell, a symbol of freedom, was held aloft by two massive columns. Both columns were anchored by wooden pilings driven 30 feet into the ground. Each had a steel framework that was covered by plaster painted a bronze color with additional gold ornamentation. The columns themselves represented America's industry and progress. (John D. Cardinell.)

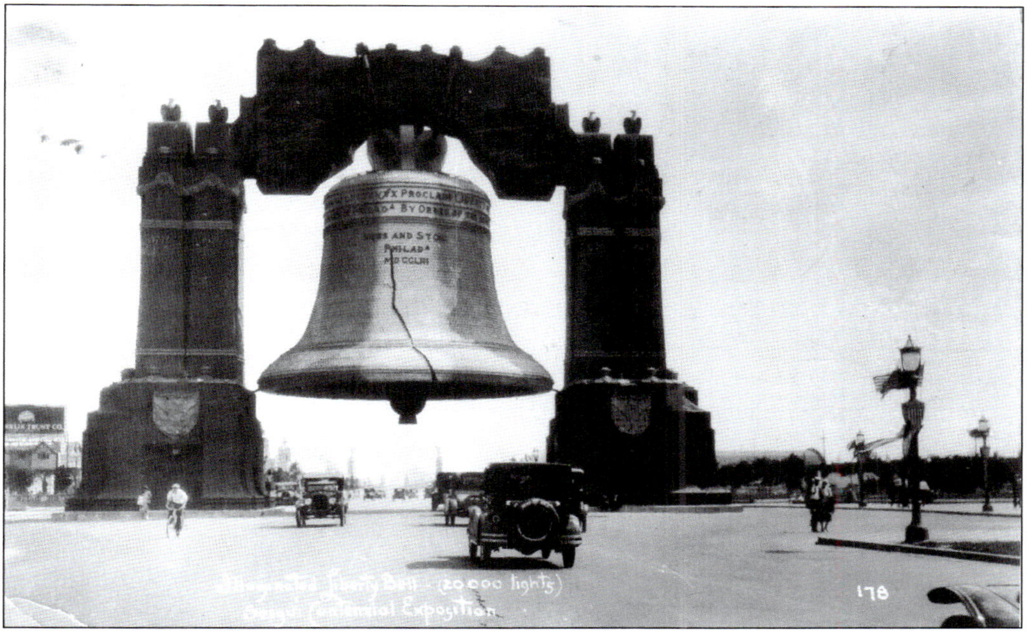

COLOSSAL LIBERTY BELL. Automobiles pass beneath the mammoth replica Liberty Bell as they travel to and from the exposition grounds along Broad Street. The giant bell was constructed in less than two months under the direction of the contractor Frank C. English and Sons. Some 97 tons of steel, several tons of sheet metal, and approximately 35,000 feet of lumber were used.

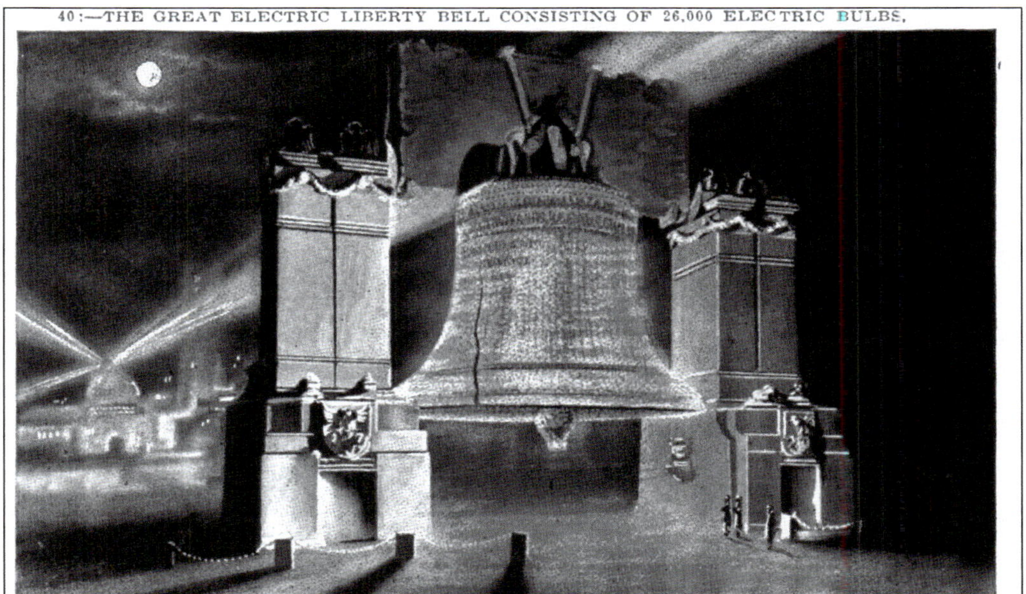

LUMINOUS LIBERTY BELL. Making the giant replica Liberty Bell even more impressive was the fact that it was illuminated at night. The sheet metal shell of the bell was covered by 26,000 15-watt lightbulbs, set six inches apart. In addition, the clapper of the bell was lit by eight 200-watt projectors. After dark, the glow in the sky created by this symbol of freedom was visible throughout the city. (John D. Cardinell.)

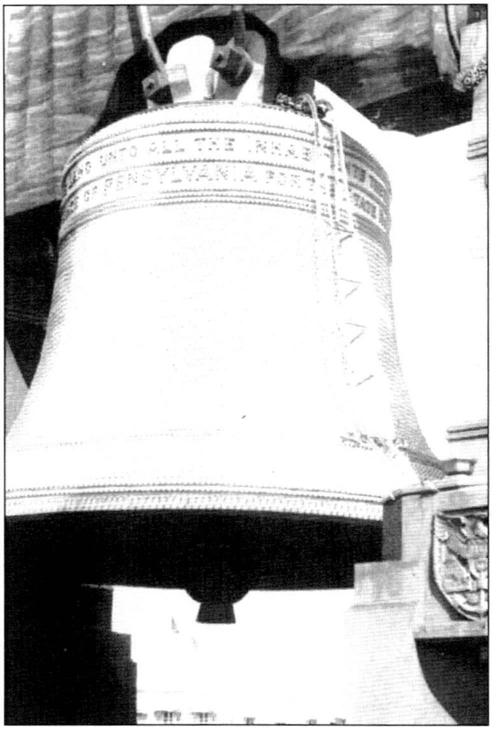

CLOSE-UP OF BELL. A close-up view of the bell itself shows the attention to detail that was taken in its construction. Even the inscription at the top of the bell was accurately duplicated. To service and maintain the thousands of lightbulbs installed on the surface of the bell, a contoured wheeled ladder was set into tracks that circled the bell at top and bottom. (W. J. Gambino.)

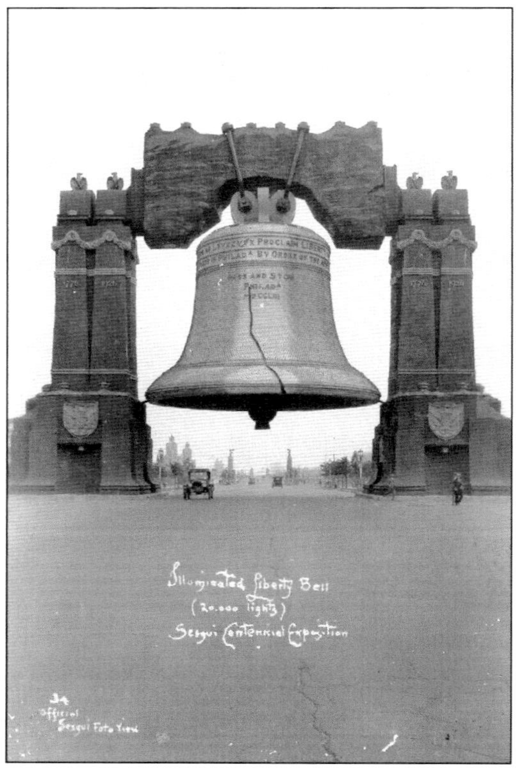

SYMBOL OF THE SESQUI-CENTENNIAL. This enormous replica Liberty Bell came to symbolize the Sesqui-Centennial International Exposition and left a lasting impression on all who gazed upon it. At the conclusion of the exposition, the momentous structure was sold at auction as scrap for the sum of $60. It remained standing until finally dismantled in August 1927. (John D. Cardinell.)

PARADE UNDER LIBERTY BELL. Crowds look on as mounted soldiers parade beneath the giant Liberty Bell as they head toward the main entrance. This was part of the Sesqui-Centennial International Exposition's opening day festivities held on May 31. Notice that scaffolding is still in place on the bell's supporting towers, as construction was not yet fully completed. (International Newsreel.)

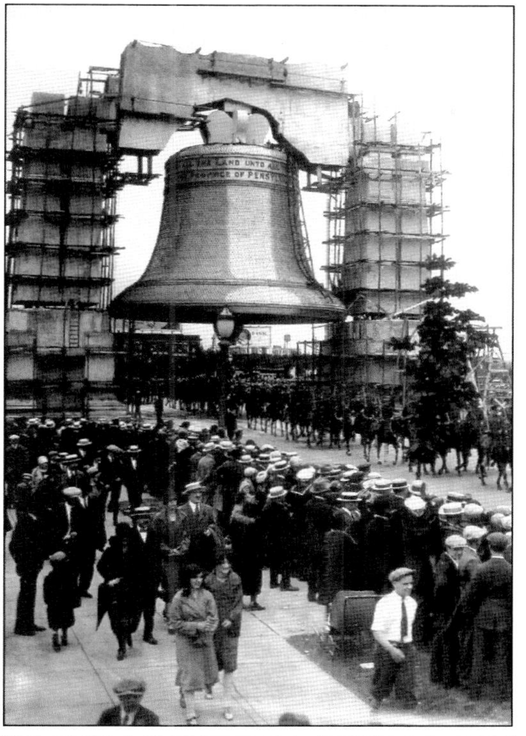

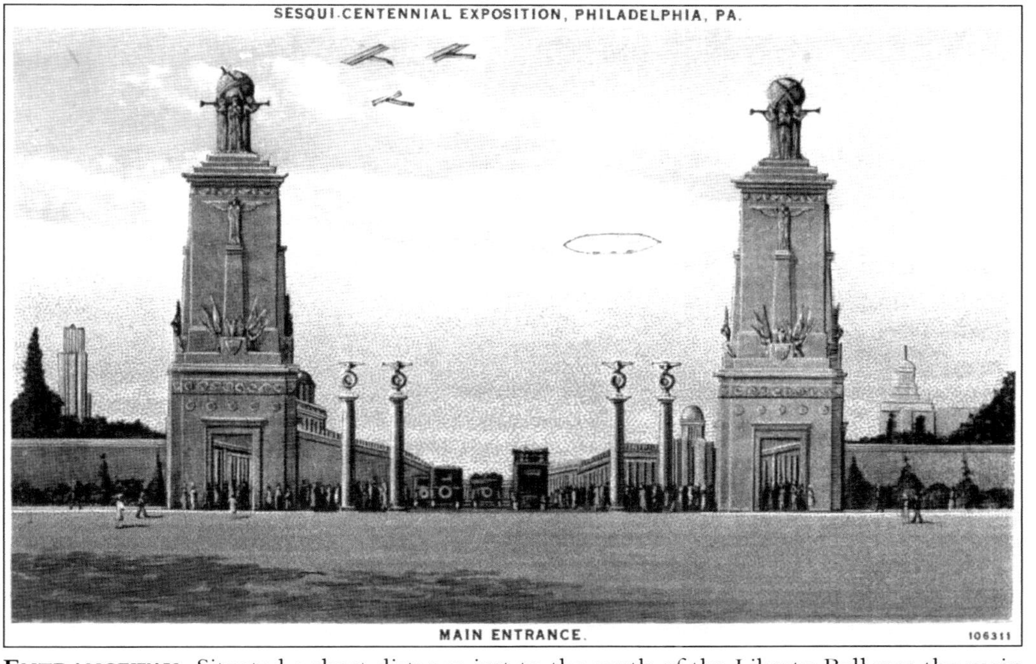

ENTRANCEWAY. Situated a short distance just to the south of the Liberty Bell was the main entrance to the exposition. The approach was designed in such a manner as to help create "a holiday character" for the visitors. Standing to each side were 25-foot-high pylons, topped by sculptures titled *Heralds of the New Dawn*. (John D. Cardinell.)

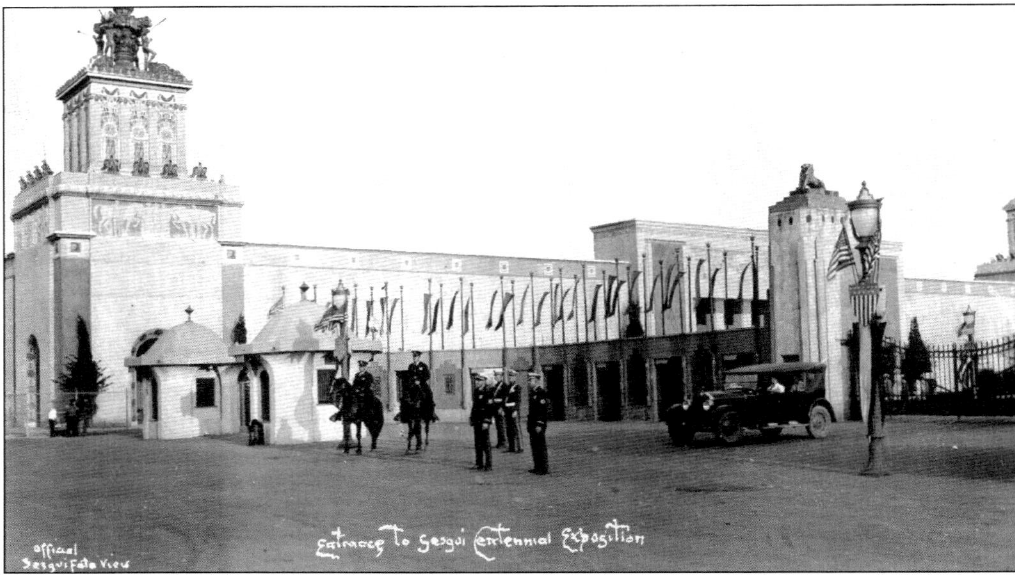

TICKET BOOTHS. Standing near several of the main entrance ticket booths are members of the special police force assigned to the exposition grounds. Supplementing policemen on foot patrol and in automobiles were horse-mounted officers like those seen here. Policemen were on duty 24 hours per day to protect and serve the safety needs of the Sesqui-Centennial International Exposition. (John D. Cardinell.)

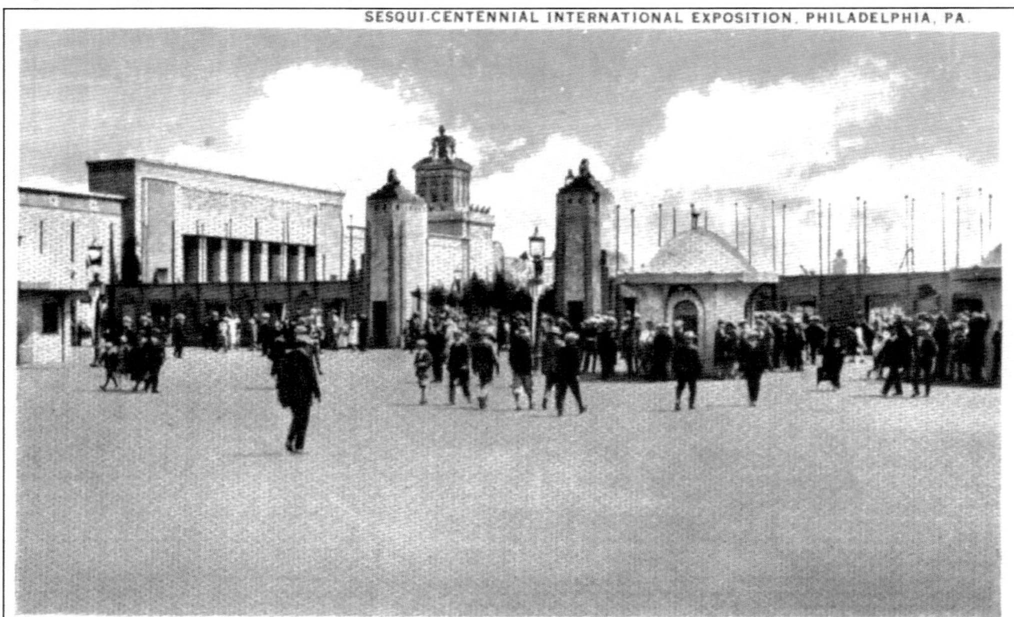

ATTENDANCE. Prior to the opening of the Sesqui-Centennial International Exposition, it had been estimated that 36 million people would attend. Actual attendance was ultimately only 6,408,289. The principal reason for the low turnout was most likely due to the unusual poor weather. During the 184 days that the exposition was open, it rained an astonishing 107 days; only 50 days were recorded by the Weather Bureau as clear. (John D. Cardinell.)

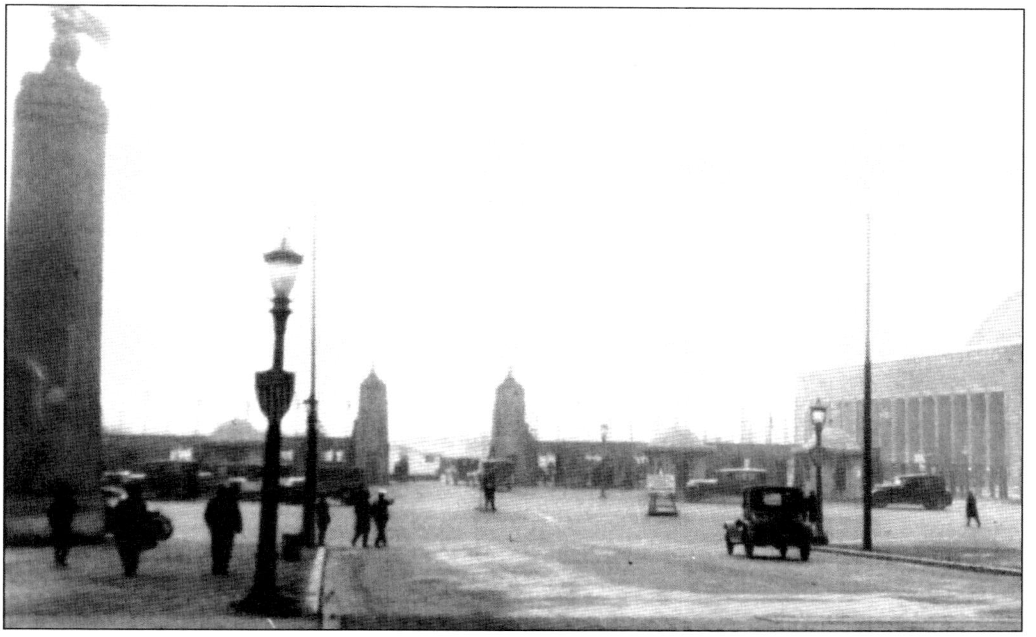

VIEW OF MAIN ENTRANCE. This view is looking south through the main gates. On the left one of the tall entrance pylons is visible, while on the right stands the auditorium. Sunday, October 3 saw the largest daily paid attendance of 107,937 visitors. The lowest number to attend the exposition on a single day was 2,687, who entered the grounds during a rain on June 7. (W. J. Gambino.)

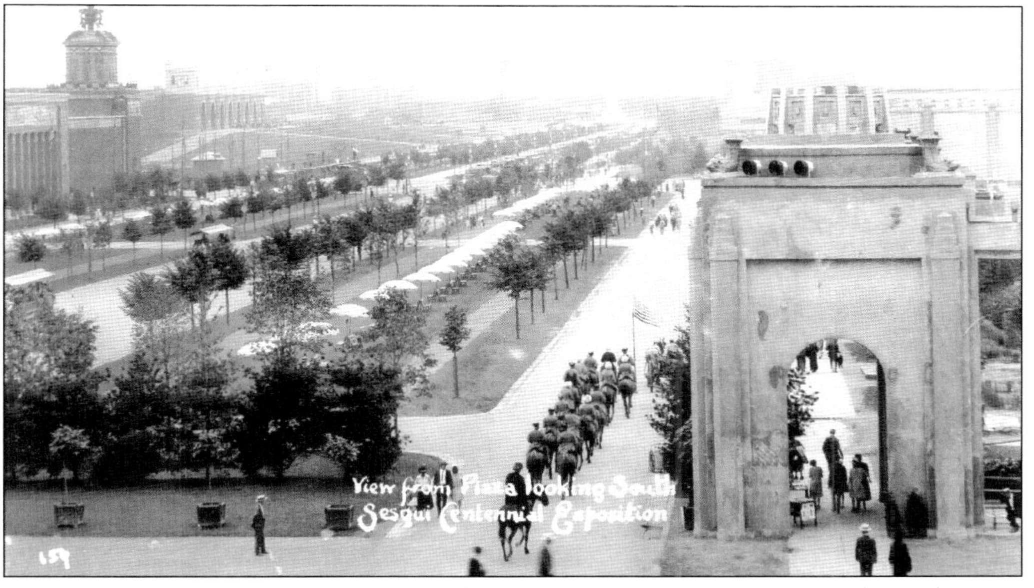

LOOKING SOUTH. A vista looking south from just inside the main entrance shows the great breadth of the tree-lined boulevard, which extended from Packer Avenue to Pattison Avenue. Horse-mounted soldiers are seen making their way along the concourse, possibly heading for the large military encampment that was located at the other end of the exposition grounds, near the navy yard.

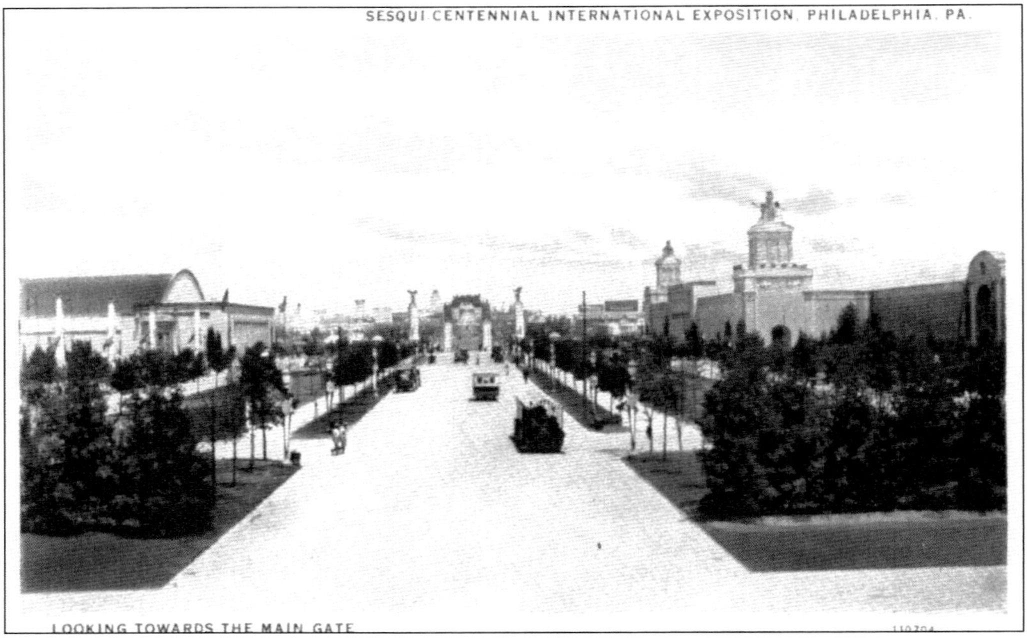

Looking Toward Main Gate. The main entrance and the giant replica Liberty Bell are visible in the center of this view looking northward up Broad Street. On the left is the auditorium, and on the right is the Palace of Liberal Arts. A party car and several other vehicles occupy the roadway. (John D. Cardinell.)

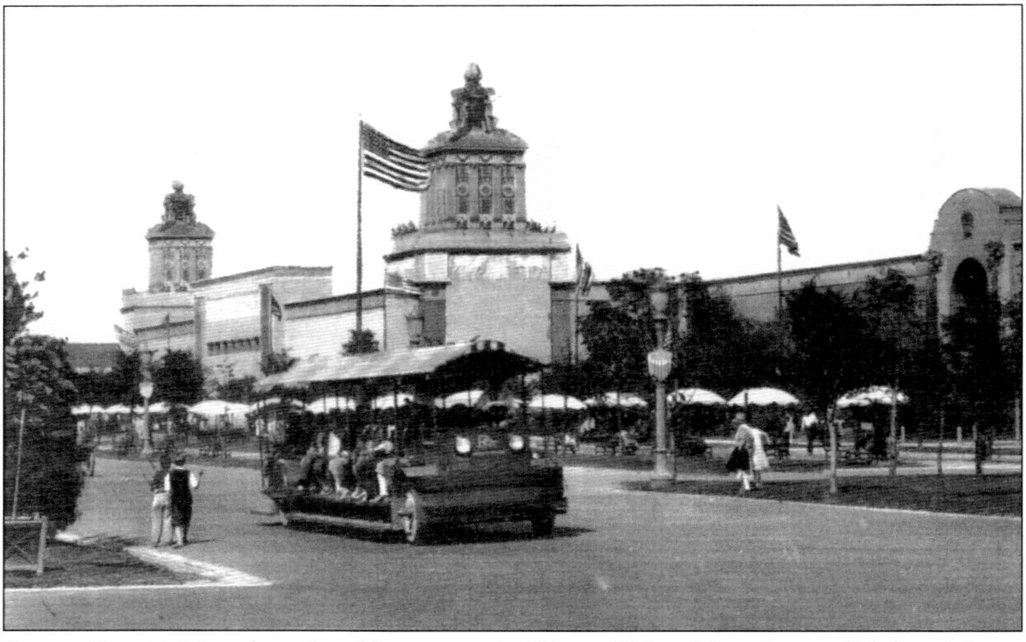

Party Car. Driving along Broad Street, past the Palace of Liberal Arts, is one of 25 electric buses that transported visitors around the exposition. Each bus, or "party car," carried 40 passengers who sat on benches facing out the side of the open-air vehicles. Capable of speeds of six to eight miles per hour, each bus had a driver and a conductor. (John D. Cardinell.)

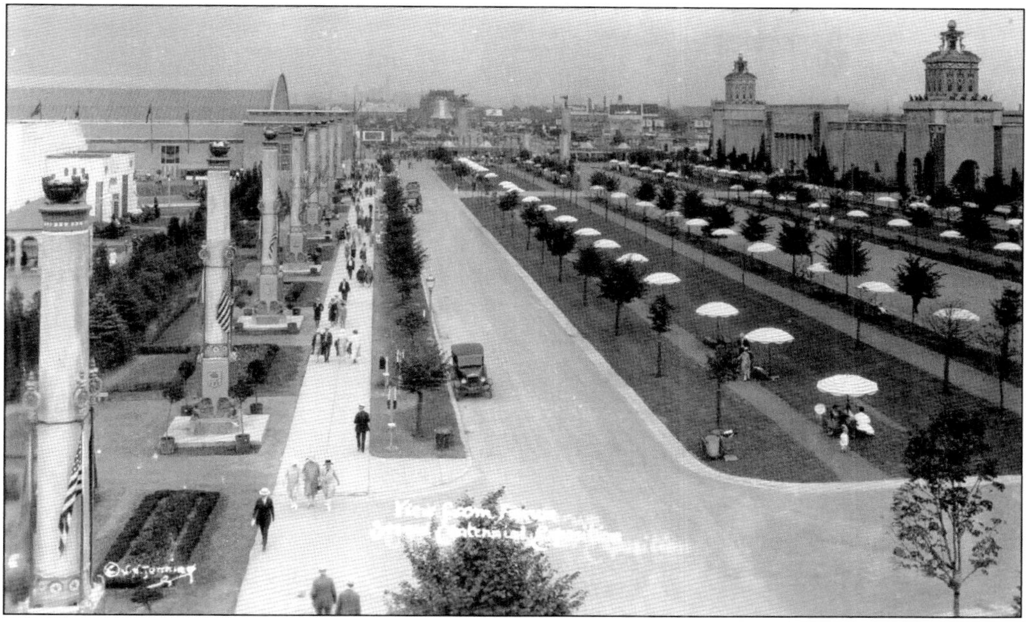

View From the Forum of the Founders. This is a view of a section of the exposition grounds immediately south of the main entrance, along a portion of Broad Street known as the "Avenue of the Colonies." Erected along the side of this thoroughfare were 13 columns or pylons honoring the original colonies. Running down the center were small shaded tables where people could sit and rest themselves. (W. N. Jennings.)

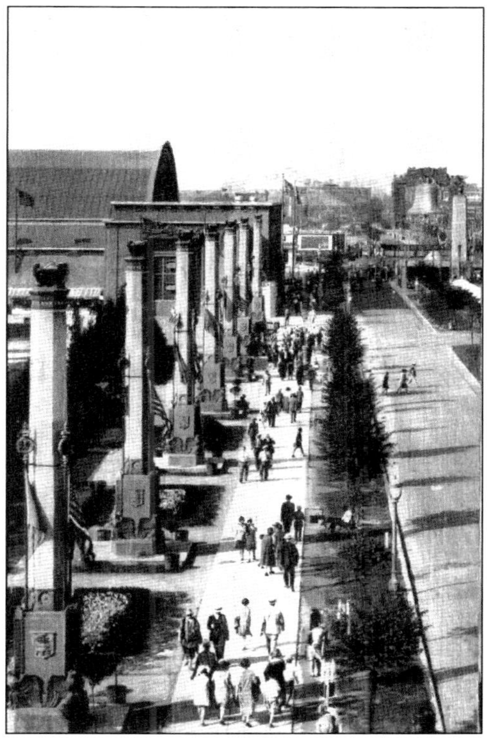

Founders Pylons. Lining the west side of Broad Street, between the Pittsburgh Building and the Pennsylvania Building, were 13 columns each representing an original colony and memorializing the 56 signers of the Declaration of Independence. In this view, the skyline of Center City Philadelphia is visible in the far distance. (John D. Cardinell.)

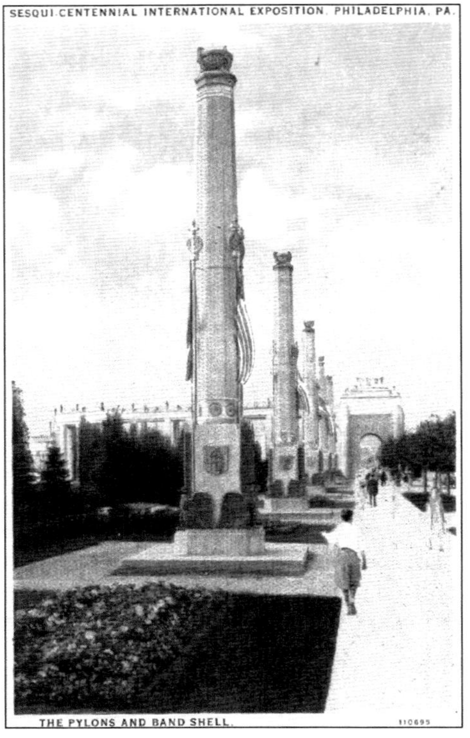

PYLONS AND BAND SHELL. Here a row of flag-decorated Founders Pylons stretch into the distance north toward the band shell. Each of the columns stood 40 feet in height and was made of steel, cement, and plaster. On every pylon was a bronze tablet bearing the names and coat of arms of that particular colony's signers of the Declaration of Independence. (John D. Cardinell.)

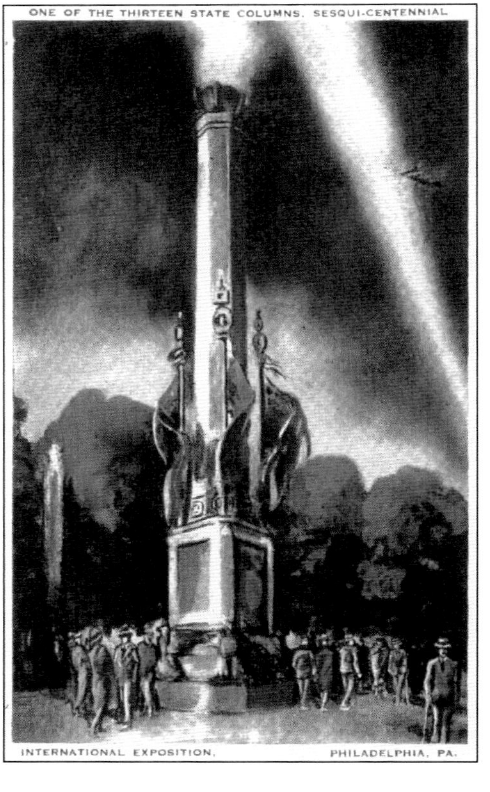

ILLUMINATED PYLON. Construction of the 13 Founders Pylons began on May 6 and was completed on June 10, 1926. Every evening each of the tall columns was illuminated with additional light projected into the sky from their tops. Such fantastic lighting effects helped create a festive atmosphere. (John D. Cardinell.)

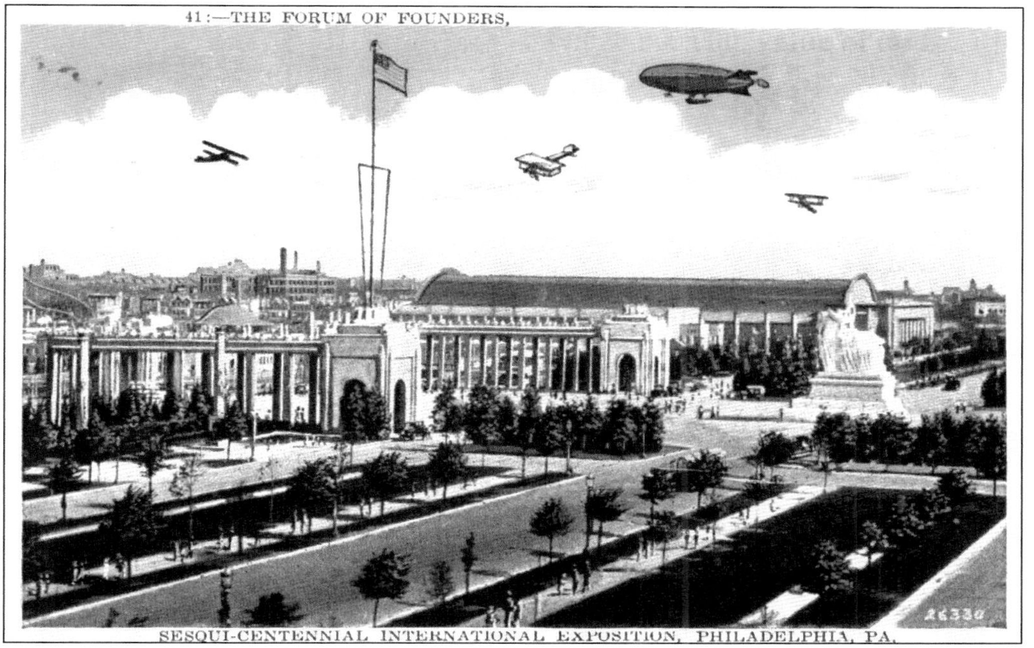

FORUM OF THE FOUNDERS. On Broad Street, midway between Packer and Pattison Avenues, was an open plaza named the Forum of the Founders. Standing in its center was the statue *Philadelphia Progressive*. Just to the west of this stood the colonnade, a series of columns 42 feet in height that stretched for 155 feet. From here visitors could, if they wished, continue on to the Gladway. (John D. Cardinell.)

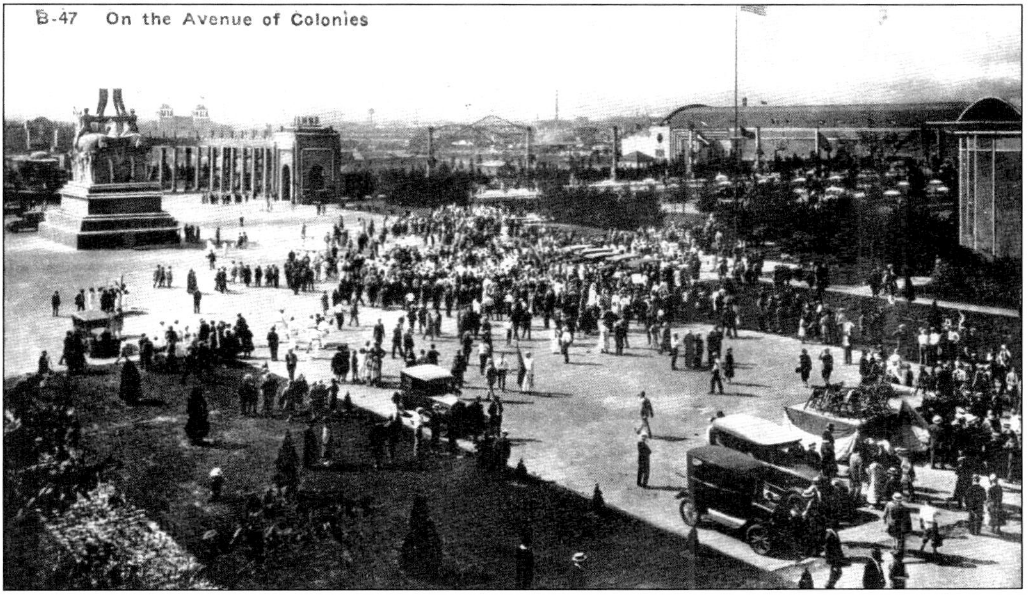

ON THE AVENUE OF THE COLONIES. A large group of people is seen gathered along a stretch of the Avenue of the Colonies near the large *Philadelphia Progressive* statue, which occupied the center of the Forum of the Founders. Off in the distance, to the right, is the auditorium. (John D. Cardinell.)

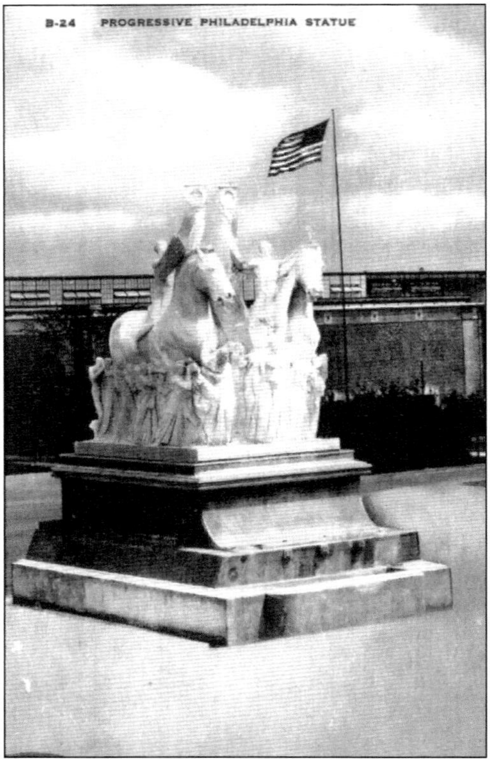

PROGRESSIVE PHILADELPHIA STATUE. Standing in the heart of the Forum of the Founders was the magnificent equestrian statuary group titled *Philadelphia Progressive.* It was designed as a tribute to the city's progress. This impressive piece of artwork was sculpted by the noted artist Charles E. Taft (1874–1951), who also served as the director of sculpture for the exposition. (John D. Cardinell.)

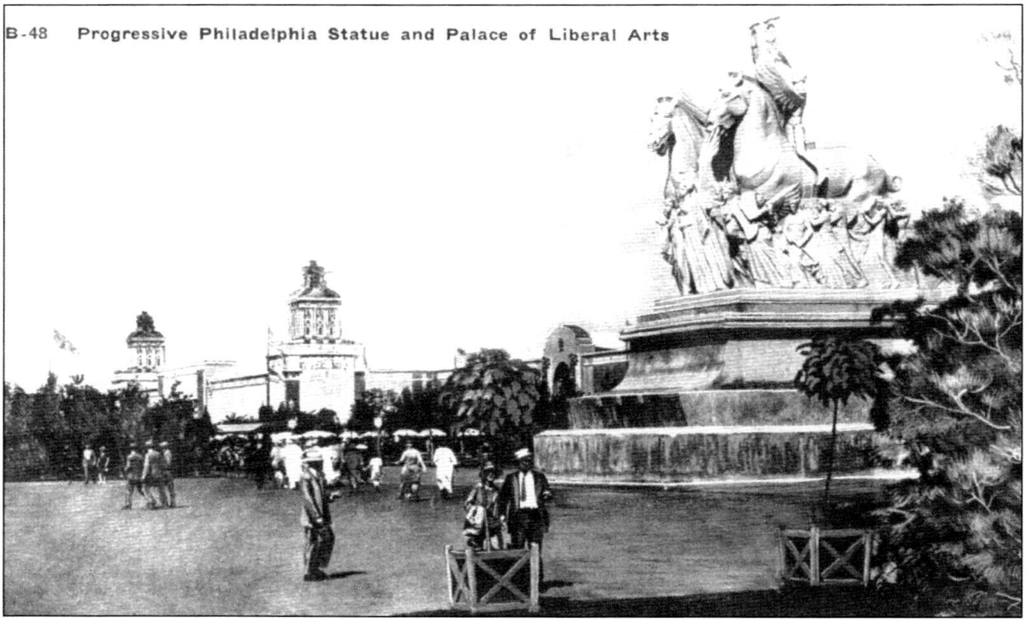

STATUE AND PALACE OF LIBERAL ARTS. From this vantage point, looking northward past the *Philadelphia Progressive* statue, the large exhibition hall known as the Palace of Liberal Arts is visible in the distance. In the evening the magnificent statue was illuminated on all four sides by strategically placed groupings of 500-watt, amber-colored floodlights. (John D. Cardinell.)

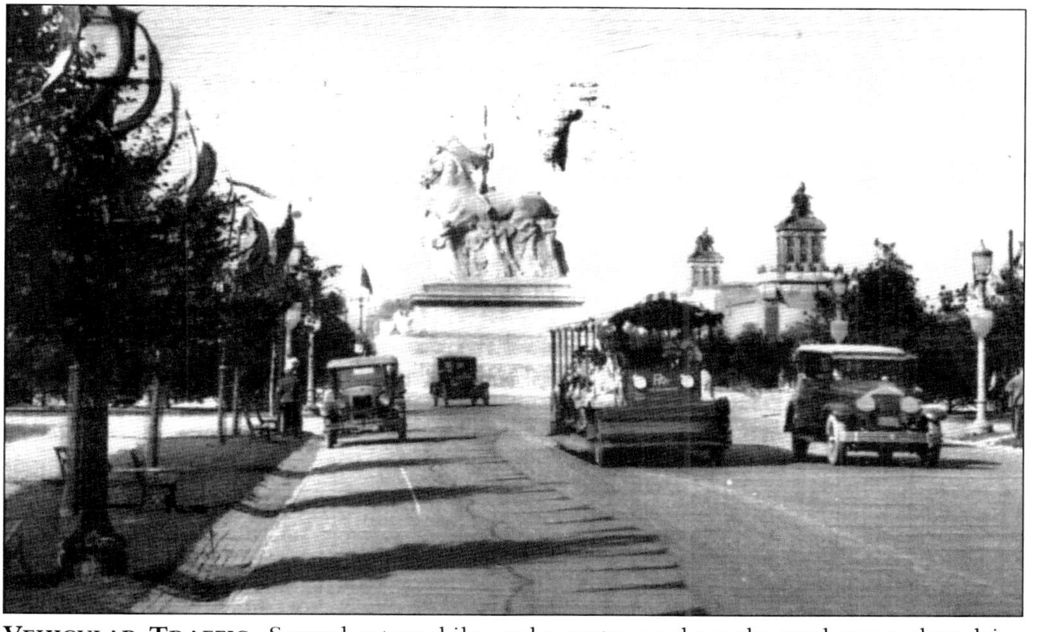

Vehicular Traffic. Several automobiles and a party car share the roadway as they drive along the Avenue of the Colonies past the *Philadelphia Progressive* statue. Beginning on August 16, automobiles were permitted entrance for a fee of $1 in addition to regular admission costs. A total of 213,745 drivers took advantage of this convenience. (John D. Cardinell.)

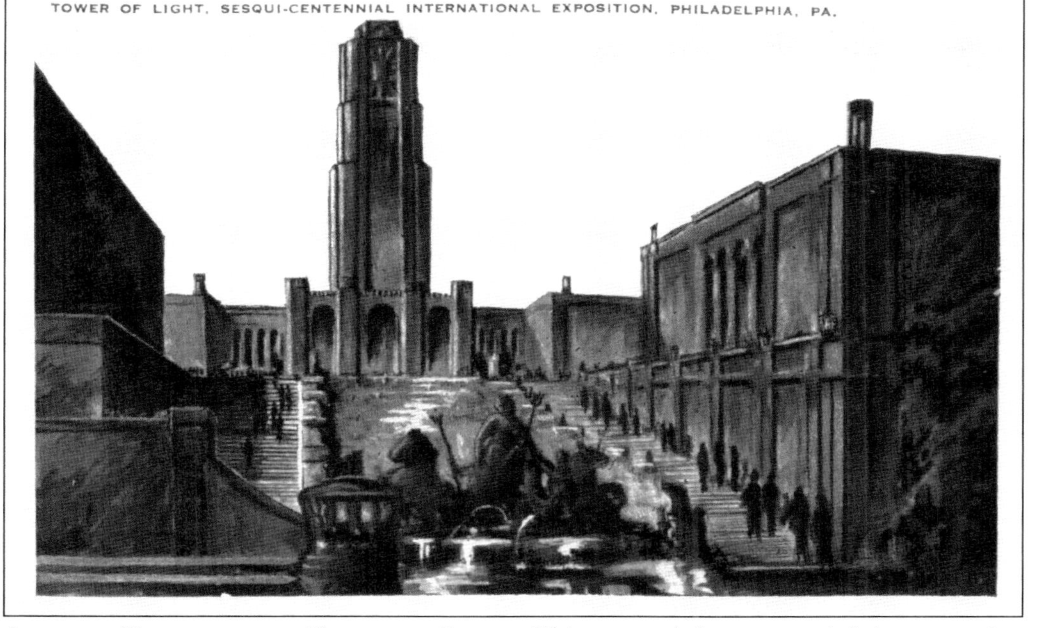

Artistic Vision of the Tower of Light. This postcard shows an artist's interpretation of what the Tower of Light would look like according to its initial design. Erected where it could occupy a central position on the exposition grounds, just off the Forum of the Founders, it unfortunately was never fully completed. (John D. Cardinell.)

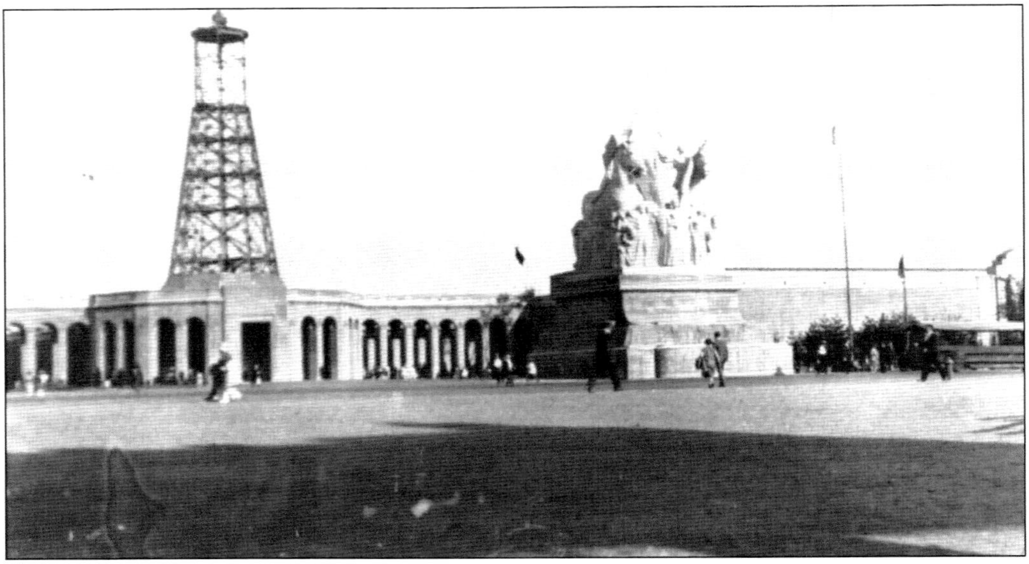

TOWER OF LIGHT. With construction beginning at the rather late date of June 6, it was finally decided by exposition officials to halt the building of the Tower of Light when it was only half completed. Its steel tower had been fully erected when work stopped on July 8, and on its top platform, a large searchlight was installed. (W. J. Gambino.)

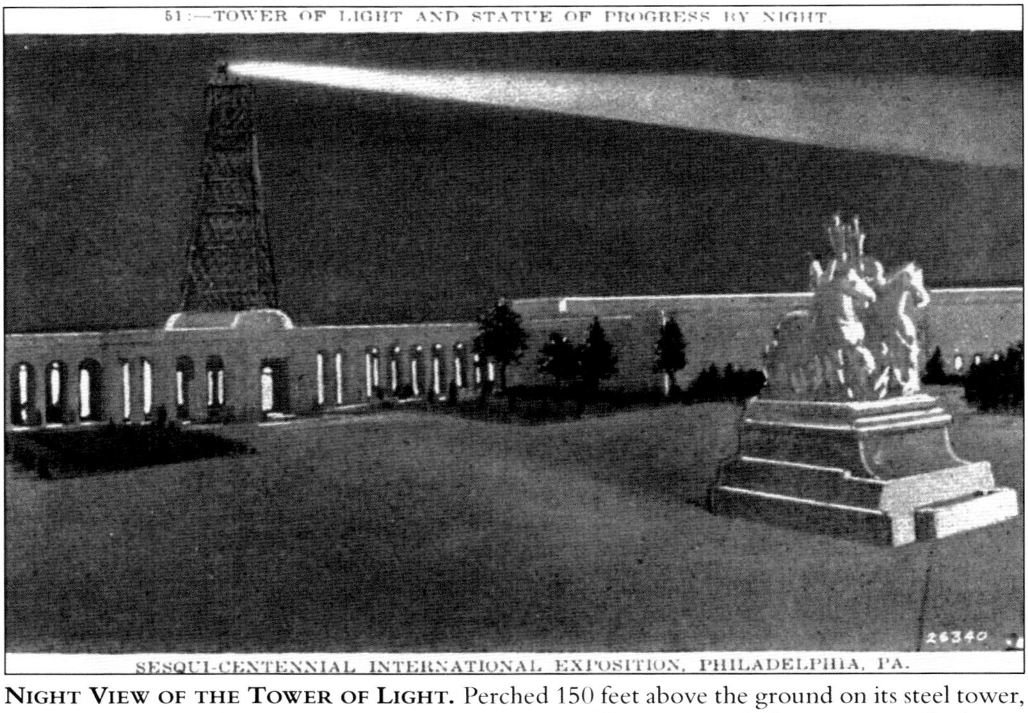

NIGHT VIEW OF THE TOWER OF LIGHT. Perched 150 feet above the ground on its steel tower, one of the nation's largest searchlights sent out its brilliant beam of illumination, which was visible for many miles in all directions. The beam, referred to as the "Light of Independence," commemorated the vision of liberty that was held by the original signers of the Declaration of Independence. (John D. Cardinell.)

Three

The Great Exhibition Halls

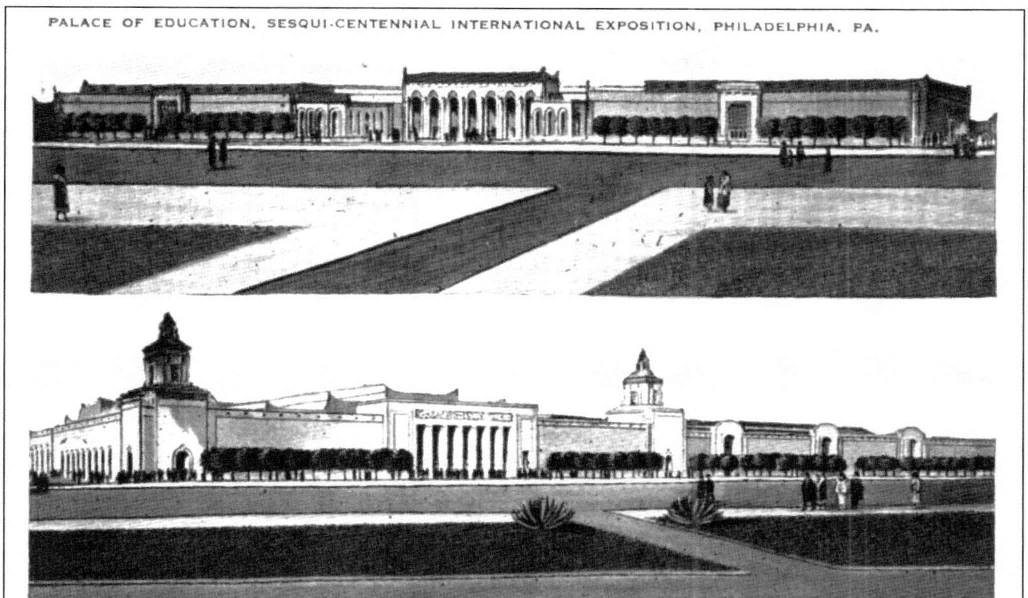

Exhibit Halls. Five major exhibition halls, referred to as "palaces," were erected to house the vast number of exhibits and displays that were to be presented. The design of these buildings was under the supervision of the exposition's appointed architect, John Molitor. Each building was dedicated to a different theme. Here is an artist's representation of two of these, the Palace of Education and the Palace of Liberal Arts. (John D. Cardinell.)

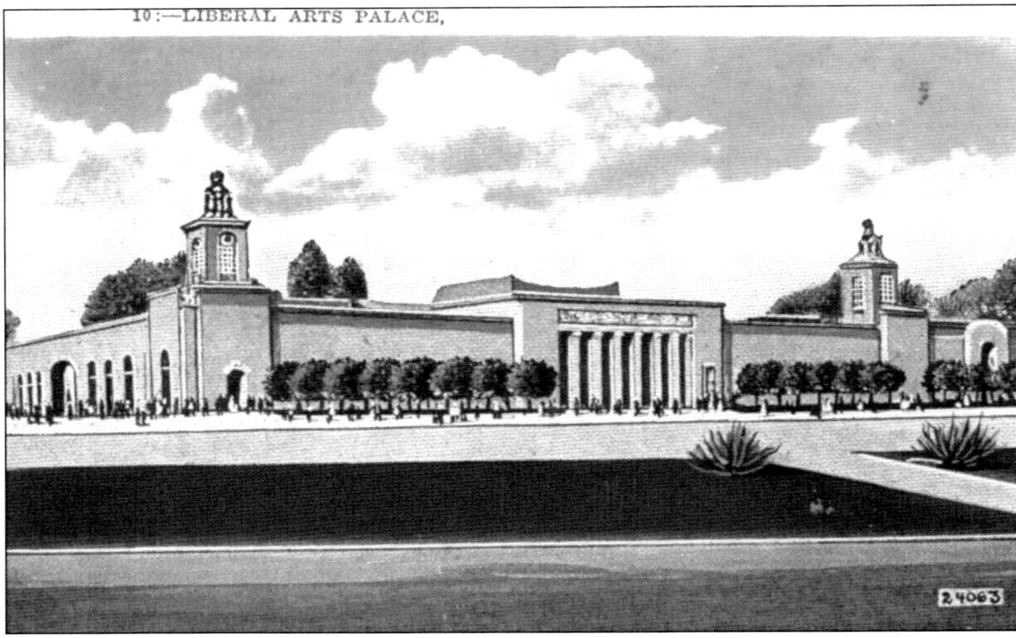

LIBERAL ARTS PALACE. The first of the great exhibition halls that visitors to the exposition encountered was the Palace of Liberal Arts. Standing immediately to the left of the main entrance, this vast building measured 962 feet in length and was 392 feet wide. Construction of this structure began on October 7, 1925, and it was completed on April 2, 1926, at a cost of $950,000. (John D. Cardinell.)

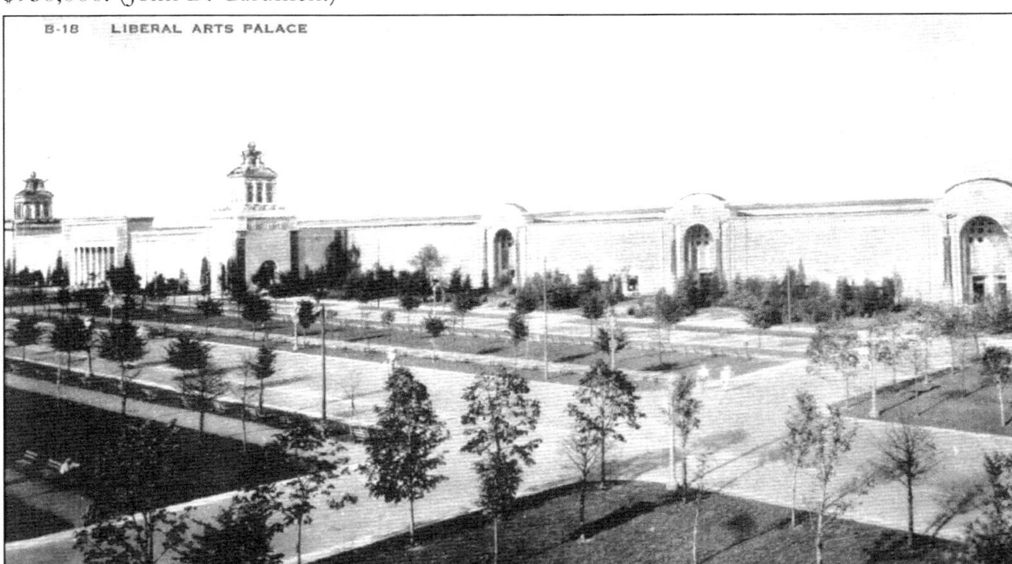

PALACE OF LIBERAL ARTS. Formally titled the Palace of Liberal Arts and Manufactures, this building, like the other great exhibit halls, was designed to provide as much exhibit space as possible. Within this particular structure there was 338,000 square feet, or approximately 7.75 acres of floor space. This was quite an impressive building when one considers that it was only meant to remain until the conclusion of the exposition. (John D. Cardinell.)

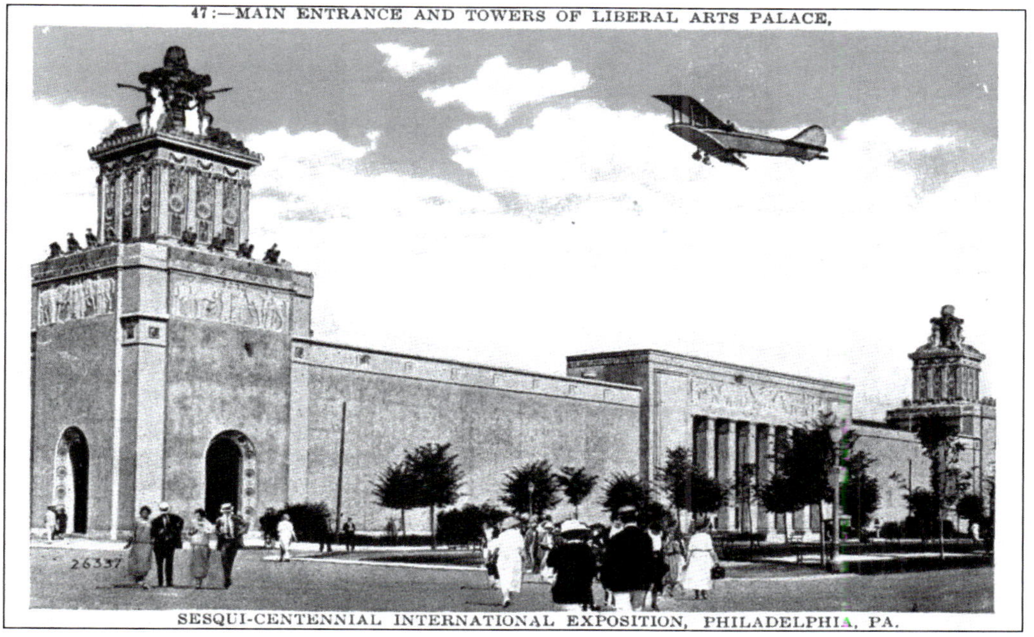

MAIN ENTRANCE AND TOWERS. A front view of the Palace of Liberal Arts, as seen from Broad Street, shows people walking to and from the exhibit hall. Two large towers flank the main entrance into the building, which was located opposite the auditorium. Being that it was situated so close to the entrance, it was often the first building that visitors would explore. (John D. Cardinell.)

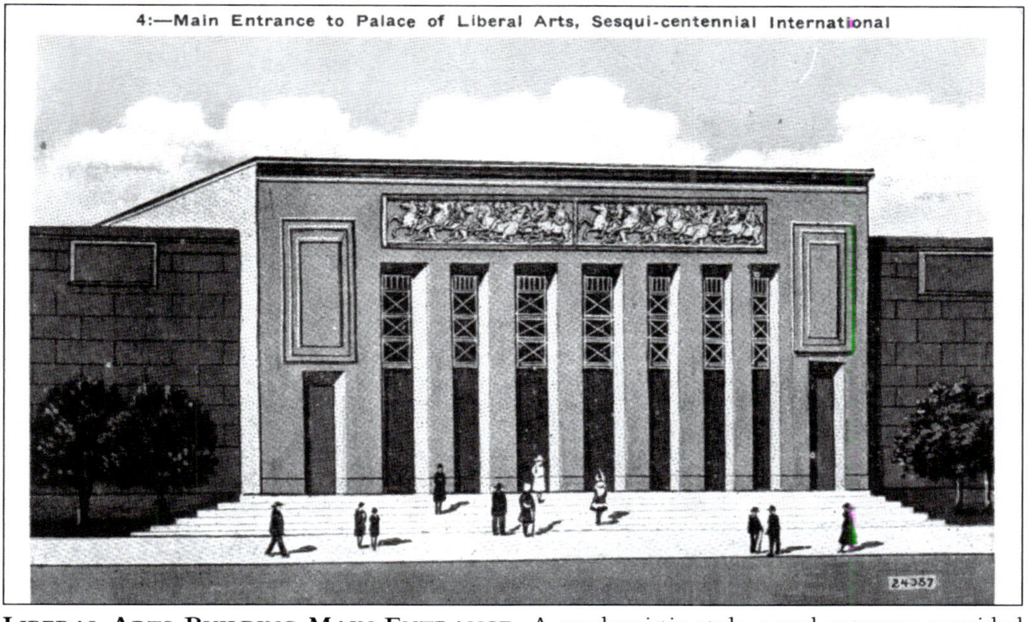

LIBERAL ARTS BUILDING MAIN ENTRANCE. A modernistic-style grand entrance provided access to the Palace of Liberal Arts. Above its tall columns was a carved bas-relief that provided a decorative touch. Thousands of people daily passed though this portal to be amazed by the quantity and quality of exhibits that awaited them. (John D. Cardinell.)

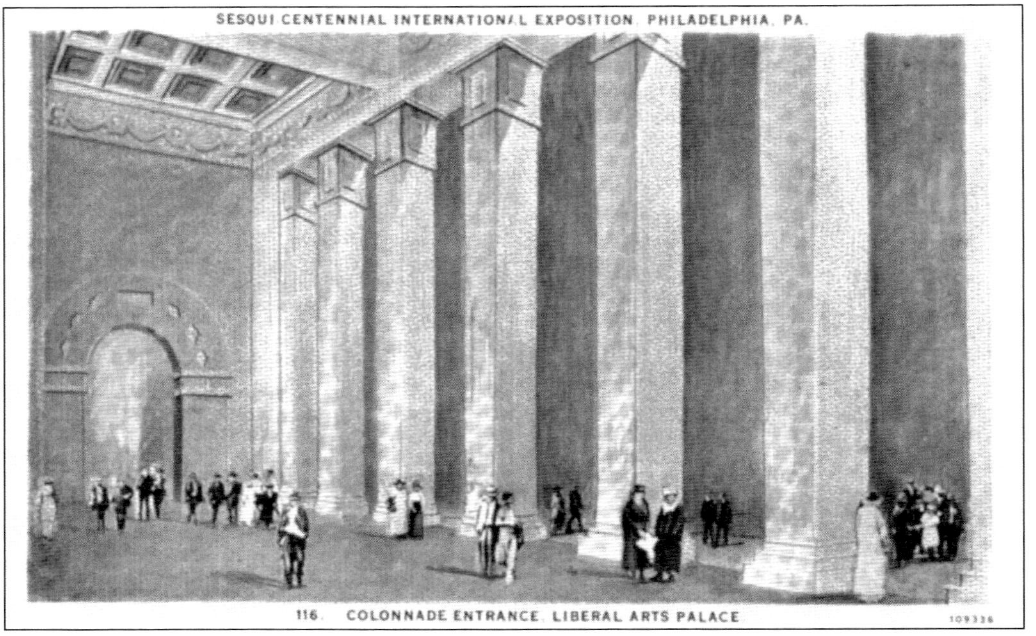

COLONNADE. A spacious, high-ceilinged vestibule, capable of accommodating a great number of visitors to the Palace of Liberal Arts and Manufactures, was located just behind the towering rectangular columns of the main entrance. This architectural feature helped to convey a feeling of grandeur and importance to the building. (John D. Cardinell.)

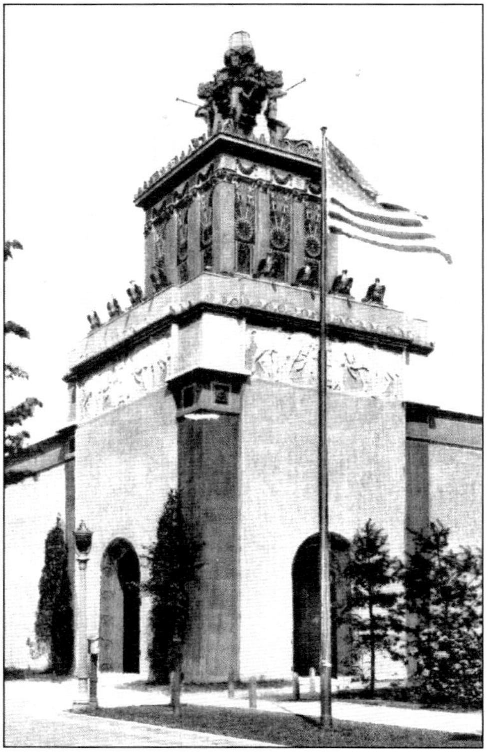

CORNER TOWER. Two massive towers were located along the front facade of the Palace of Liberal Arts. This particular tower occupied the corner at the north end of the building. At its base was a pair of arched entranceways. The upper portions of the tower were heavily decorated and embellished. (John D. Cardinell.)

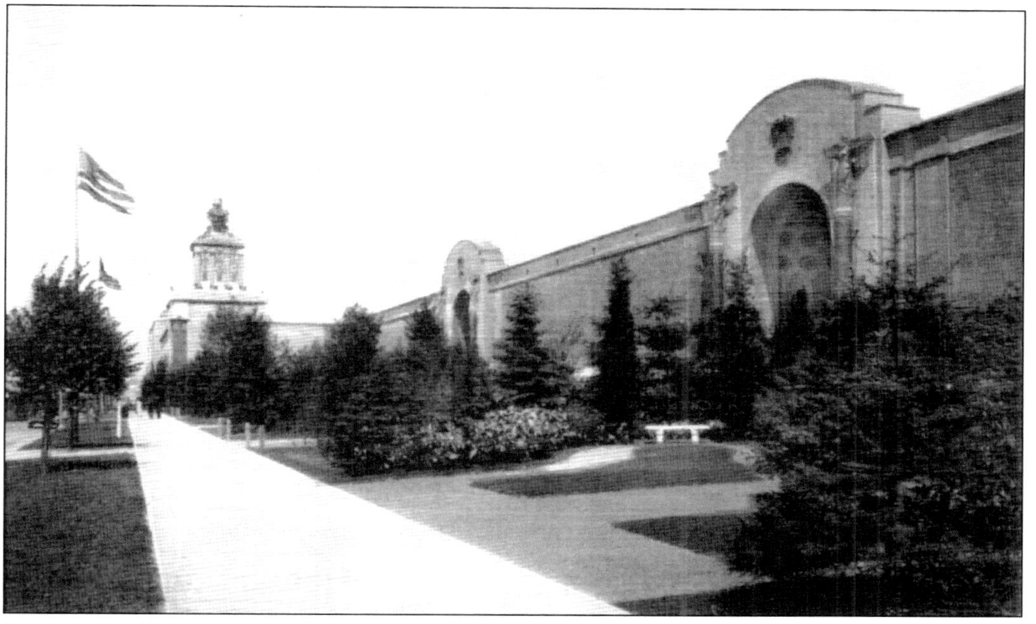

FACADE OF LIBERAL ARTS BUILDING. To make the building somewhat more pleasing to the eye, some portions were enhanced by landscaping. At night, powerful floodlights created deep, lush colors at the entrance, while the towers were set off by even more colorful and brighter lighting effects. In addition, each tower was also topped by a radiant glowing beacon. (John D. Cardinell.)

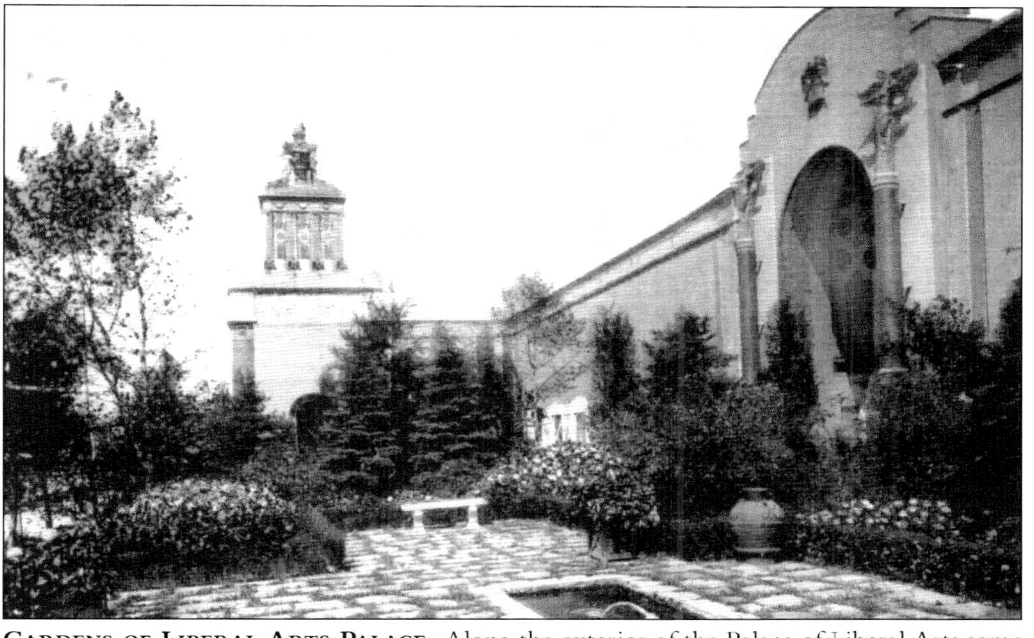

GARDENS OF LIBERAL ARTS PALACE. Along the exterior of the Palace of Liberal Arts some attempt was made to create some places of beauty and serenity. Here was such an inviting spot where a person could sit on a bench and relax for a time among the plots of colorful flowers and greenery. (John D. Cardinell.)

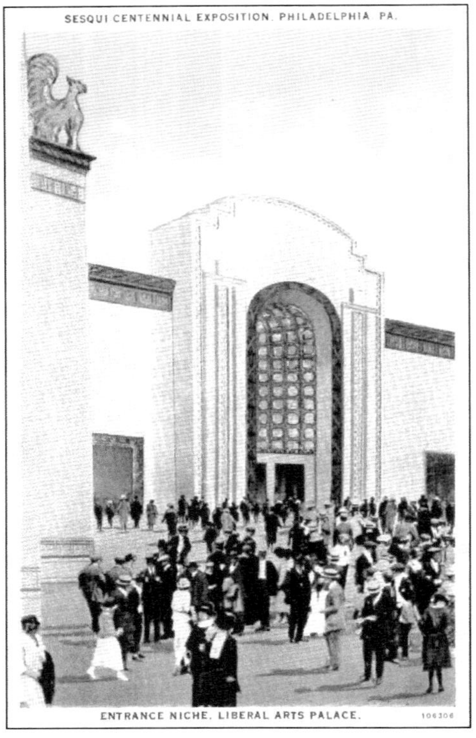

ENTRANCE NICHE. Strategically placed along the length of the building were a number of smaller entranceways. Once inside the Palace of Liberal Arts, visitors would find almost 200 exhibits to inspect. These ranged from simple booths to extensive and elaborately constructed displays. It was reported that it cost over $1 million just to install these exhibits. (John D. Cardinell.)

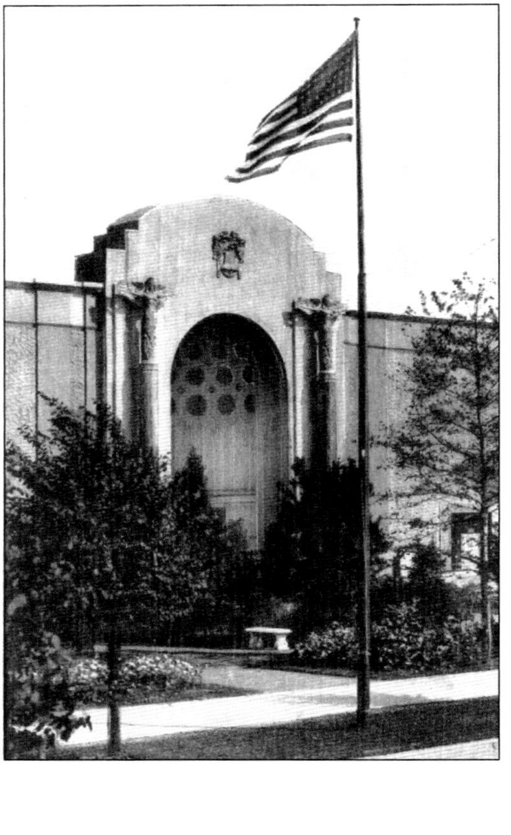

ONE OF THE ENTRANCES. This is a view showing yet another entrance to the Palace of Liberal Arts. The exhibits housed inside the building demonstrated the most up-to-date products, processes, and technologies developed by the nation's leading manufacturers and businesses. So diverse and extensive were the exhibits, it was unlikely that a person could completely investigate all in a single visit. (John D. Cardinell.)

THOMAS A. EDISON. Located on the main aisle of the Palace of Liberal Arts was an oversized model of Thomas A. Edison's invention, the Ediphone. This giant version of Edison's business dictation machine stood more than 18 feet high, while real versions of the machine were on hand and their uses demonstrated daily. Those visiting the exhibit received this souvenir postcard showing a portrait of the famous inventor. (John D. Cardinell.)

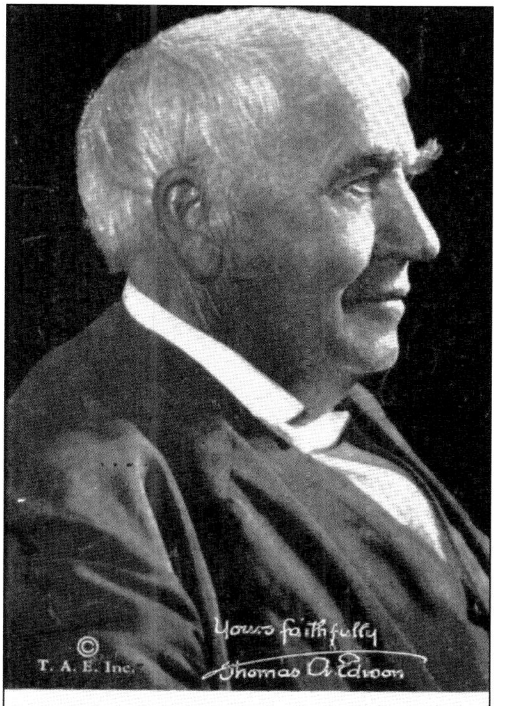

The Ediphone, Edison's New Dictating Machine
Officially adopted for the Exposition

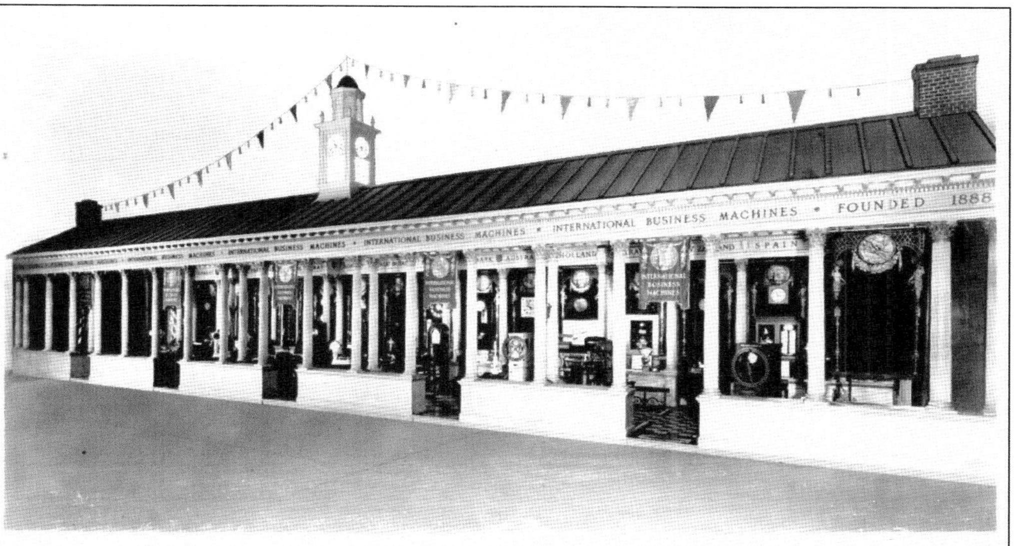

Exhibit of International Business Machines Corporation, Palace of Liberal Arts and Manufactures, Sesquicentennial Exposition, Philadelphia

IBM DISPLAY. Placed on exhibit by IBM for the public to examine were 40 different types of machines the company produced to help businesses save time, labor, and money. Included among the devices were accounting machines, time stamps, watchmen's systems, industrial scales, and even meat slicers and cheese cutters. At the time, IBM had over 300 offices and service locations worldwide and had only adopted its now familiar name in 1924.

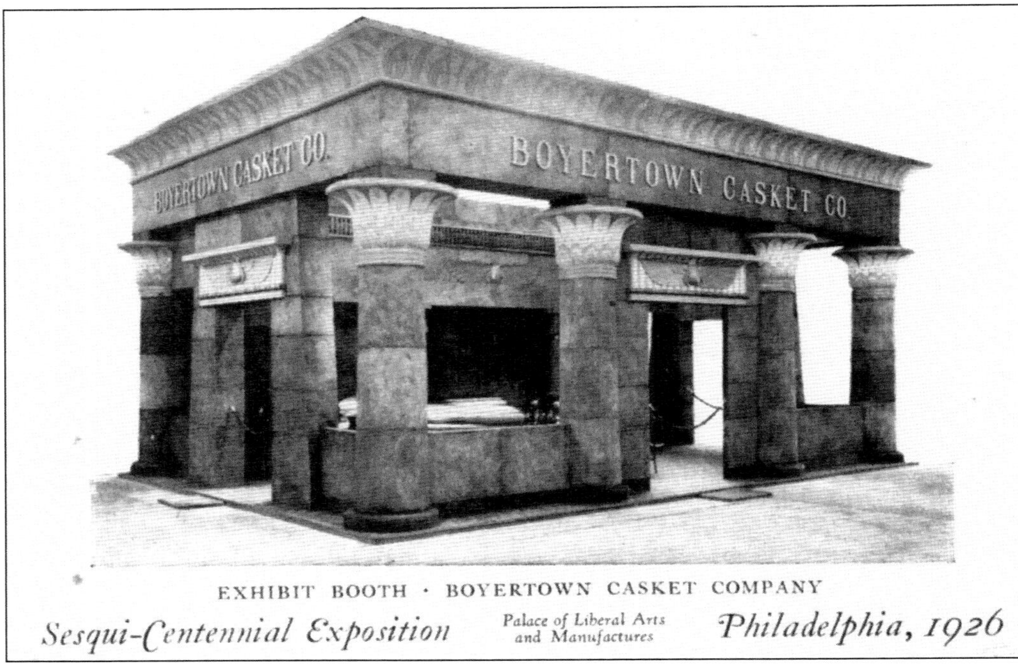

BOYERTOWN CASKET COMPANY. This mausoleum-like exhibit booth was used by the Boyertown Casket Company to display a number of its burial casket models to the public. Dating back to 1893, this company headquartered in Boyertown was one of the country's leading manufacturers of caskets and had been a major supplier to the military during World War I.

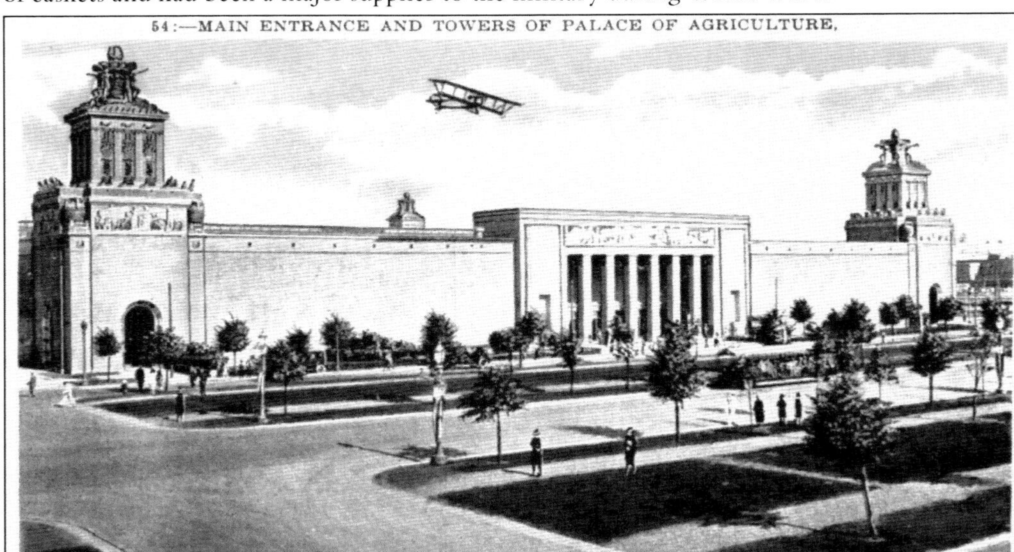

PALACE OF AGRICULTURE AND FOREIGN EXHIBITS. Construction of this enormous exhibit hall was begun on September 15, 1925, and was completed on March 6, 1926. Largest of all the buildings to be built for the exposition, it cost approximately $1 million to erect. Its dimensions were 970 feet by 460 feet, which gave it 367,500 square feet, more than eight acres, of floor space for its exhibits. (John D. Cardinell.)

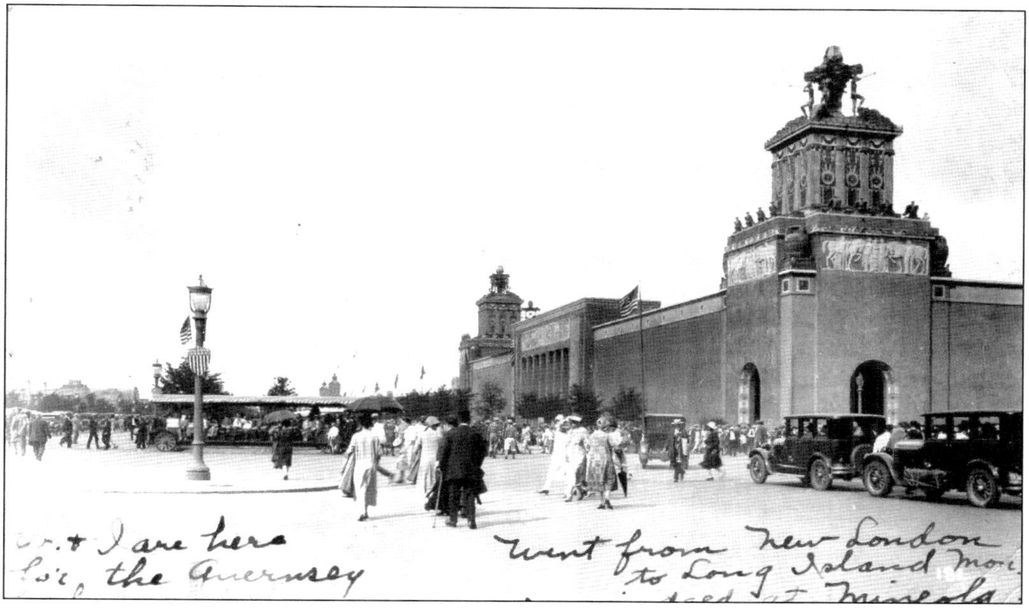

PALACE OF AGRICULTURE. This marvelous exhibition hall was placed just south of the Palace of Liberal Arts, with the Tower of Light positioned between them. Its exterior design was almost identical to that of its neighboring exhibition hall. Housed within its walls were displays related to all types of agricultural products as well as varied goods from around the world.

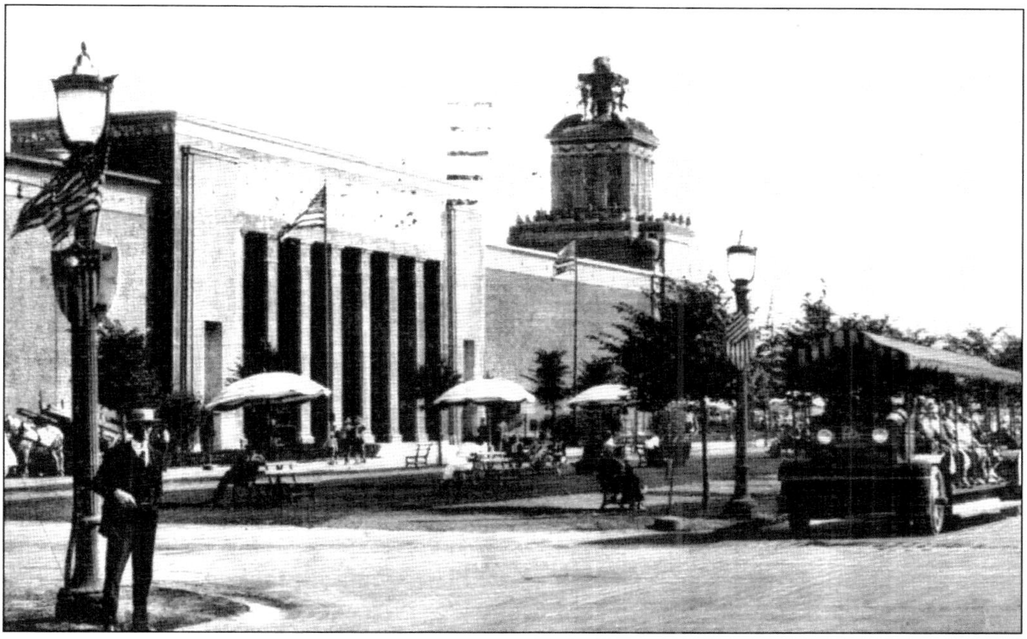

AGRICULTURAL BUILDING. This postcard view shows the main entrance to the vast Agricultural and Foreign Exhibits Building. A truly international building, it housed exhibits from 14 foreign nations as well as from regions all around the United States, including four states, six cities, and two counties. The displays were very diversified and in many cases quite elaborate. (John D. Cardinell.)

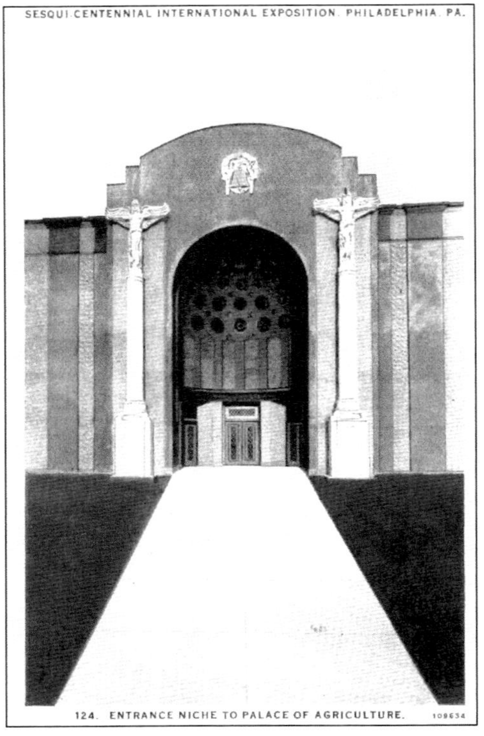

ENTRANCE. Upon entering the great Palace of Agriculture, there was much to see. At the northern end of the building were the foreign exhibits, ranging from Japanese silk making to merchandise typical of the finest French stores. The central area of the hall was devoted to displays by numerous civic organizations. While in the southern end of the building could be found all those exhibits related to food and agriculture. (John D. Cardinell.)

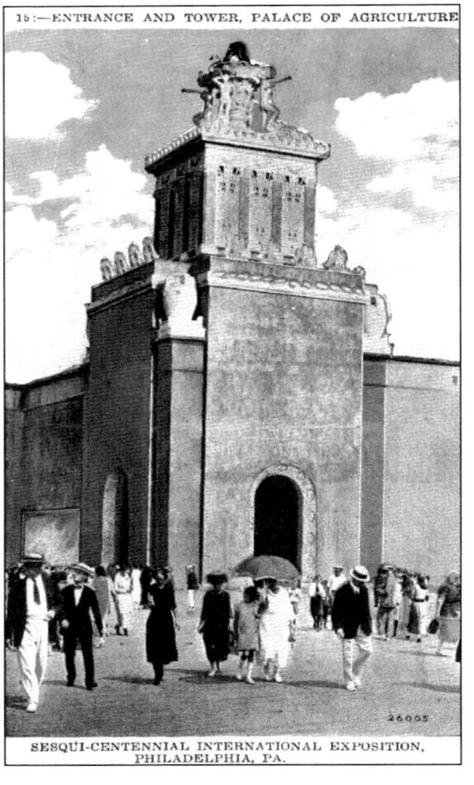

ENTRANCE AND TOWER. At the corners of the Palace of Agriculture were massive towers, which also included entrances into the building. There was no cost to the public to enter and experience the magnitude of exhibits that were housed here. The official tour book stated that there was more in this building than could be seen in a single day's visit. (John D. Cardinell.)

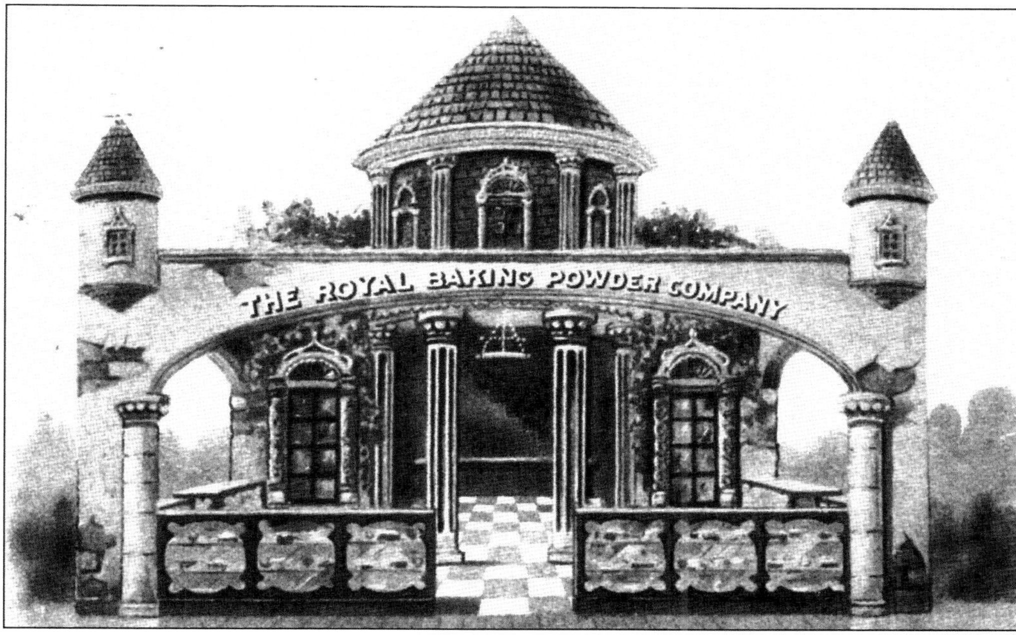

ROYAL BAKING POWDER COMPANY. Resembling a 17th-century French Renaissance castle, the Royal Baking Powder Company display was eye-catching. Here eight costumed young ladies distributed souvenir advertising fans and also served up molds of Royal fruit-flavored gelatin to passersby. This same company had exhibited its products at the Centennial Exposition a half century earlier.

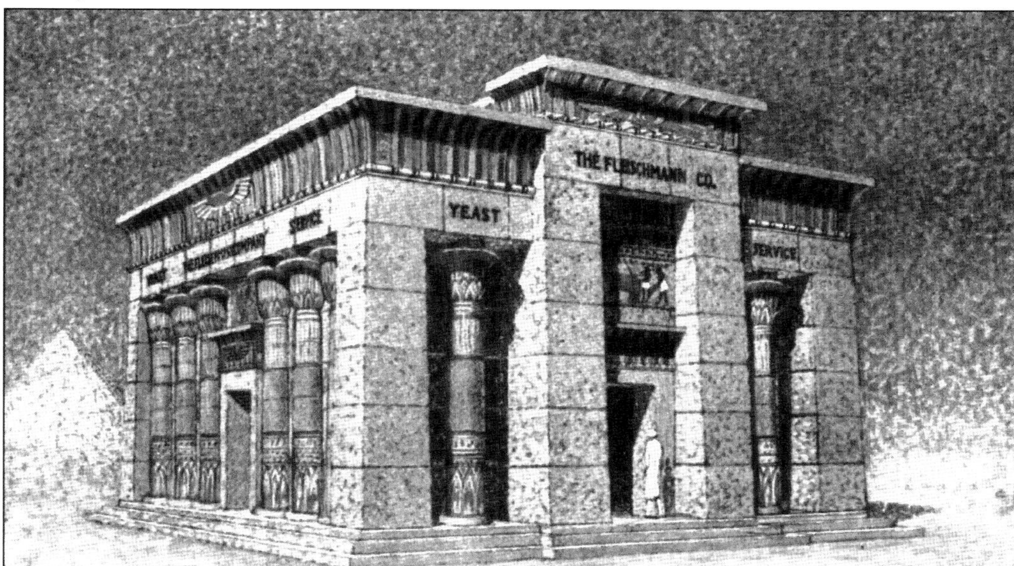

FLEISCHMANN COMPANY DISPLAY. The Fleischmann Company, renowned producers of yeast and related products, sponsored an interesting and educational exhibit that it housed inside a miniature Egyptian temple. A detailed mural chronicled the story of baking, and the uses of yeast, throughout the history of mankind. In addition, there was a display of balsa wood, which the company used in preserving and shipping yeast. (Fleischmann Company.)

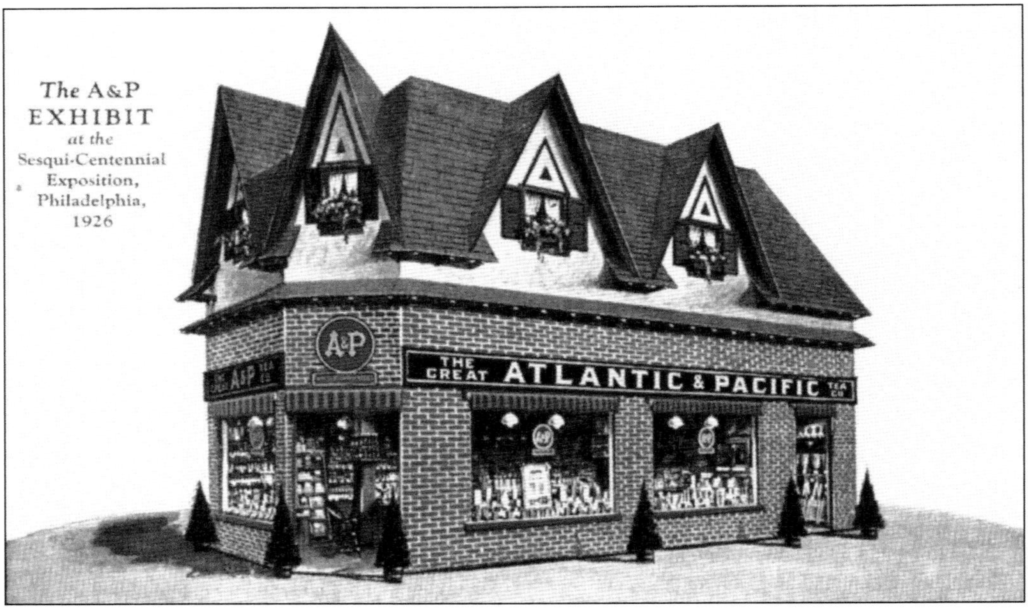

A&P Exhibit. Constructed on the floor of the Palace of Agriculture was a mock-up of an A&P grocery store. Within the store were samples of virtually every product normally found in one of its sales outlets. This exhibit gave people an indication as to the great variety of items that they might find in one of their neighborhood Great Atlantic and Pacific Tea Company stores.

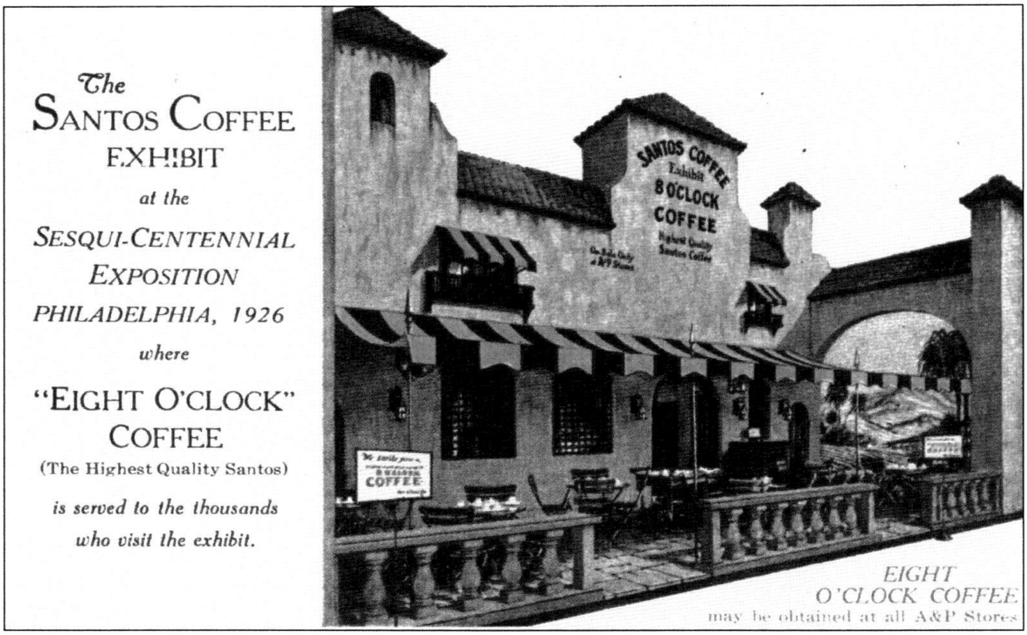

Santos Coffee Exhibit. A second exhibit sponsored by the A&P Company was for Santos Coffee, the producer of the well-known brand of Eight O' Clock Coffee. This display was a charming replica of a Brazilian coffeehouse. As a means of advertising its product, the public was invited to sit and enjoy a free cup of coffee.

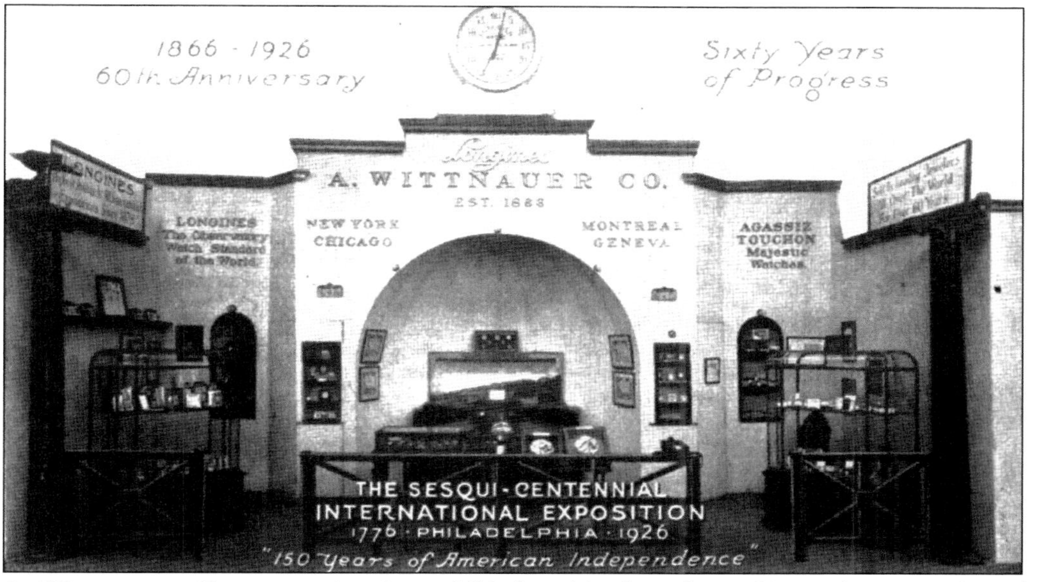

A. Wittnauer Company. Another exhibit found in the Palace of Agriculture was that of the A. Wittnauer Company of New York, manufacturers of Longines watches. It imported $250,000 worth of timepieces from Switzerland for its display. Also available for viewing were watches and clocks made by the company's European subsidiaries. A fine collection of antique chronometers helped to make this an interesting exhibit. (A. Wittnauer.)

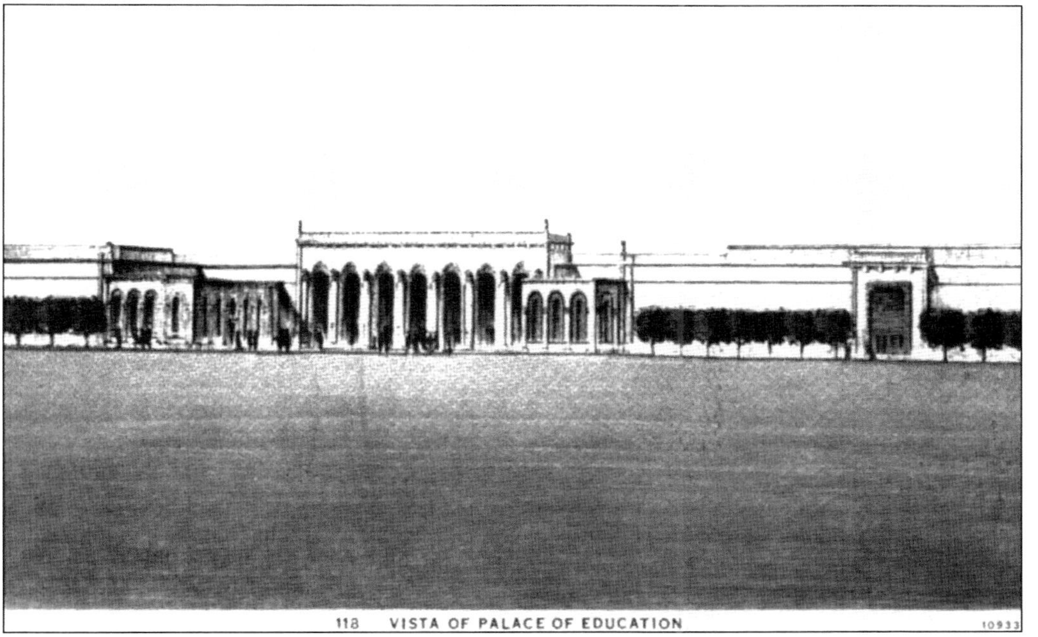

Palace of Education and Social Economy. Located on Pattison Avenue just west of Broad Street, this exhibit hall measured 526 feet by 210 feet and had over 100,000 square feet of floor space. Exhibits here represented the evolution, history, and progress of education as well as those concerns related to the "betterment, advancement, and enhancement of humanity." (John D. Cardinell.)

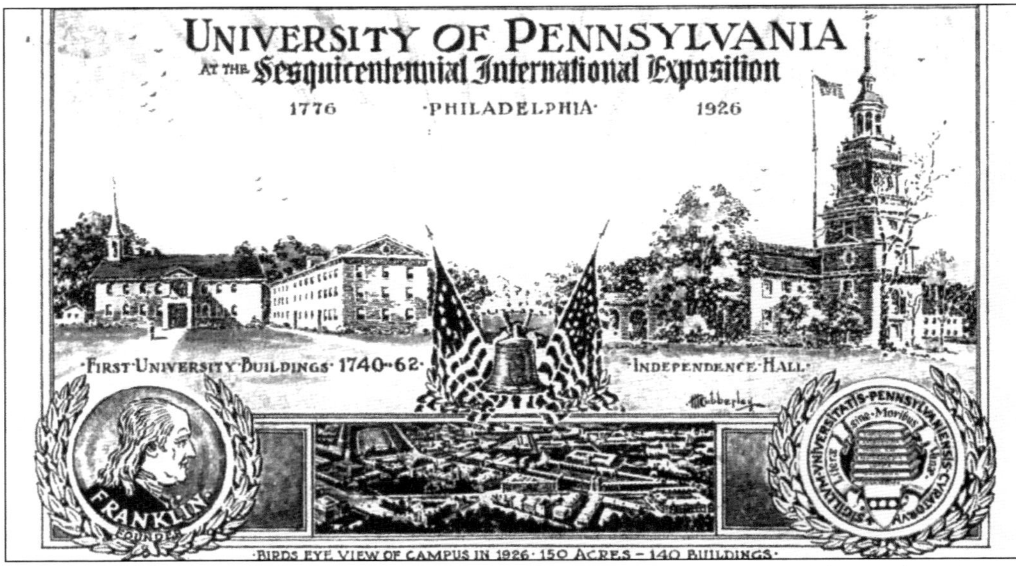

UNIVERSITY OF PENNSYLVANIA. Numerous colleges and universities had exhibits in the Palace of Education. The University of Pennsylvania had quite an extensive and diverse exhibit that included scientific instruments and specimens, original papers of famous men of the Colonial period, historic law documents, and even a page from a Gutenberg Bible. Each of the university's departments, as well as many student organizations, were represented. (Gragor-Connery Company.)

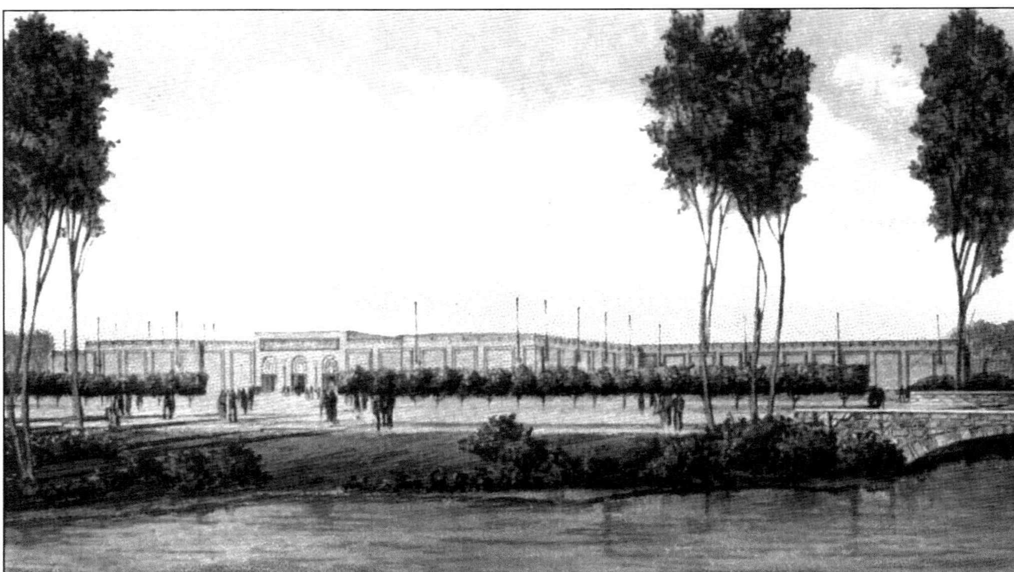

PALACE OF FINE ARTS. Devoted to the exhibition of national and international artwork, this building was situated so that its main entrance faced the Russian Pavilion on Edgewater Lake. The interior was divided into 48 galleries, which provided over one mile of wall space. This allowed for the display of more than 8,000 paintings as well as countless prints, sculptures, carvings, and tapestries. (John D. Cardinell.)

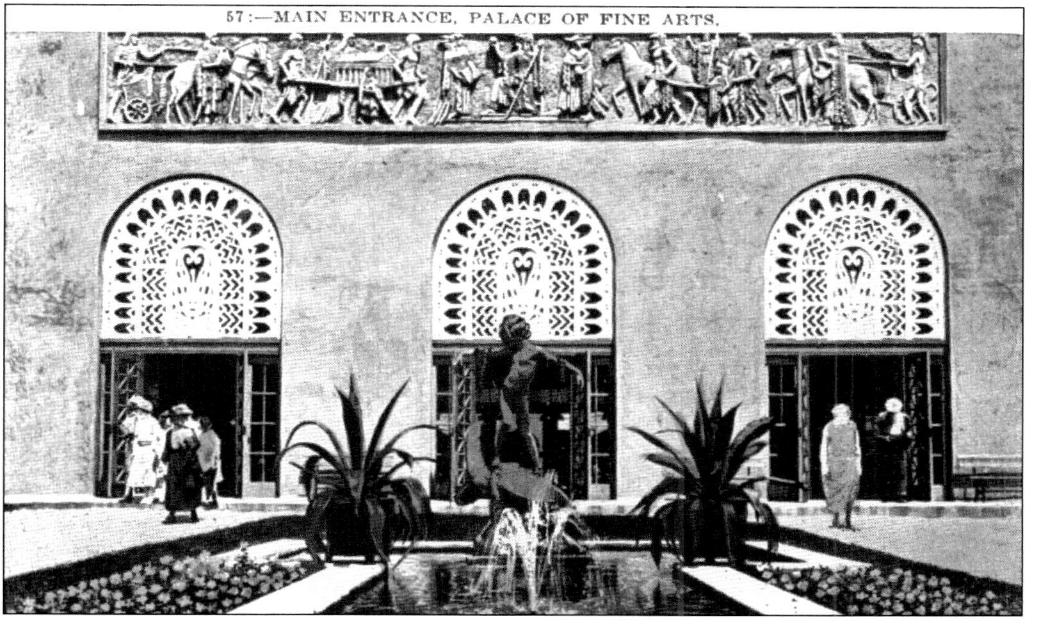

ENTRANCE TO FINE ARTS BUILDING. Leading up to the main entrance of the Palace of Fine Arts was a landscaped walkway. In front of the building was an ornamental pool containing the statue titled *A Seaweed Fountain*, the work of Beatrice Fenton (1887–1983) of Philadelphia. After the exposition, this was placed in Fairmount Park. On the wall above the doors was an intricate bas-relief created by Raphael Sabatini (1898–1985). (John D. Cardinell.)

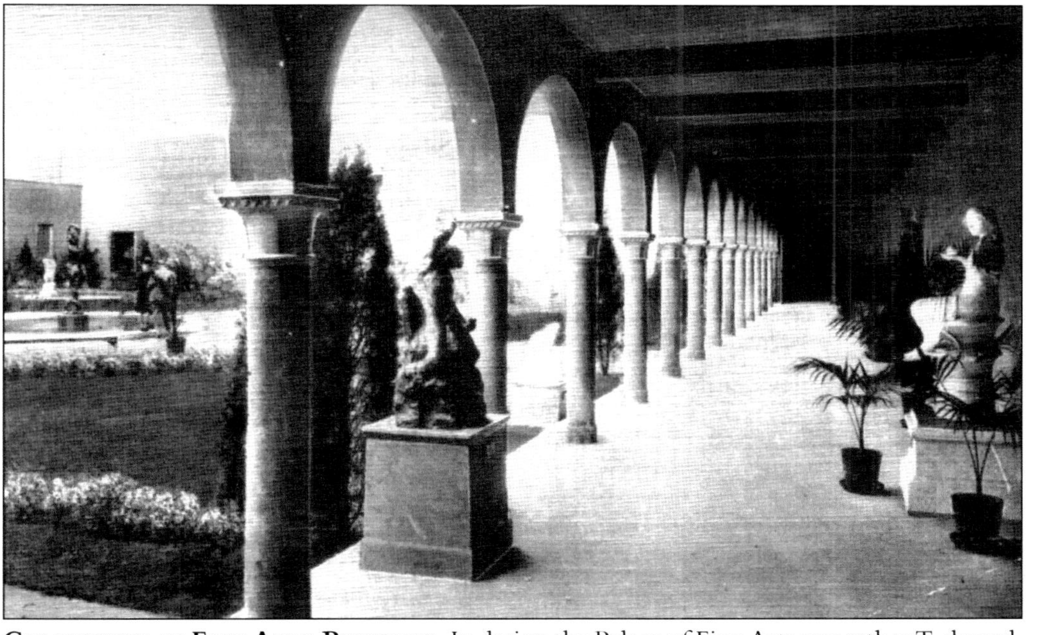

COLONNADE AT FINE ARTS BUILDING. In design the Palace of Fine Arts was rather T-shaped, with great attention being taken to provide for the best possible lighting. An open central courtyard, measuring 120 feet square, was found at the very heart of the building. Seen here is a colonnade that was built along one side of this courtyard. (John D. Cardinell.)

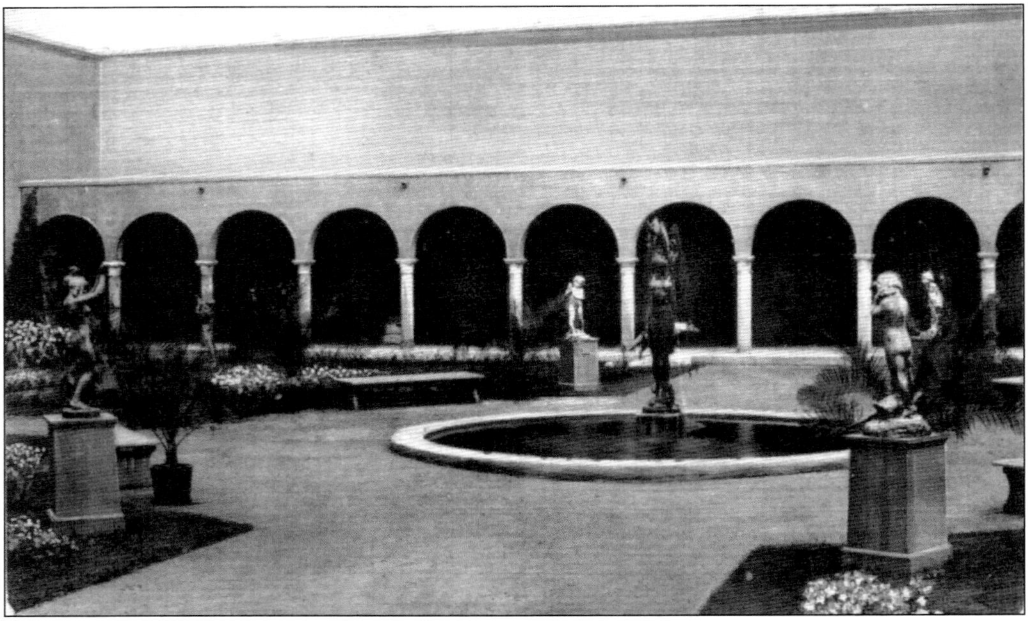

COURTYARD OF FINE ARTS BUILDING. This view looks toward the colonnade from the main entrance to the courtyard. In the middle of this open space was a small circular fountain, which was surrounded by landscaped grassy areas and colorful flower beds. Placed here and there about the open quad were a number of sculptures by various artists. (John D. Cardinell.)

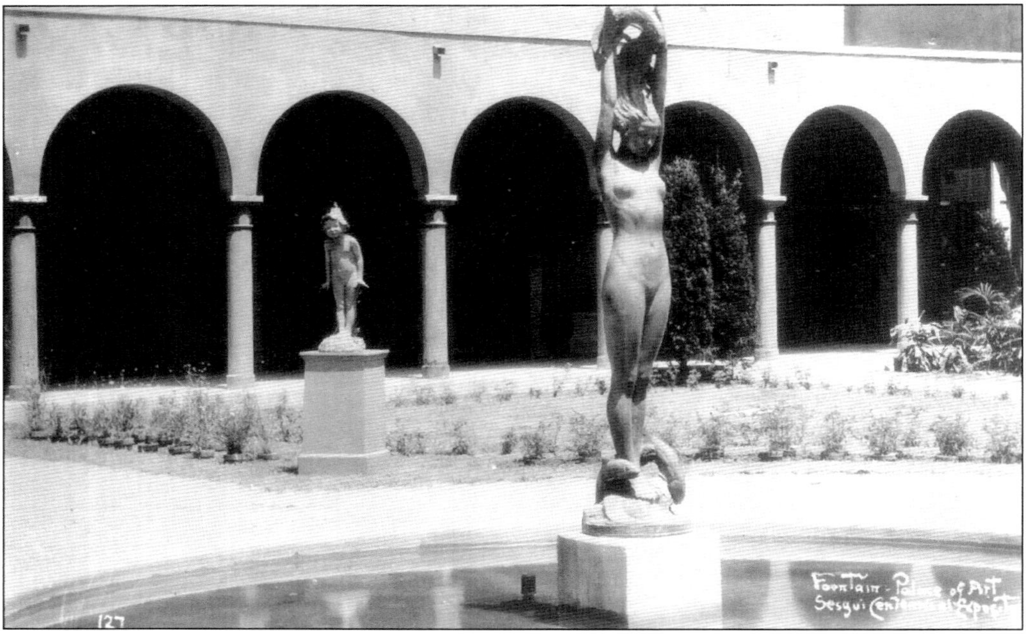

FOUNTAIN AT PALACE OF FINE ARTS. The sculpture titled *Glint of the Sea*, by Chester Beach (1881–1956), stood in the fountain found in the central courtyard of the Palace of Fine Arts. This was but one of over 400 pieces of sculpture exhibited in and around this building, many by some of the most renowned names in the art world.

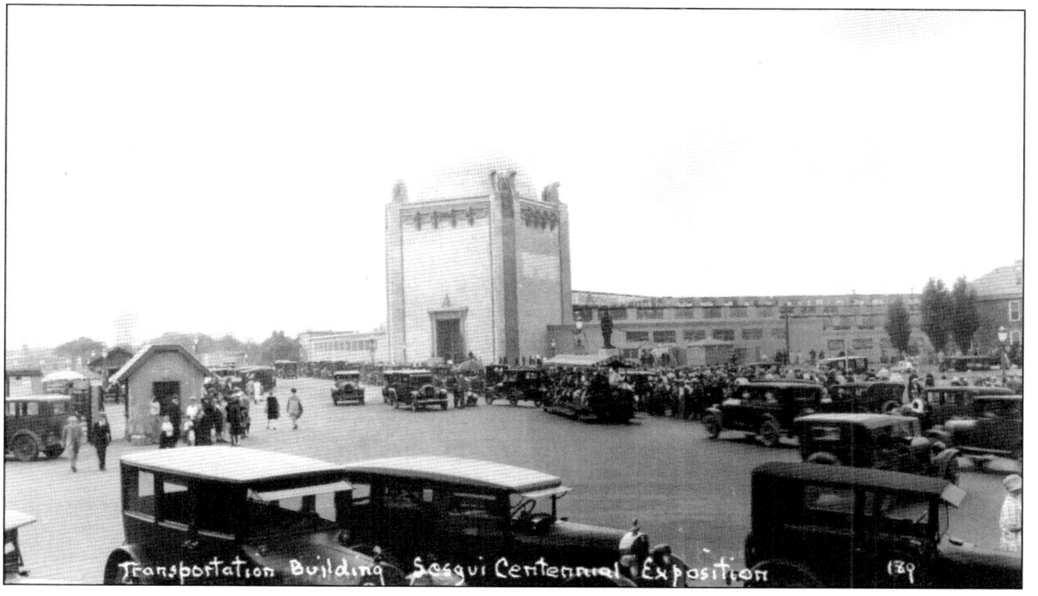

U.S. GOVERNMENT BUILDING. At the south end of Broad Street, near the entrance to the navy yard, was the Palace of the United States Government, Machinery, and Transportation. With half of its 321,800 square feet of floor space devoted to government exhibits, and the rest used for industrial displays sponsored by more than 30 manufacturers, this exhibition hall was more commonly referred to as either the Government or Transportation Building.

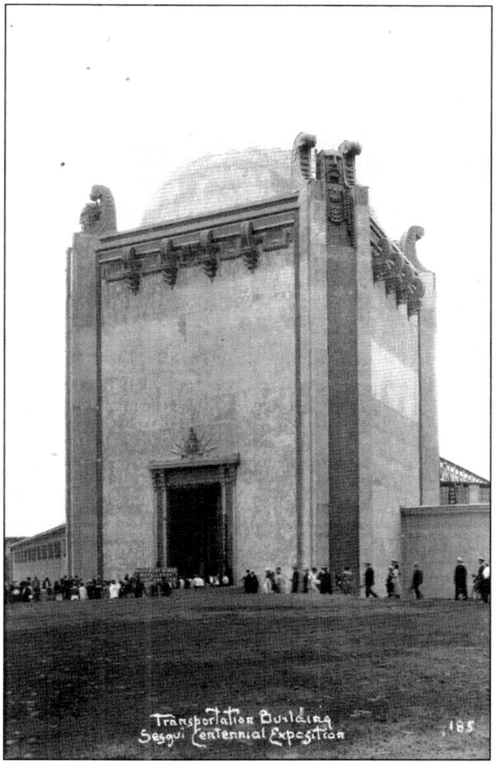

TRANSPORTATION BUILDING. Completed in late July at a cost of $850,000, this building measured 880 feet by 400 feet. It had three entrances, including this one in its great tower. The massive tower was visible from most areas of the exposition grounds. With its extensive and diverse exhibits, the building was enormously popular with visitors.

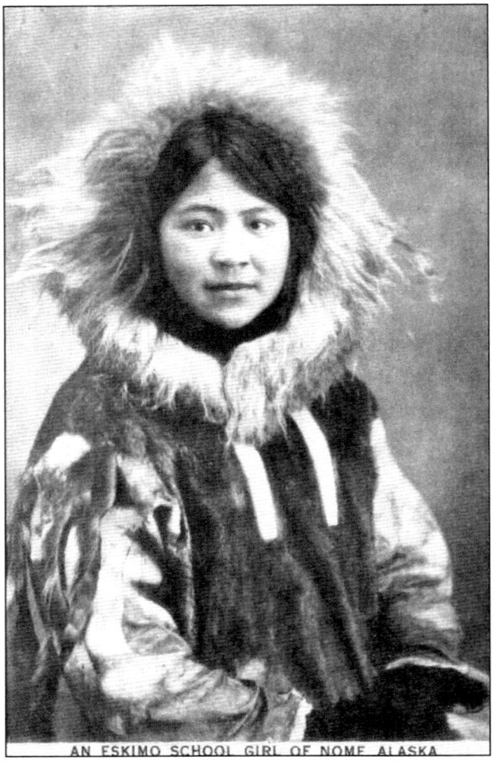

ESKIMO SCHOOLGIRL. One of the displays set up by the U.S. Department of the Interior in the Government Building pertained to the duties of its Bureau of Education. Among the responsibilities of this bureau was the supervision of education and medical care for the native Alaskan peoples. Shown on this government-produced postcard is the image of a young Eskimo schoolgirl from Nome, Alaska. (U.S. Department of the Interior.)

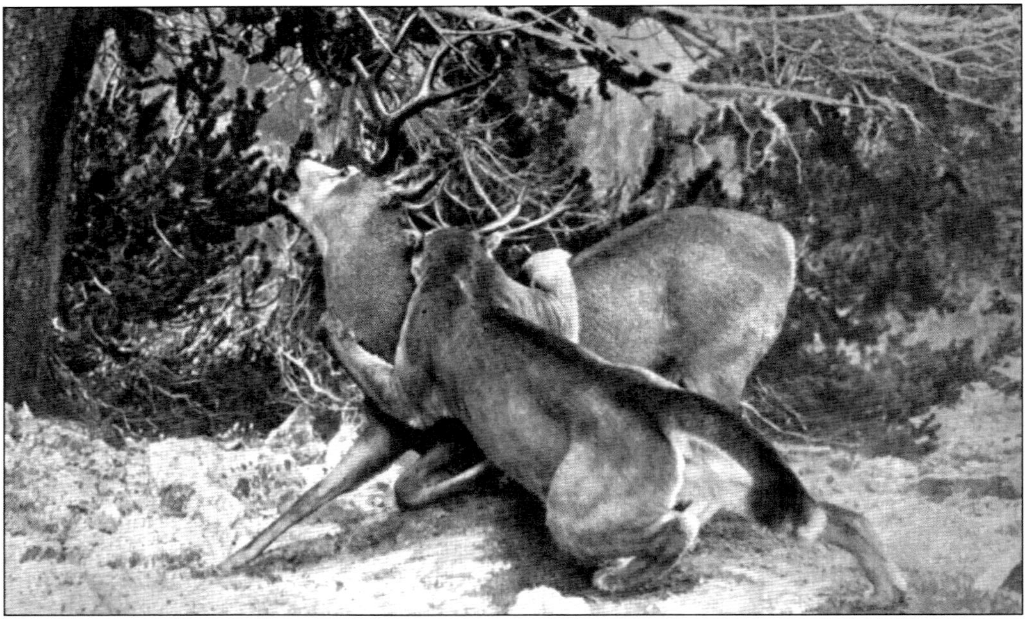

"DESTROYER OF GAME." One of the displays created by the U.S. Biological Survey, a division of the Department of the Interior, included specimens of native wildlife. Part of the exhibit was this very realistic scene of a mountain lion killing a deer entitled "Destroyer of Game." These animals were professionally mounted by the Jonas Brothers of Denver.

Four

State and Foreign Nations Buildings

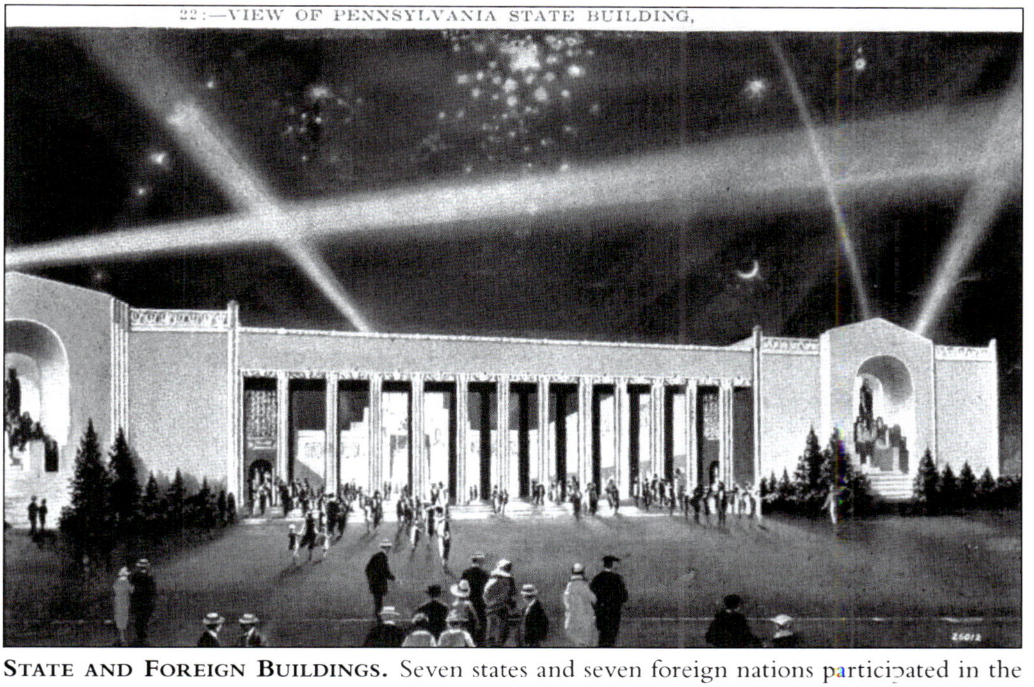

State and Foreign Buildings. Seven states and seven foreign nations participated in the Sesqui-Centennial International Exposition by officially erecting buildings. Others were represented by structures found within the large exhibit palaces. Many states were prevented from participation because their legislatures were not in session to appropriate funds when the site for the exposition was finally selected. Seen here is the building representing the host state of Pennsylvania. (John D. Cardinell.)

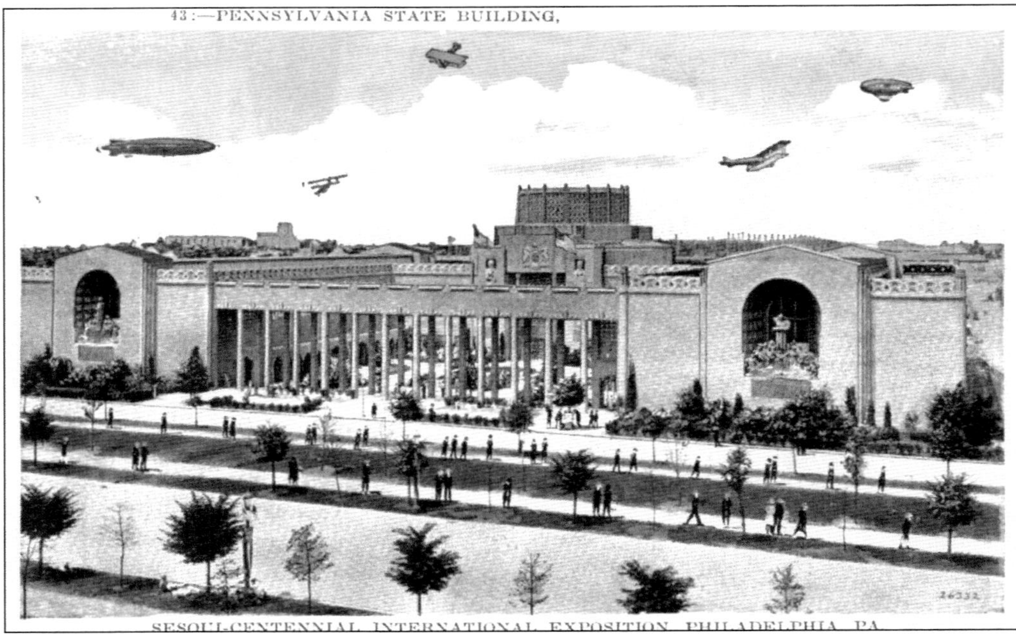

VIEW OF THE PENNSYLVANIA BUILDING. Erected on the corner of Broad Street and Pattison Avenue, the Pennsylvania Building occupied a prime location. To pay for its construction, the state approved $750,000 in funding, of which $460,000 went to its actual building. The architect chosen for the project was Ralph B. Bencker (1883–1961), whose design utilized modernistic styling. (John D. Cardinell.)

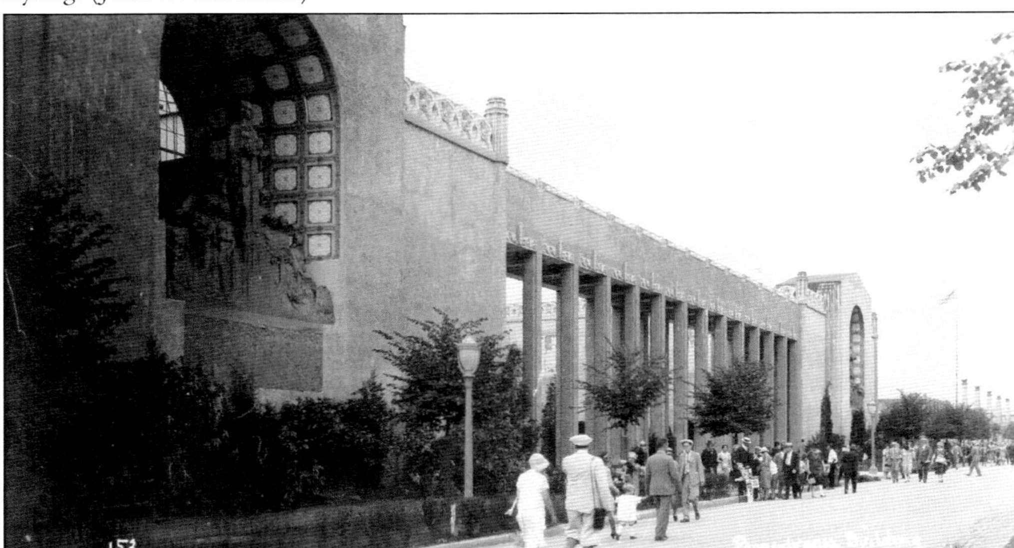

PENNSYLVANIA BUILDING. The contract for putting up the building was awarded to the F. W. Mark Construction Company. Formally opened on June 14, 1926, the Pennsylvania Building was referred to as "the gem of the exposition" by the president of the Sesqui-Centennial Exhibition Association. It consisted of two large exhibit halls situated at each end of the building, an auditorium, administrative offices, and a spacious central courtyard.

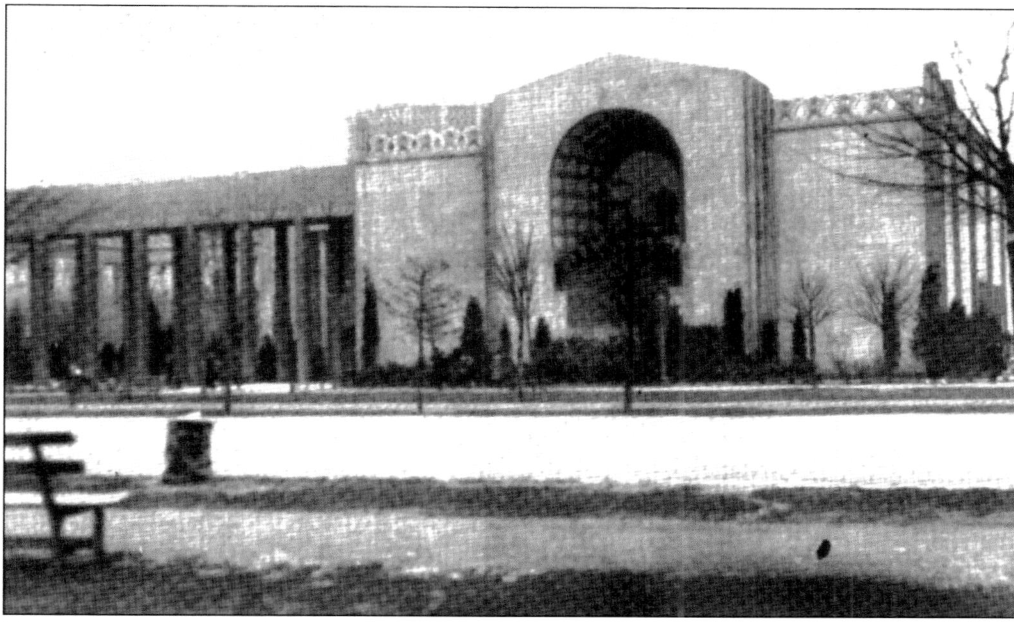

EXHIBITION HALLS. The two exhibition halls, which were positioned at opposite ends of the building, each measured 225 feet in length and 93 feet in width with a height of 43 feet. Inside these portions of the building, the walls were decorated with painted murals, while the floor space was devoted to displays related to the state's history, industries, agriculture, transportation, natural resources, and more. (W. J. Gambino.)

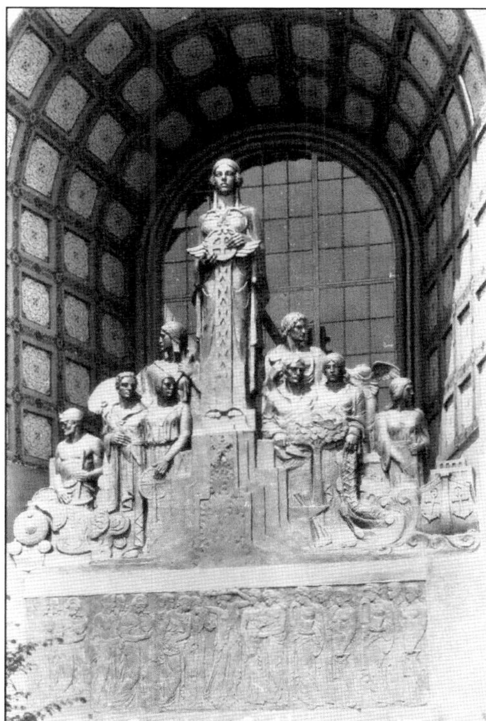

SCULPTURE OF *INDUSTRY*. Built into the exterior wall of the Pennsylvania Building's exhibition halls were large niches designed to hold sizeable groupings of sculpture. At the one gable end was this sculptural group, symbolic of the diversity and importance of industry in the commonwealth of Pennsylvania. These significant pieces of artwork surely captured the interest of many of those who passed by.

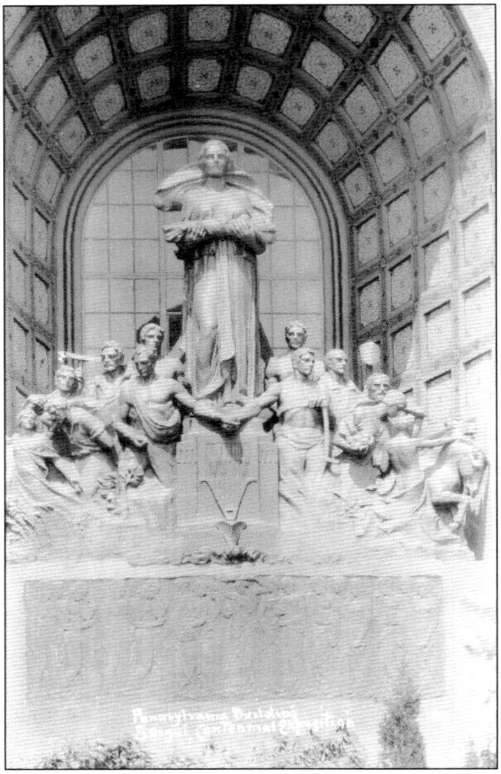

SCULPTURE OF *AGRICULTURE*. Placed into the recess at the opposite end of the building from the statues dedicated to industry was this sculpted group of figures titled *Agriculture*. Its purpose was to represent the role and significance that agriculture plays in the state of Pennsylvania. This was yet another masterful piece of artwork that was put on view for the public to appreciate.

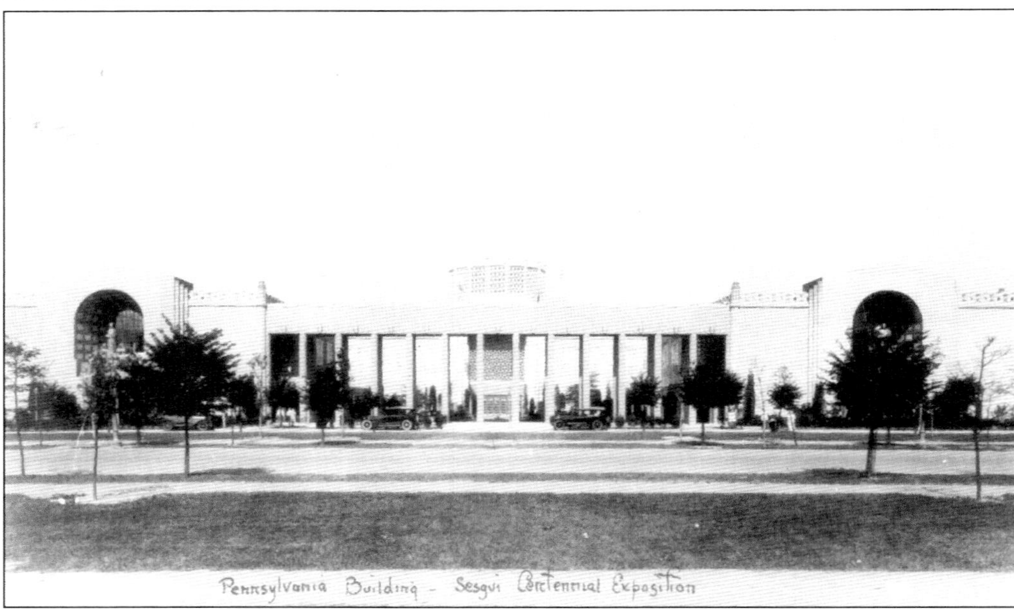

COLONNADES OF THE PENNSYLVANIA BUILDING. As seen from Broad Street, the Pennsylvania Building had 13 distinctive colonnades, each of which represented one of the original colonies. Once passing through this row of tall pillars, visitors entered an open courtyard that measured 120 feet square. From here it was on to the main entrance to the building.

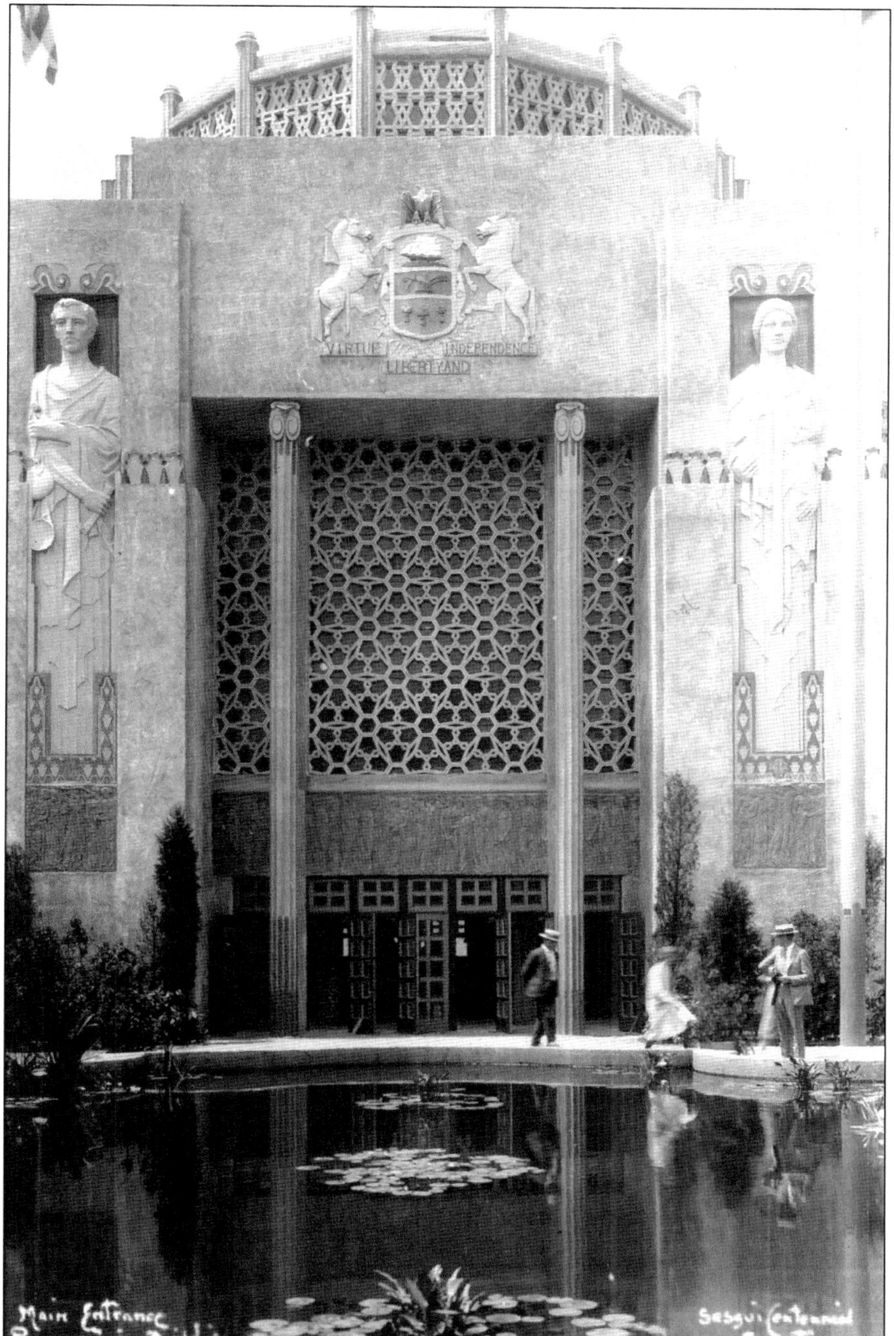

MAIN ENTRY. An impressive, towering main entrance led into the reception rotunda. On either side of the doorway stood two enormous sculpted figures of a male and female, which symbolized the equality of the sexes. Above the doors the plastered facade was embellished with "interwoven Keystone designs filled with glass." While high above the portal, carved into the colorful cement, was the coat of arms of the Commonwealth of Pennsylvania.

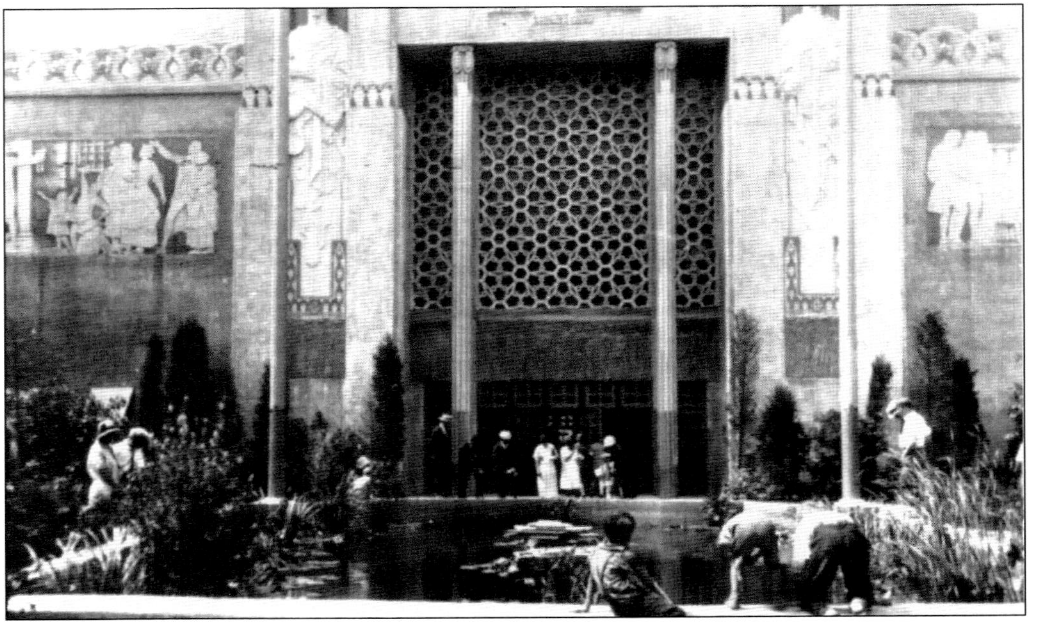

Reflecting Pool. A major feature of the courtyard was the relatively large, keystone-shaped reflecting pool that was placed directly in front of the main entrance. The pool was filled with decorative aquatic plants as well as colorful goldfish, which evidently captured the interest of the three young boys seen here at the water's edge. (W. J. Gambino.)

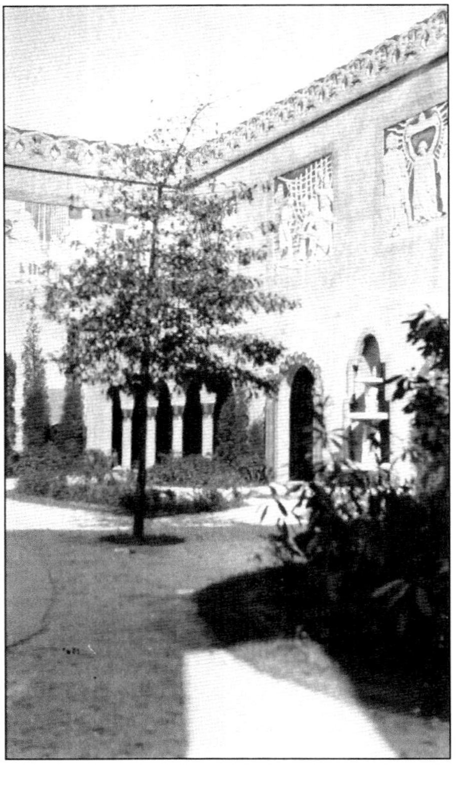

Courtyard of Pennsylvania Building. This postcard view, looking toward one corner of the central courtyard, shows some of the landscaping that was done to make the area more aesthetic. On the upper walls can be seen some of the many carved murals that embellished the exterior of the building. It was the attention given to details in the building's decoration that helped to make it one of the finest at the exposition.

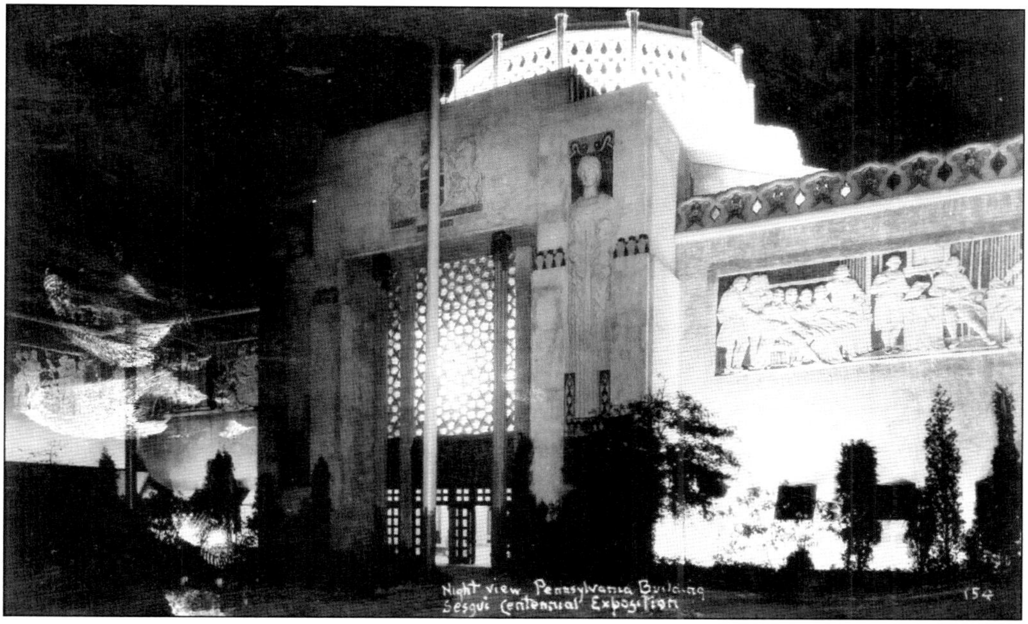

NIGHT VIEW OF PENNSYLVANIA BUILDING. At nighttime, the Pennsylvania Building took on quite a different quality when its rose-colored exterior walls were illuminated by reflected lights. The 16-sided, 75-foot-tall rotunda was given special lighting to create the impression that the tower was a glowing torch. Also highlighted at night were the exterior murals depicting important events in the history of the state.

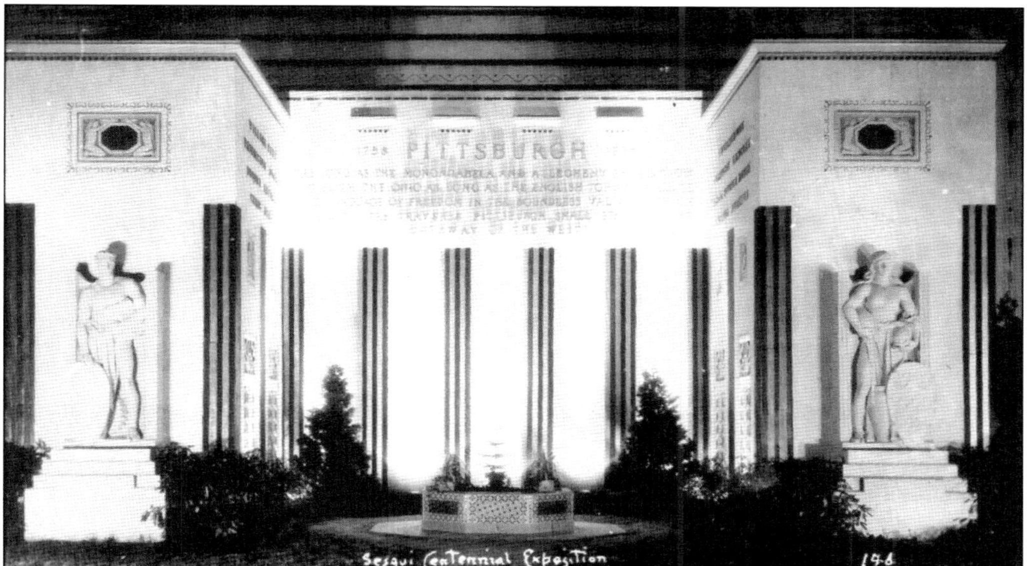

PITTSBURGH BUILDING. Seen here illuminated by floodlights at night is the Pittsburgh Building, the only building to be erected by an individual city on the grounds. Near the main entrance and just south of the auditorium, this structure was designed in what was considered to be the modern American architectural style. Costing nearly $100,000 to construct, it was regarded as one of the gems of the exposition.

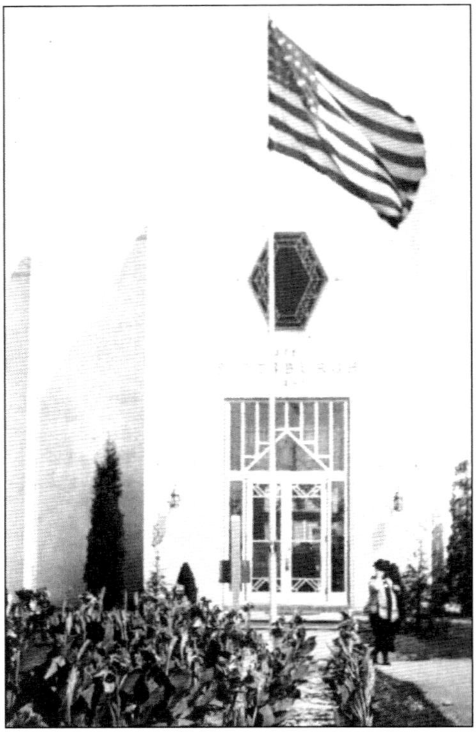

Entrance to Pittsburgh Building. Upon entering this building, visitors encountered a relatively large lobby from which they could access any of the three additional rooms on the first floor. One of these rooms was a small auditorium where movies detailing the city's industries were shown, while two additional exhibit rooms held displays related to famous people who came from Pittsburgh. The second floor held a lounge and restrooms. (W. J. Gambino.)

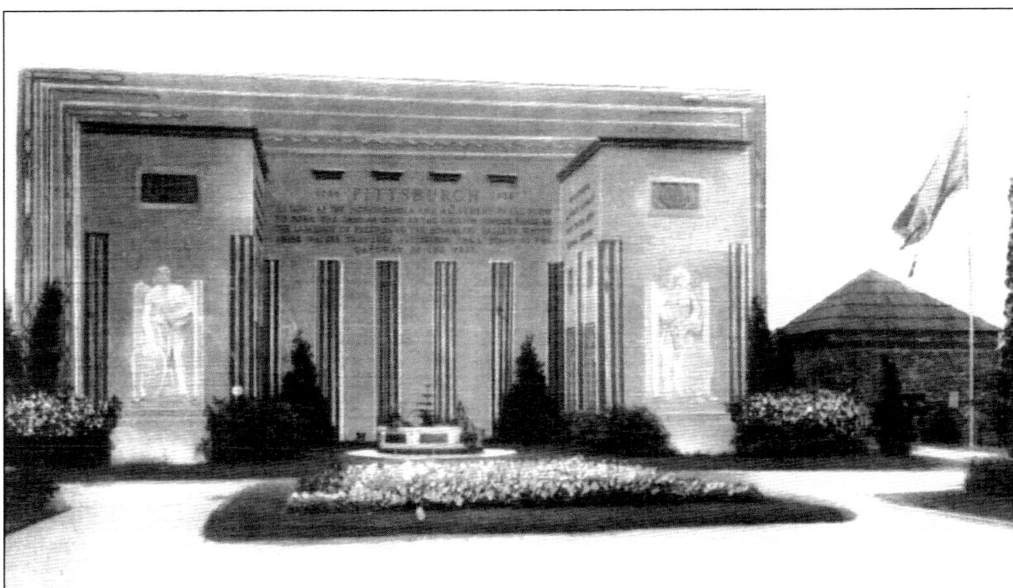

Blockhouse. Just to the right of the Pittsburgh Building stood a second structure sponsored by the city. This was a reconstruction of a blockhouse, similar to those that had been present at Fort Pitt during the French and Indian Wars. Here a re-creation of a Native American attack was held on September 23 as part of a pageant honoring Pittsburgh Day at the Sesqui-Centennial International Exposition. (John D. Cardinell.)

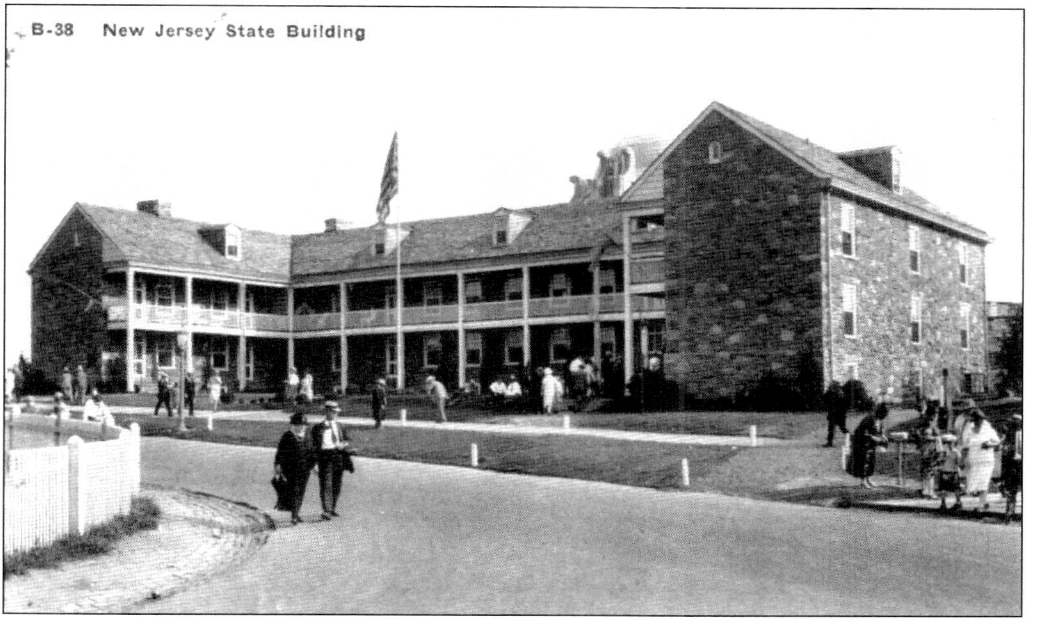

NEW JERSEY BUILDING. The first state building for which funds were granted, the New Jersey Building was a replica of the Trenton barracks first used by the British and later by the Continental army under George Washington. Sited near the entrance to the navy yard, it was constructed of Germantown fieldstone and given a slate roof. Originally planned to be a permanent structure, it was not to be. (John D. Cardinell.)

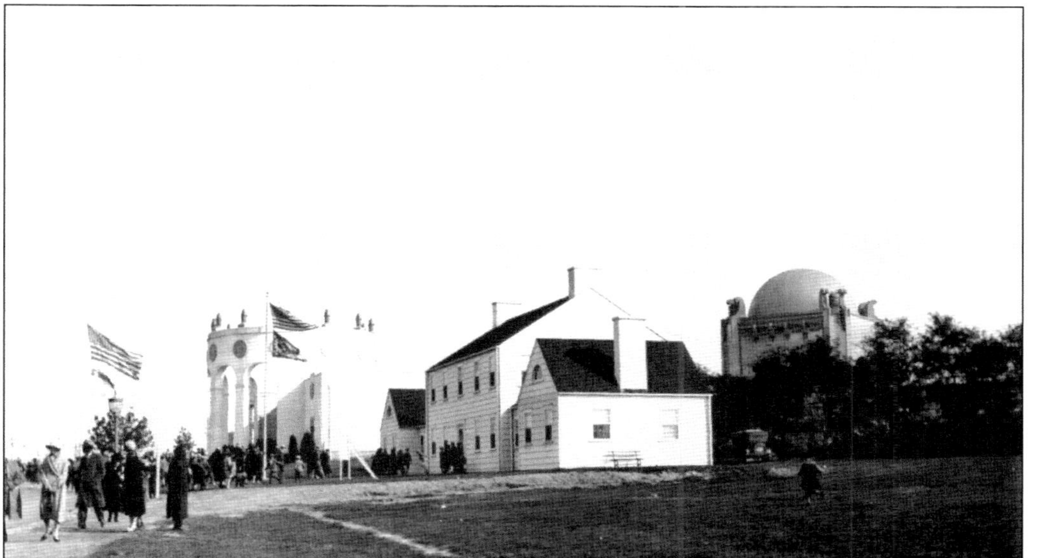

ILLINOIS AND OHIO BUILDINGS. Erected adjacent to the New Jersey Building were the buildings representing the states of Illinois and Ohio. These structures occupied a site not far from the Palace of Transportation, whose distinctive tall domed tower is visible in the distance.

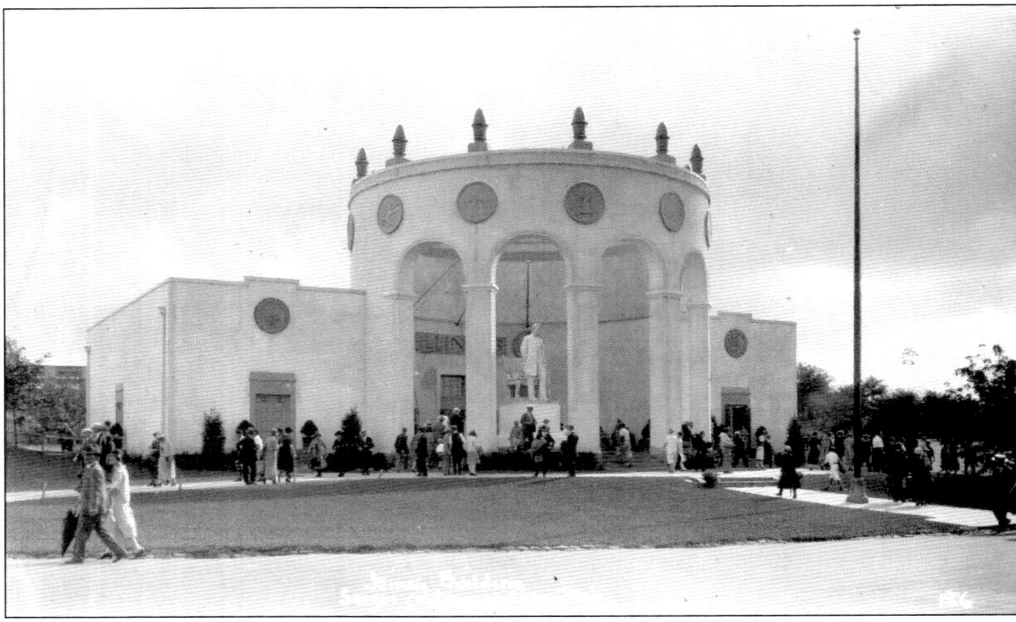

ILLINOIS BUILDING. Dedicated on September 21 by its governor, Len Small, the Illinois Building stood between that of Ohio and New Jersey. Built in the form of a U, it had two square ends and a circular courtyard in front with five arched entrances. In the courtyard, which was more than 50 feet in diameter, was a 19-foot-tall copy of St. Gauden's famous statue of Abraham Lincoln.

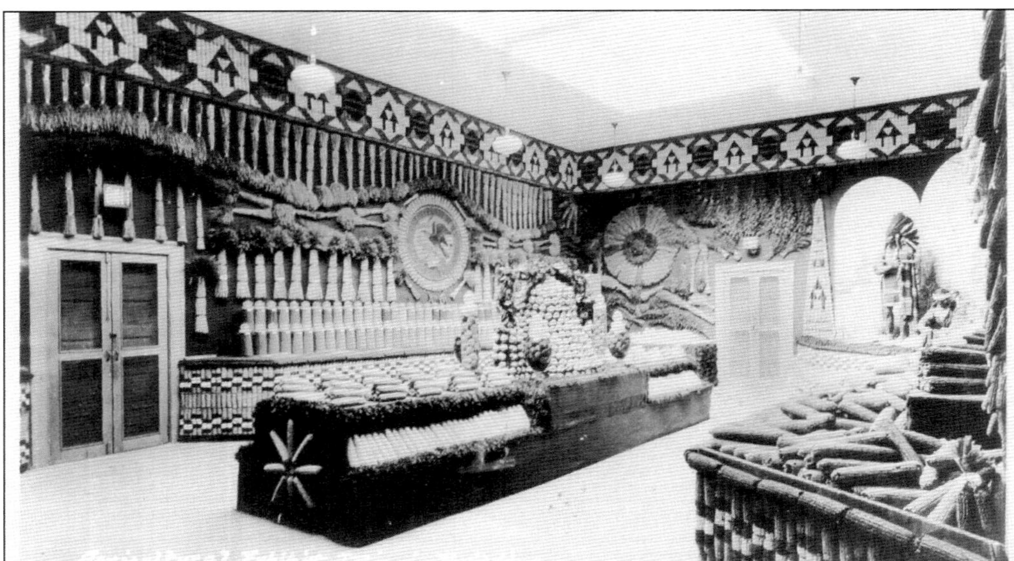

AGRICULTURAL EXHIBIT IN ILLINOIS BUILDING. Here is a view showing the extensive exhibit highlighting agricultural products, especially corn, grown in the state of Illinois. Items related to developments in some of the state's other industries, including mining and commerce, were also displayed. Of greatest interest to visitors were the two rooms, on either end of the building, where relics associated with the life of Abraham Lincoln were on display.

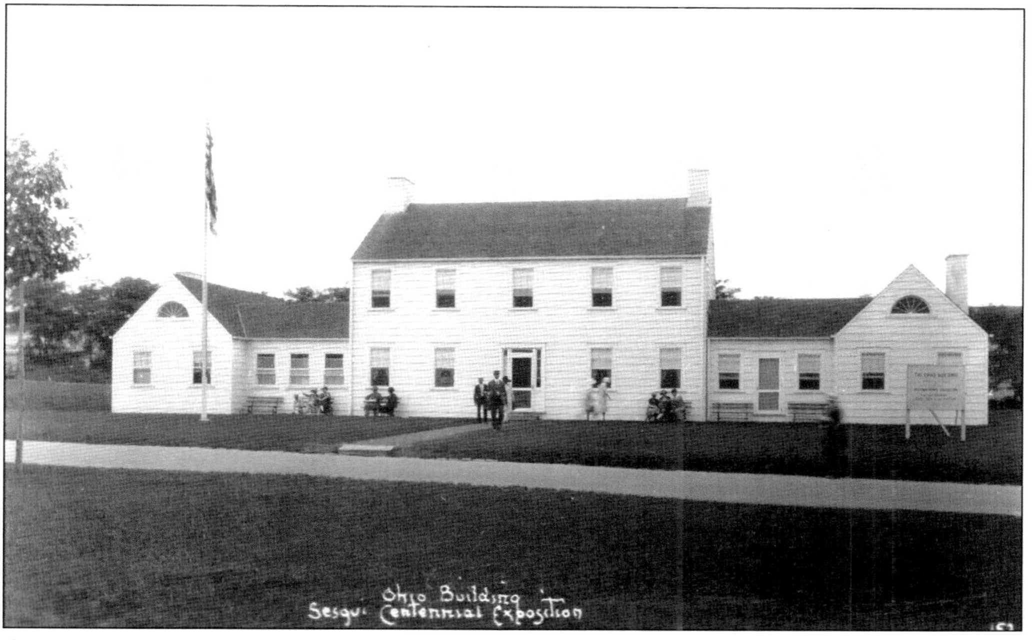

OHIO BUILDING. Located next to the Illinois Building was the Ohio Building, which was designed as a replica of the home of Pres. William Henry Harrison, who was a native of the state. The two-story, clapboard-sided home measured 106 feet in length and was 43 feet wide. Interior furnishings included some of President Harrison's original furniture. The state appropriated $150,000 for this building.

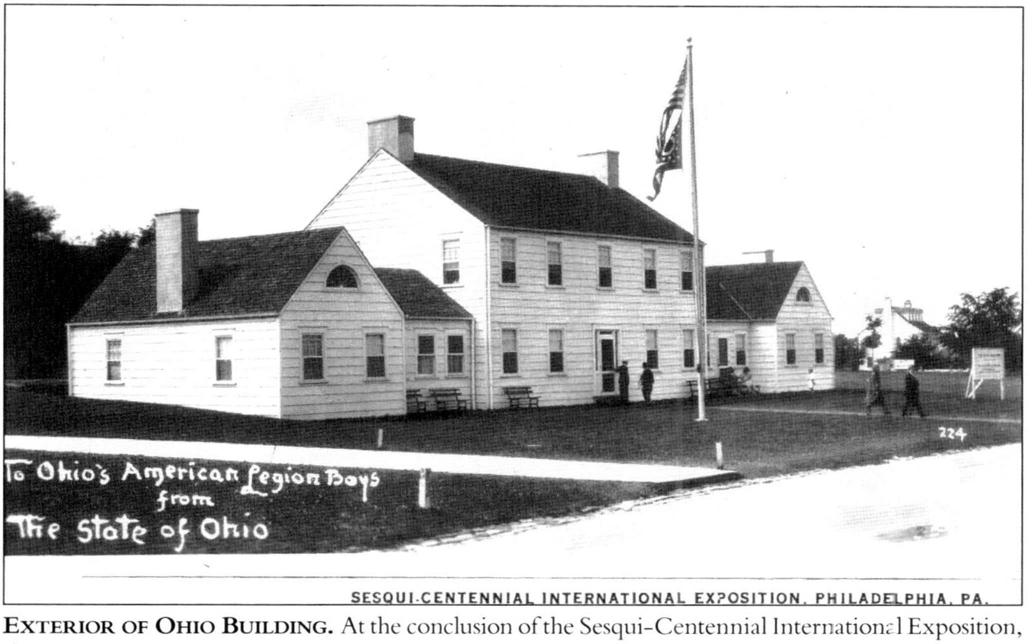

EXTERIOR OF OHIO BUILDING. At the conclusion of the Sesqui-Centennial International Exposition, this handsome building was carefully dismantled and shipped back to Ohio, where it was reerected just east of Heritage Hall on the state fairgrounds in Columbus. There the home stood until the late 1980s or early 1990s, when it was finally torn down due to its deteriorating condition.

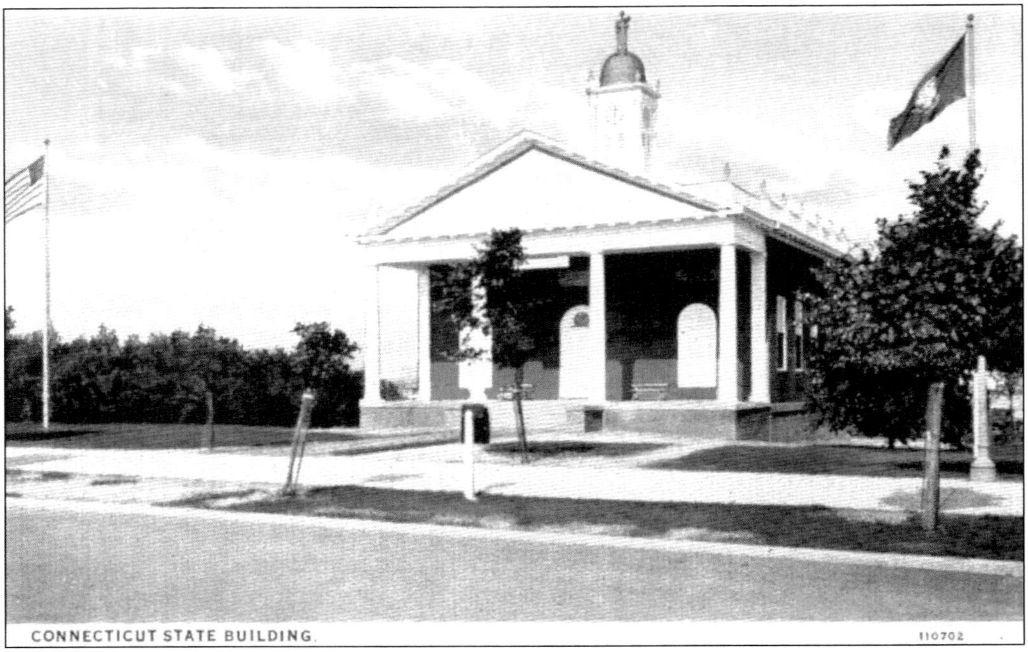

CONNECTICUT BUILDING. To represent the state of Connecticut, a reproduction of the old statehouse in Hartford, which had been designed by Charles Bulfinch (1763–1844) architect of the U.S. Capitol in Washington, D.C., was erected on Broad Street facing the stadium. The building was accented by a sloping grass lawn measuring 150 square feet. The cost for constructing this fine building was nearly $50,000. (John D. Cardinell.)

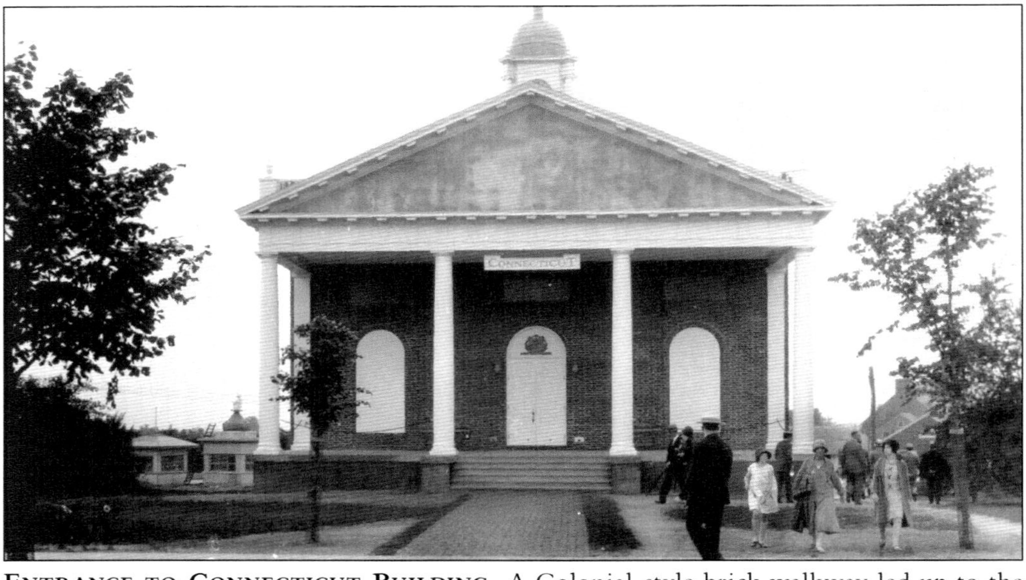

ENTRANCE TO CONNECTICUT BUILDING. A Colonial-style brick walkway led up to the Connecticut Building, which had a classically designed porch that was 45 feet long and 14 feet in depth. Another feature of the structure was a copy of the original statehouse dome on its roof. Placed on the dome was the figure of *Justice*, which contained a clock manufactured by the Seth Thomas Clock Company. (John D. Cardinell.)

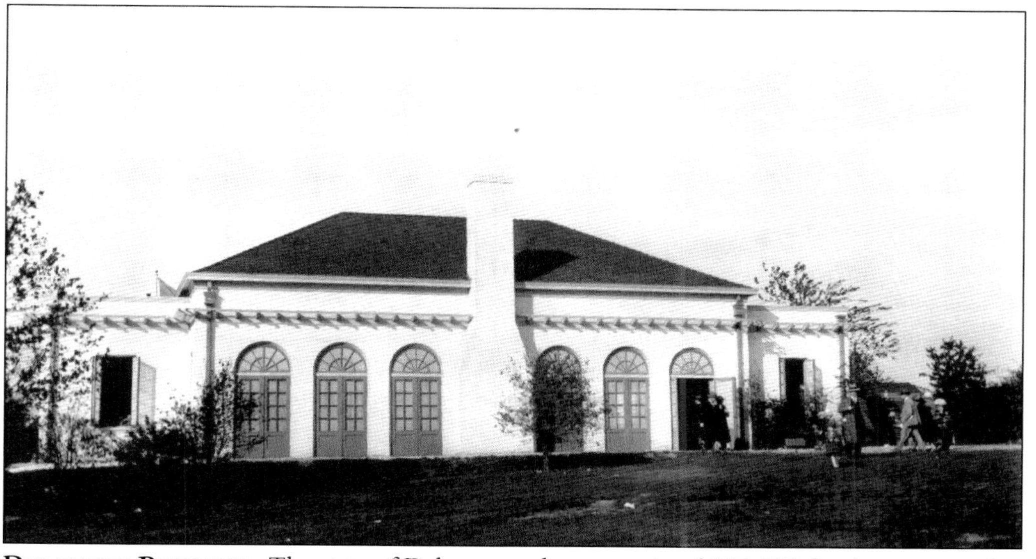

DELAWARE BUILDING. The state of Delaware only appropriated $25,000 for the construction of its representative building. Built of relatively inexpensive materials, it nevertheless presented a grand appearance and displayed architectural features found in many of the state's historic buildings. It possessed a large central room, 56 feet long by 30 feet wide, having a ceiling with a height of 16 feet and accented by a brick-patterned floor.

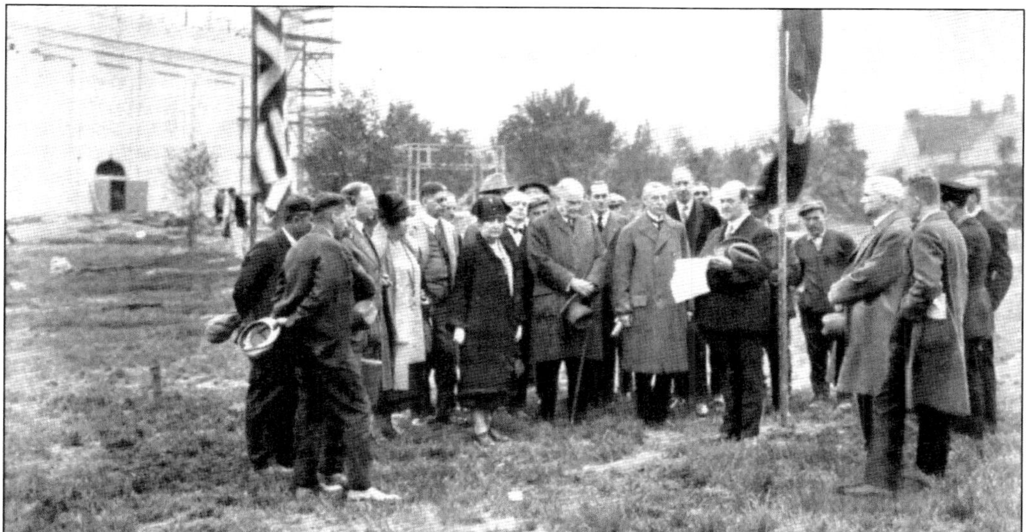

Dr. Clarence J. Owens, Special Commissioner of the Sesqui-Centennial International Exposition reading the Proclamation of Governor Alfred E. Smith at the Dedication of the Site for the New York State Buildings at the *Sesqui-Centennial International Exposition* — PHILADELPHIA 1926

DEDICATION CEREMONY. On August 11, this group of dignitaries, including New York governor Alfred E. Smith, participated in dedication ceremonies for the breaking of the ground to construct two buildings to represent the state of New York. Shown here reading a special proclamation is Dr. Clarence J. Owens, special commissioner for the exposition.

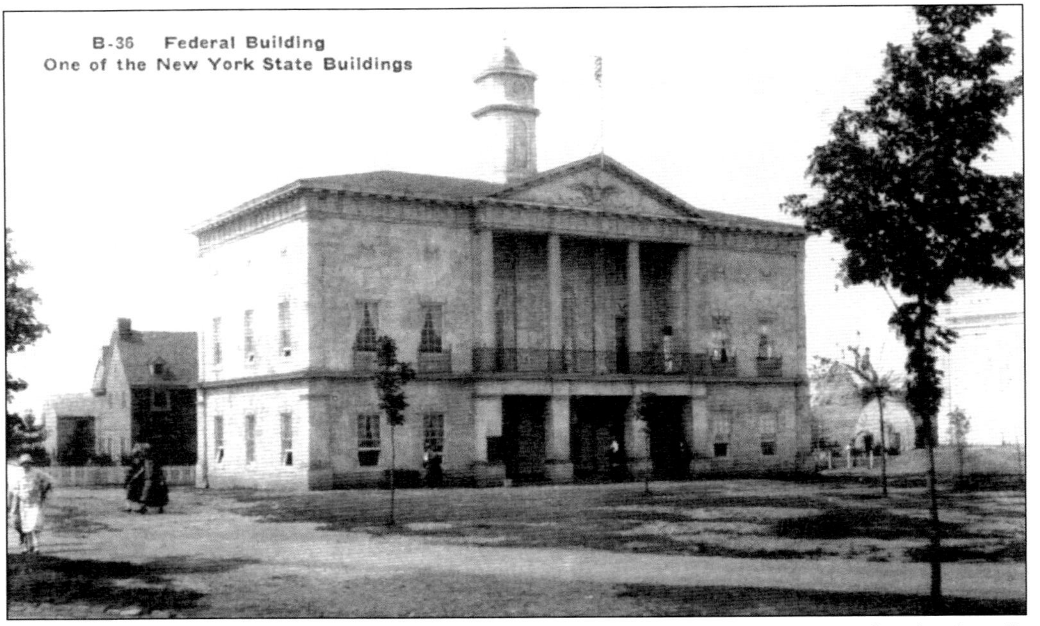

FEDERAL HALL. One of New York's buildings was this fine representation of Federal Hall, which once stood in New York City. It was at Federal Hall that George Washington was sworn in as the first president of the United States on April 30, 1789. The state's second building was a replica of Washington's headquarters at Newburgh, New York. (John D. Cardinell.)

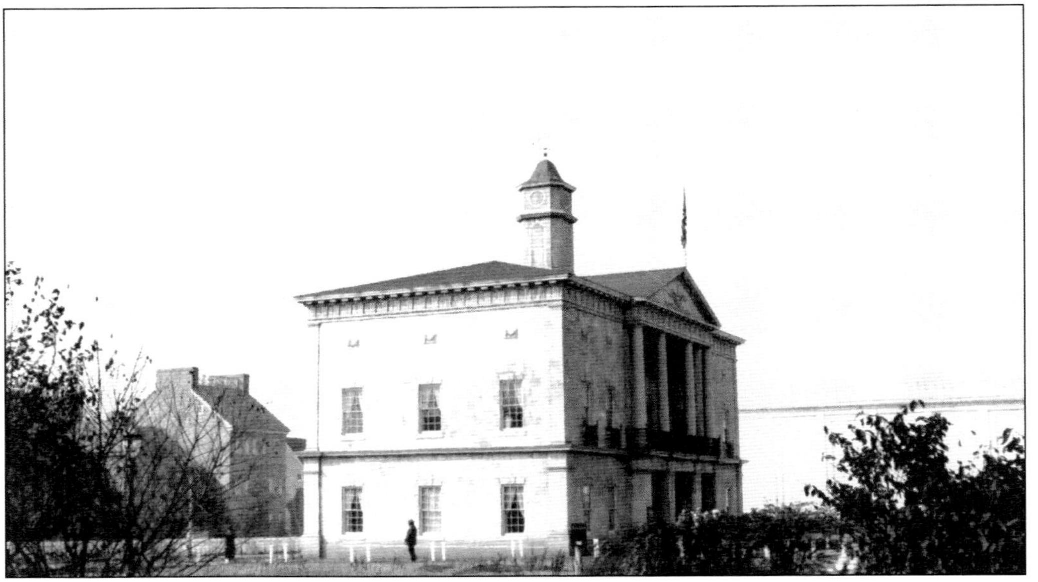

NEW YORK STATE BUILDING. Erected between High Street and the India Building, this facsimile of Federal Hall measured 40 by 80 feet. The exterior was made to look like it was made of sandstone blocks, while the stately columns were imitation marble. The interior contained a collection of relics from the American Revolution and was furnished with antiques from that same time period.

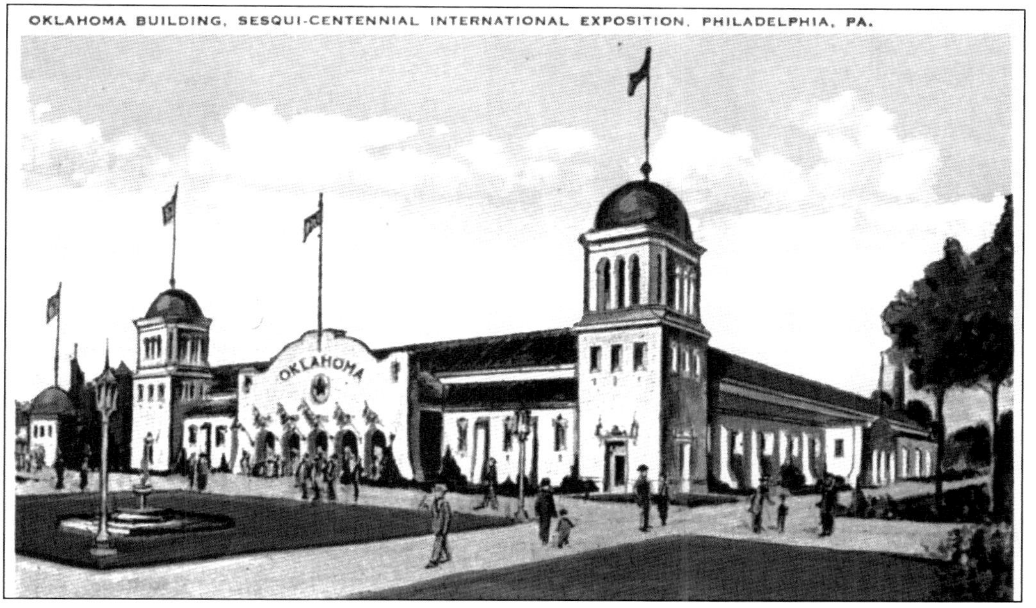

OKLAHOMA BUILDING. A number of states, although expressing interest in participation in the Sesqui-Centennial International Exposition, never fulfilled their plans for erecting buildings or completing exhibits. This was often due to time constraints and budgetary problems. One such state was Oklahoma. Here a postcard depicts an artist's conception of this state's building, which unfortunately never became a reality. (John D. Cardinell.)

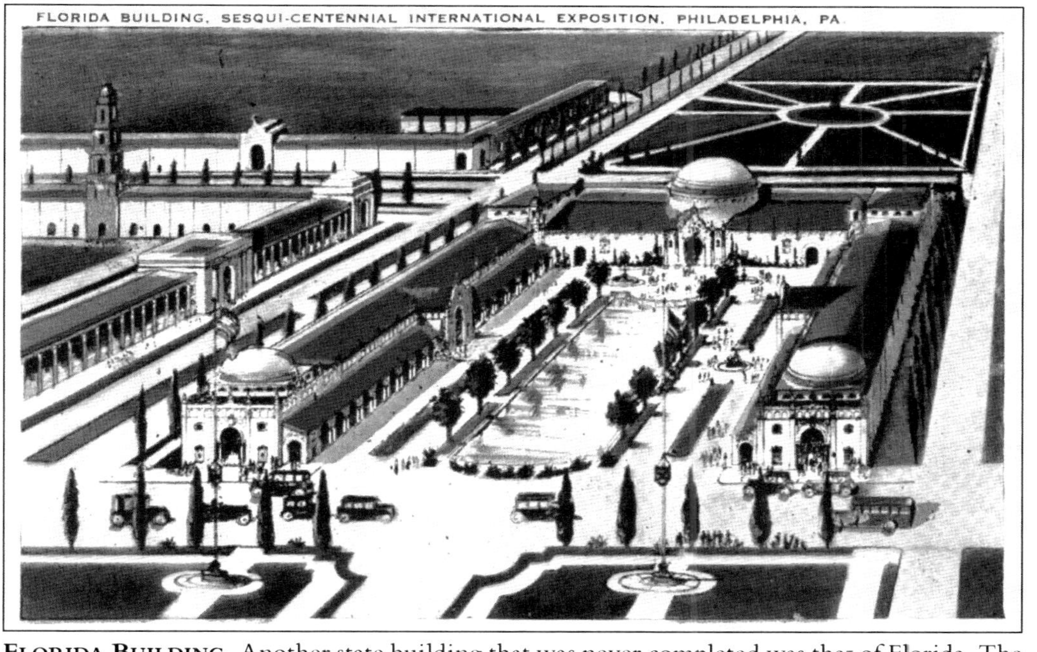

FLORIDA BUILDING. Another state building that was never completed was that of Florida. The wonderful structure depicted on this postcard never got beyond the planning stage. In lieu of this building, the state sponsored a motion picture exhibit that was placed in the Palace of Education. It was reported that this visual display was well received. (Tichnor.)

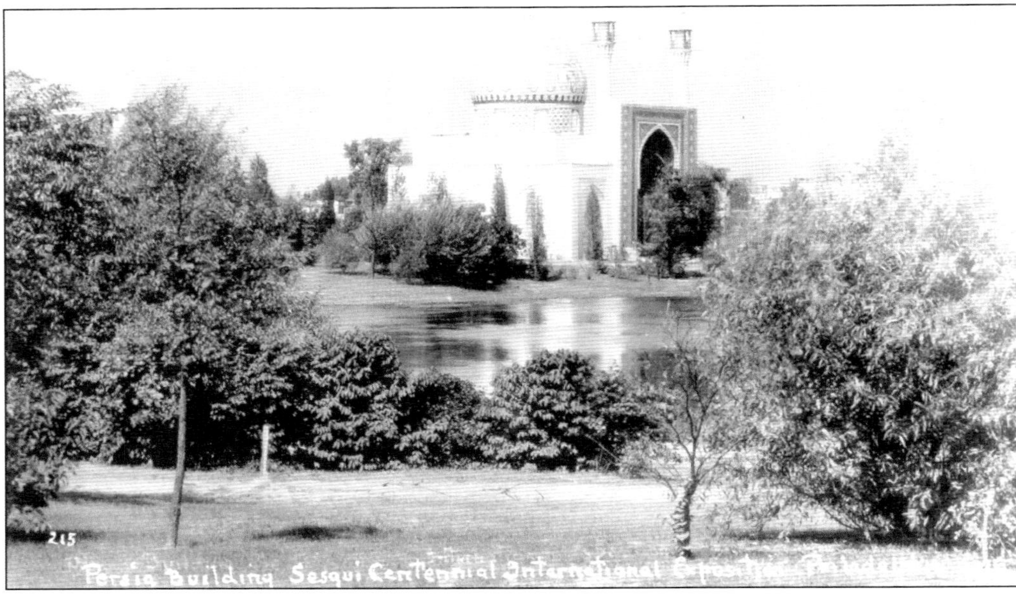

PERSIA BUILDING. The official pavilion of the government of Persia (now Iran) was a most exceptional and striking structure. Situated on Edgewater Lake, along with the other foreign buildings, this was truly an impressive sight. Designed by architect Carl Zeigler, it was meant to be representative of an ancient mosque. It was said that this was the finest example of Persian-style architecture found in the United States.

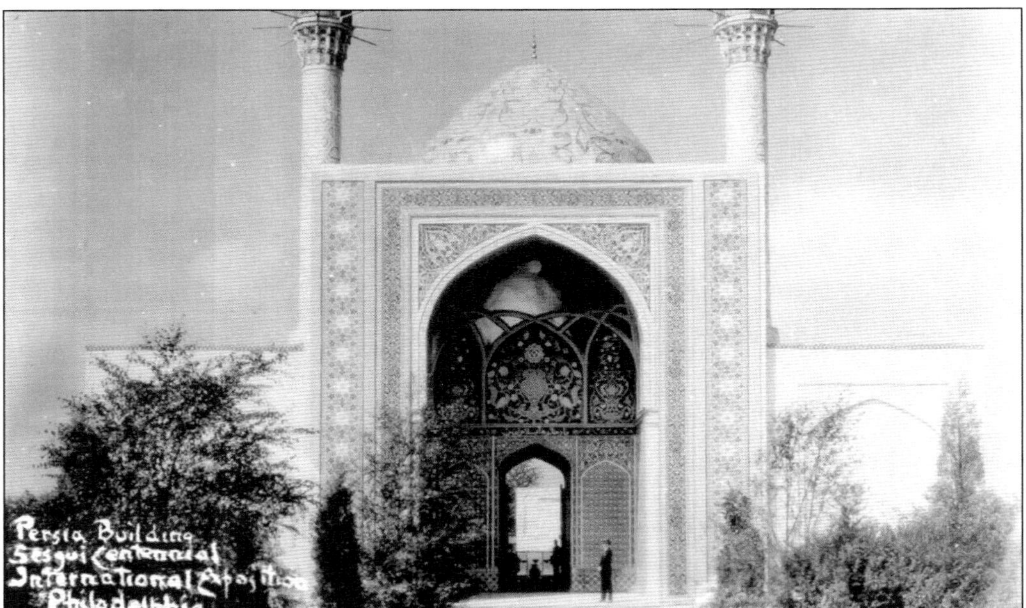

PERSIAN PAVILION. Officially dedicated on October 6, this extraordinary pavilion exhibited a high degree of architectural detail. Two tall towers flanked the main entrance. The exterior stucco walls were enhanced by molded and stamped designs having exquisite patterns, which in turn were brilliantly colored. It was the incorporation of elements such as these that made this one of the most beautiful buildings at the exposition.

DOME OF PERSIA BUILDING. A striking feature of the Persia Building was its magnificent dome complete with classic ornamentation. Here an automobile is seen parked on the drive in front of what is actually the rear entrance to the building. Nearby, the government of Persia also erected a fine reproduction of one of the ancient columns from the Great Hall of Xerxes, the original of which dates from 480 BC.

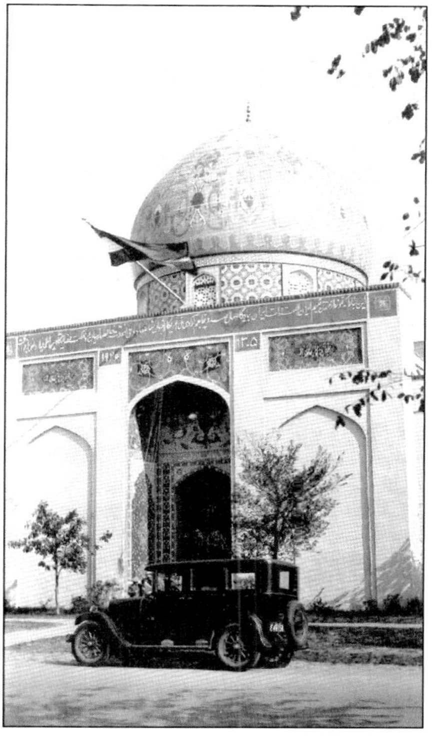

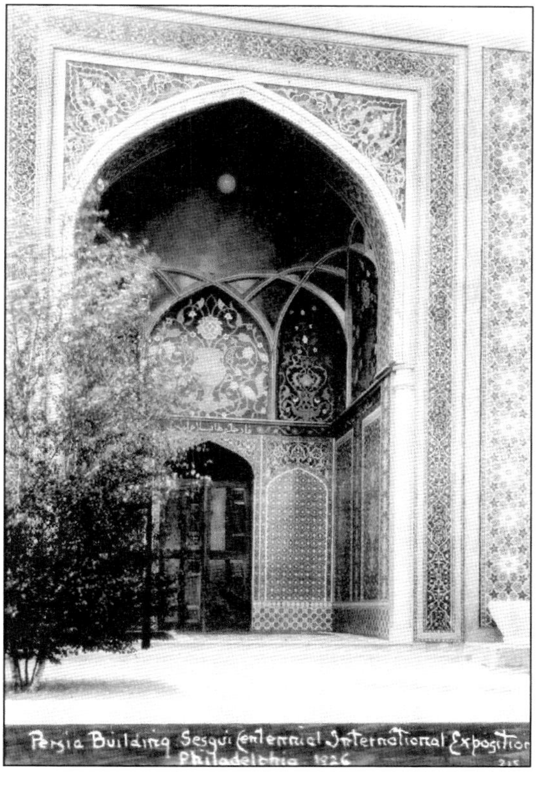

ENTRANCE TO PERSIA BUILDING. The main entrance to the Persia Building faced the waters of Edgewater Lake. Surrounding the large antique doors, which were centuries old, were mosaics having arabesque designs in gleaming turquoise, black, gold, and ivory. Once inside, visitors could inspect a wide range of items on display. This included handmade rugs, tapestries, pottery, metalwork, wood carvings, jewelry, and rare manuscripts.

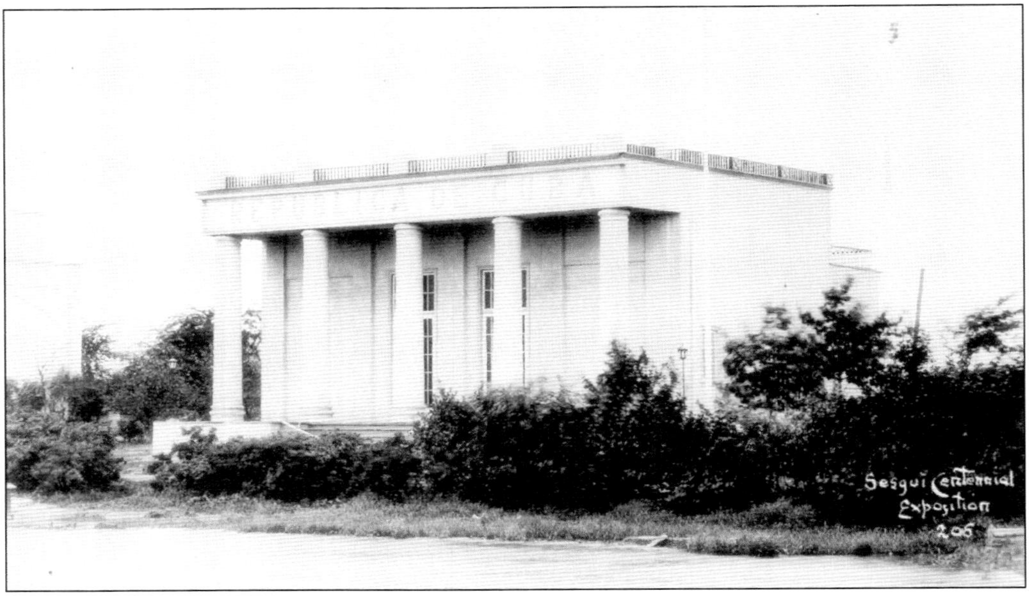

CUBA BUILDING. Five stately columns stood in front of the building housing Cuba's contribution to the exposition. Besides this fine pavilion, the Cuban government also placed exhibits within the Palace of Education, where its educational display was awarded the grand prize.

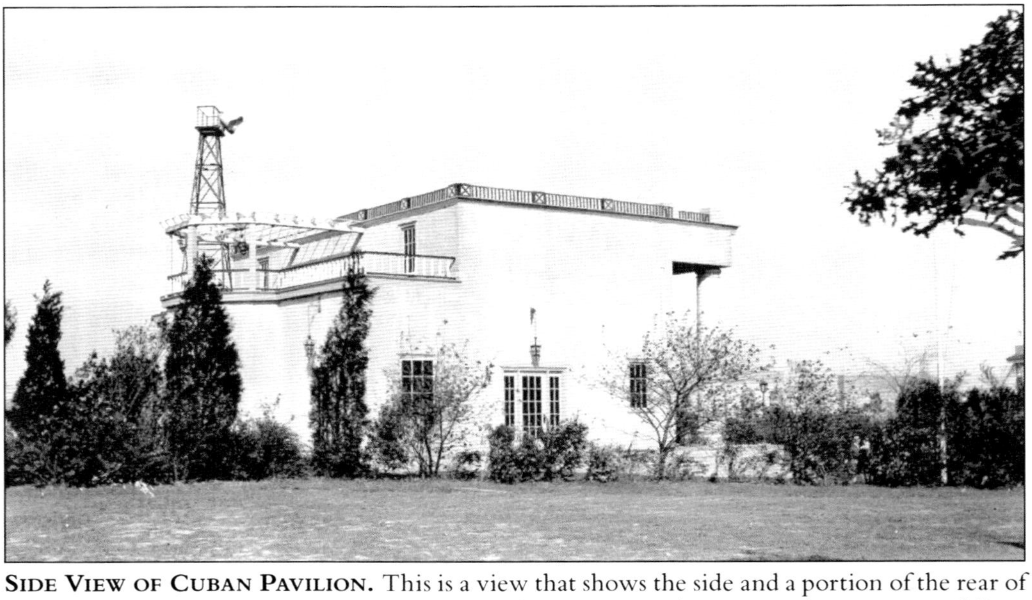

SIDE VIEW OF CUBAN PAVILION. This is a view that shows the side and a portion of the rear of the Cuban Pavilion. Located on the shoreline of Edgewater Lake, next to the Persian Building, its official opening ceremonies were not held until September 10, 1926. During the short time that it was open to the public, a number of fine entertainments were held here.

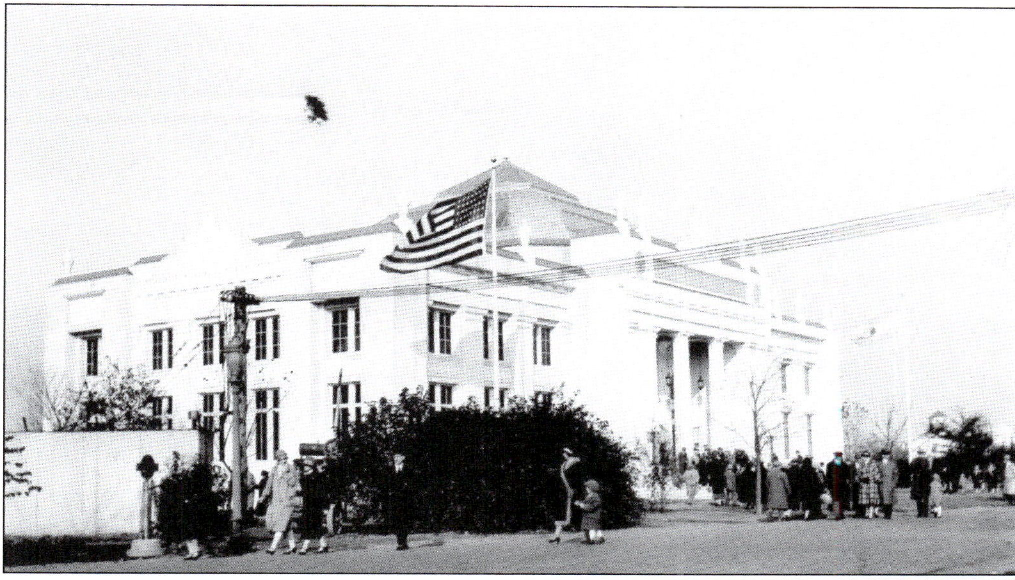

ARGENTINE BUILDING. As in the case of the Cuban, Persian, and Spanish pavilions, the Argentine Building was also situated along the shores of Edgewater Lake. This building was not officially opened until October 30, 1926. It was 300 feet long and 120 feet deep and had a spacious rotunda topped by a 40-foot-diameter glass dome at its center. A wide double driveway led up to the front steps.

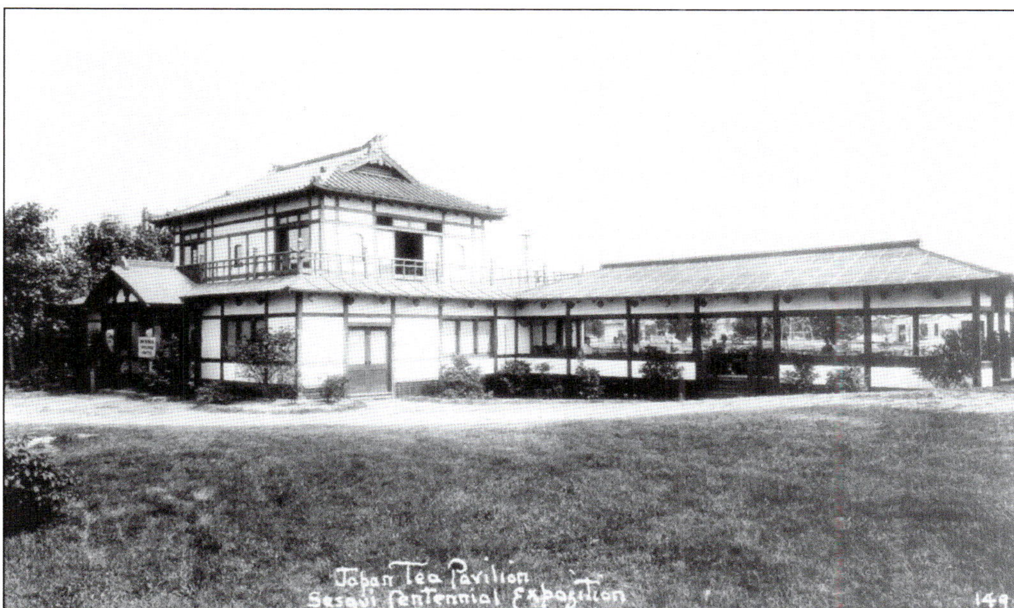

JAPANESE TEAHOUSE. The official pavilion of the government of Japan was this teahouse located along Edgewater Lake. Here visitors could enjoy a cup of Japanese green tea. Besides this building, there were two others erected nearby by private concerns; together they comprised what was known as the Japanese Garden. Additionally, Japan had varied and extensive exhibits within the Palace of Fine Arts and Palace of Education.

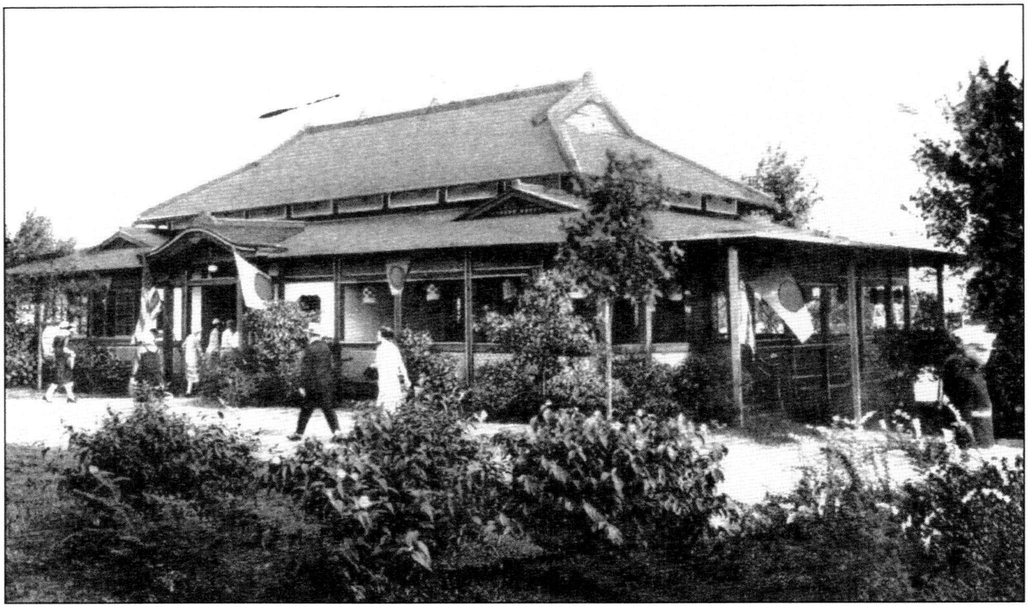

FORMOSA TEA HOUSE. As one of the three buildings comprising the Japanese Garden, the Formosa Tea House added yet more oriental charm and appeal. The island of Formosa, which was ruled over by Japan at the time, was represented by this replication of an authentic country teahouse. (John D. Cardinell.)

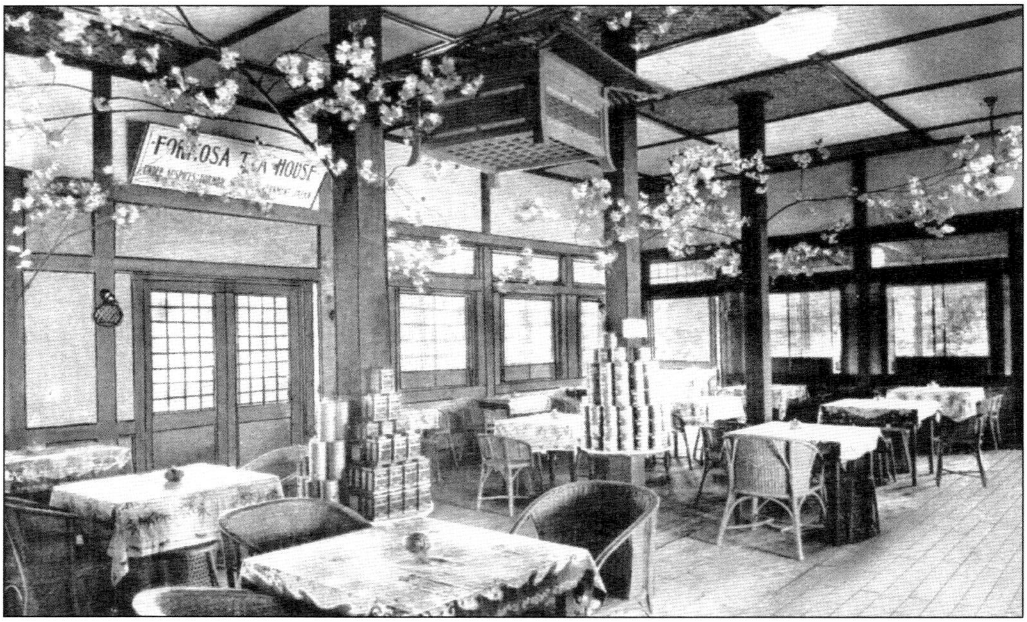

INTERIOR OF TEAHOUSE. An interior view of the Formosa Tea House shows what awaited those who entered. Here visitors could partake of hot cups of Formosa's famous oolong tea while seated at the small tables in this traditional tearoom. Adding to the ambiance were branches of cherry blossoms suspended from the ceiling. (John D. Cardinell.)

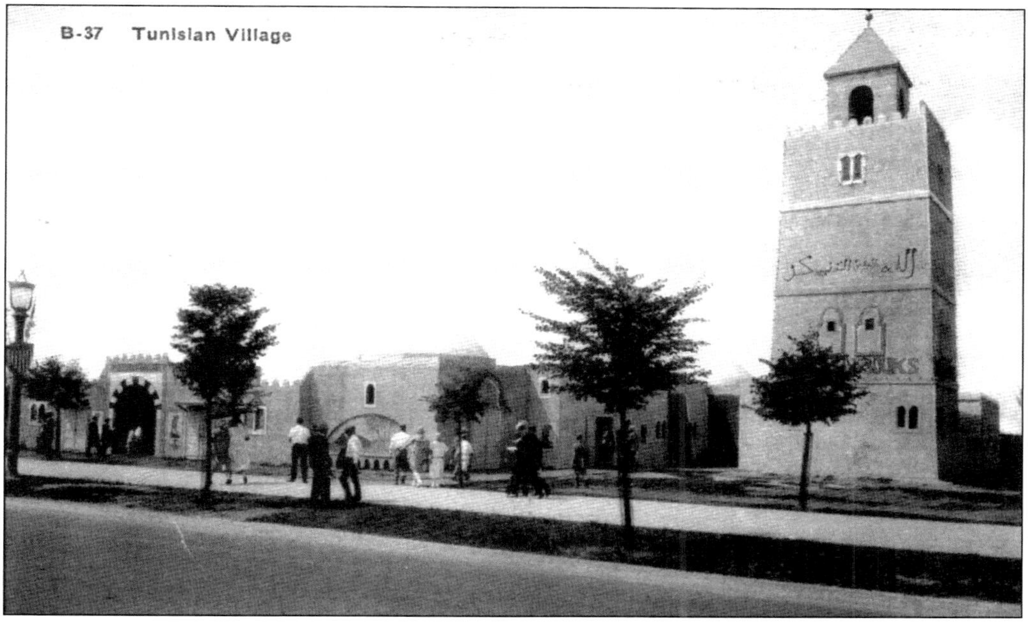

TUNISIAN VILLAGE. Tunisia, a protectorate of France at the time, sponsored a North African–style village. Within its walls, visitors were treated to displays of native handiwork such as hammered brass, jewelry, handmade furniture and rugs, and other goods. A photographic gallery depicting Arab life in the desert was of special interest to many. (John D. Cardinell.)

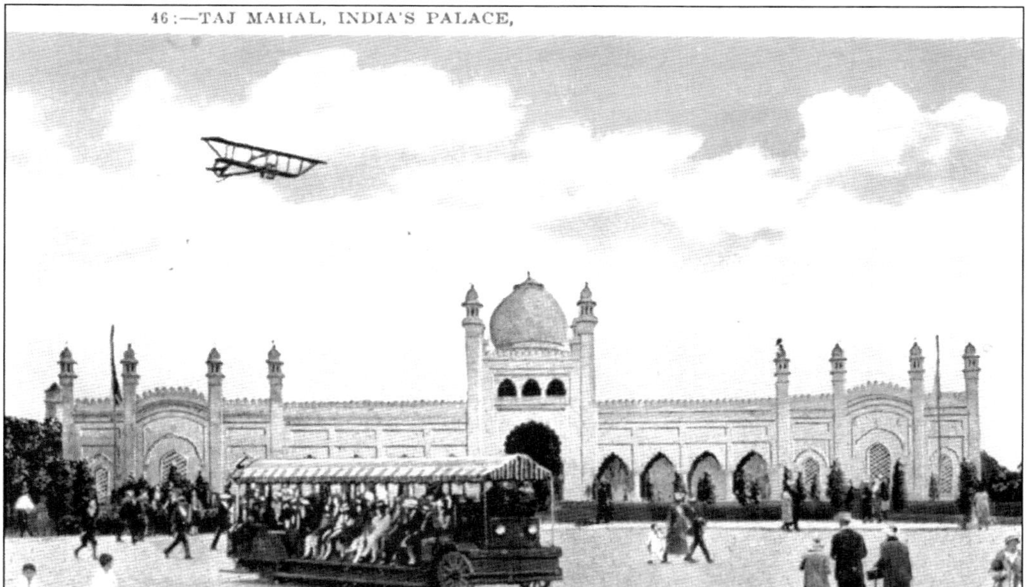

INDIA PAVILION. A party bus passes by the elaborate India Pavilion. This beautiful white building was designed using detailed proportions and architectural features typical of the Moghul style of the 16th and 17th centuries. It especially resembled India's best-known building, the Taj Mahal. Not officially sponsored by the government of India, the structure was under the supervision of the Taj Mahal Trading Company of London. (John D. Cardinell.)

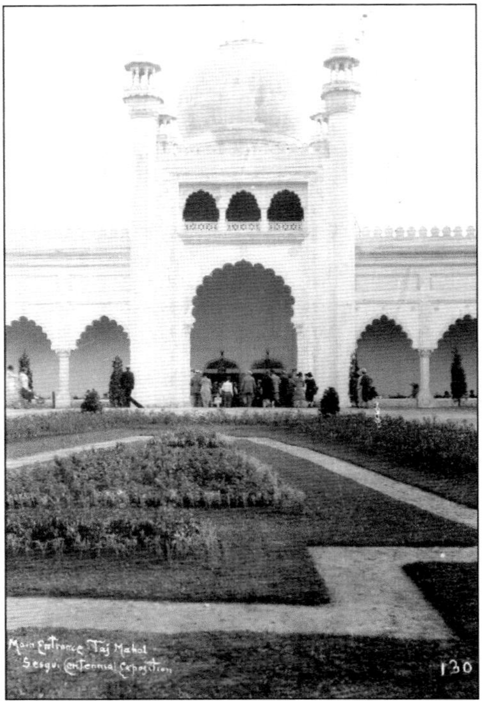

ENTRANCE TO TAJ MAHAL. The India Pavilion was also referred to as the Taj Mahal, which it was intended to resemble. Immediately upon walking through the entrance, visitors were greeted by the richness and abundance of items on exhibit. All manner of goods from this nation, as well as from Burma and Ceylon, were displayed. Included among the items were examples of brassware, carpeting, furniture, inlaid woodwork, jewelry, and artwork.

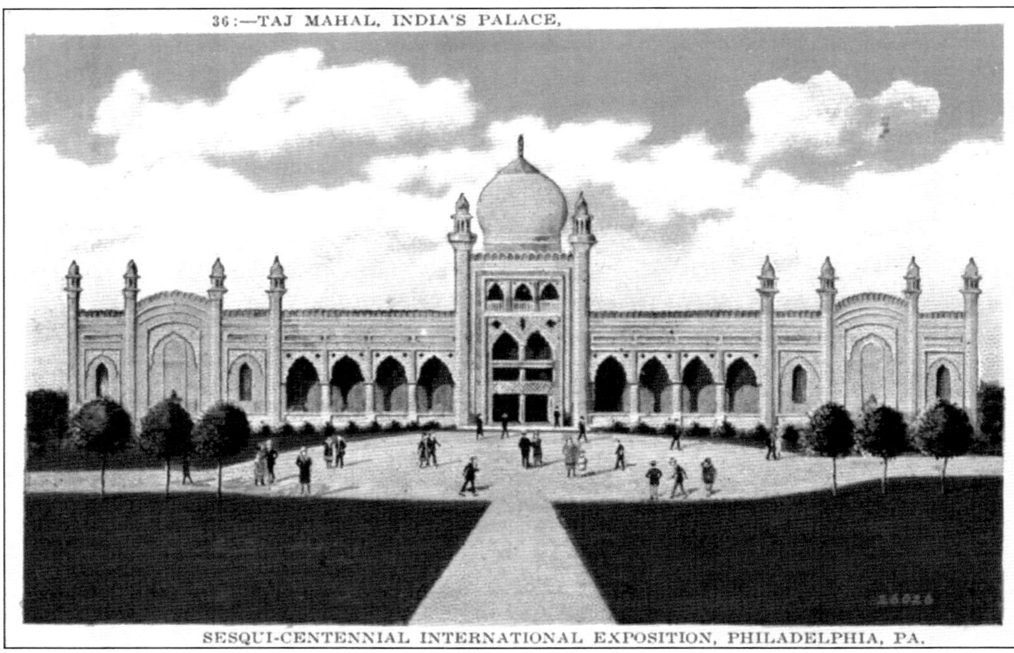

TAJ MAHAL. Besides the abundance of merchandise presented, the building housed a number of other attractions within its 60,000-square-foot area. A restaurant capable of seating 1,000 people featured both native and American cuisine. There was also a tea-sampling room, a reading room with current Indian newspapers and periodicals, and even an imitation Indian jungle, which was said to be both educational and entertaining. (John D. Cardinell.)

Five

SPECIAL BUILDINGS AND EXHIBITS

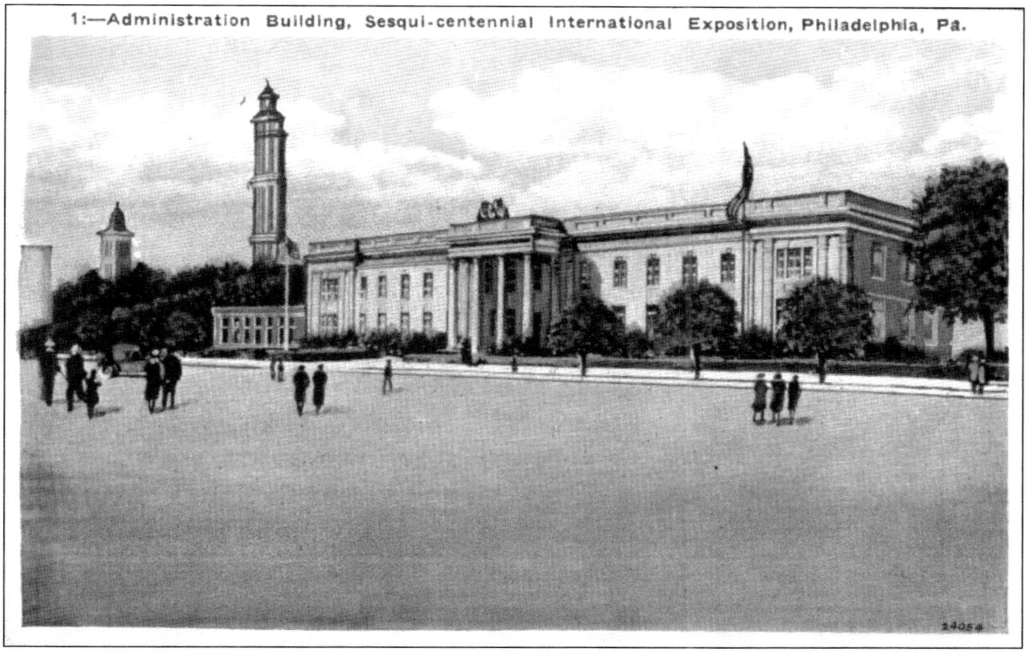

SPECIAL BUILDINGS. Nearly 70 significant special buildings and hundreds of smaller booths, kiosks, and concession stands were located on the grounds of the exposition. These structures were varied in their purposes and design and provided all manner of services, entertainment, and opportunities for visitors to enjoy their Sesqui-Centennial International Exposition experience. Among those specialized buildings was the exposition's administration building. (John D. Cardinell.)

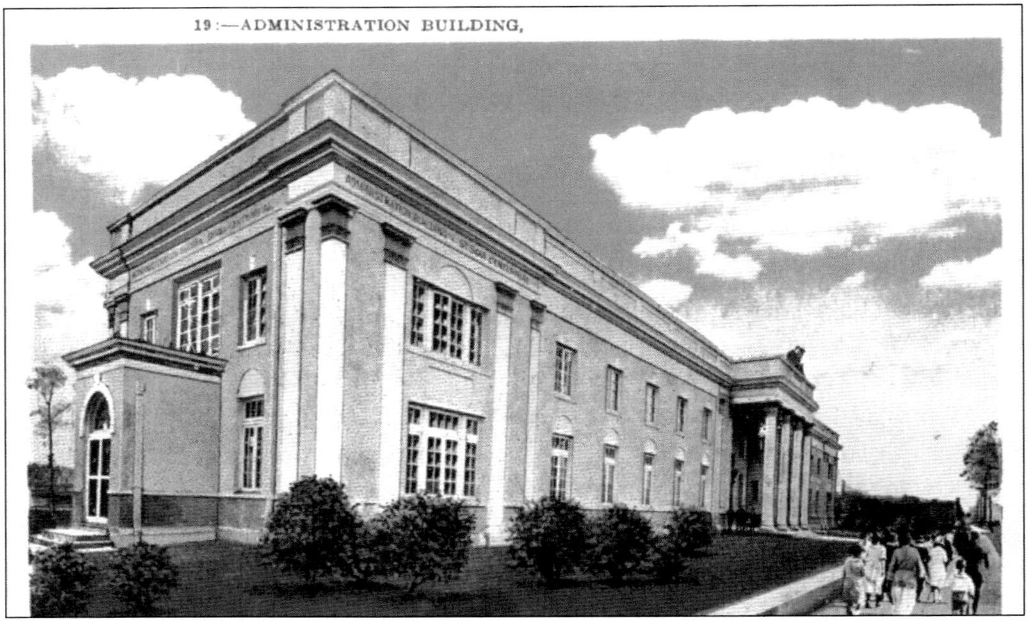

ADMINISTRATION BUILDING. Erected just outside the main entrance, the administration building was the first building especially constructed for the event. Completed on October 6, 1925, it served the important role of accommodating the staff that managed and oversaw all the operations of this great exposition. The building itself measured 200 feet by 40 feet and offered 17,600 square feet of floor space. (John D. Cardinell.)

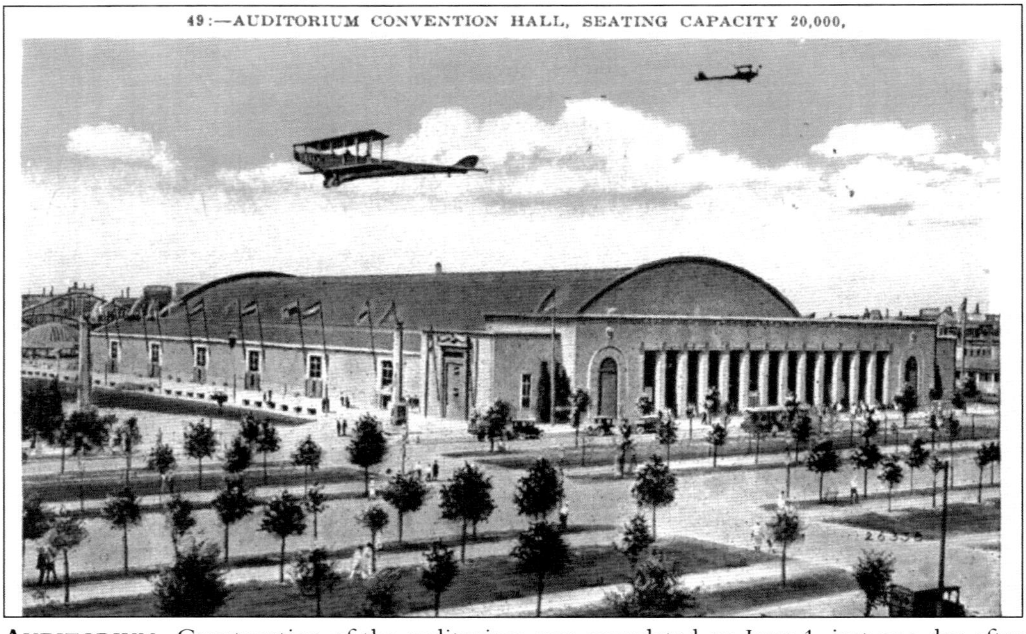

AUDITORIUM. Construction of the auditorium was completed on June 1, just one day after the official opening of the exposition. Conveniently situated just inside the main entrance, the building was 274 feet by 450 feet and had a floor area of 113,300 square feet. It was capable of accommodating upward of 10,000 people for most events. (John D. Cardinell.)

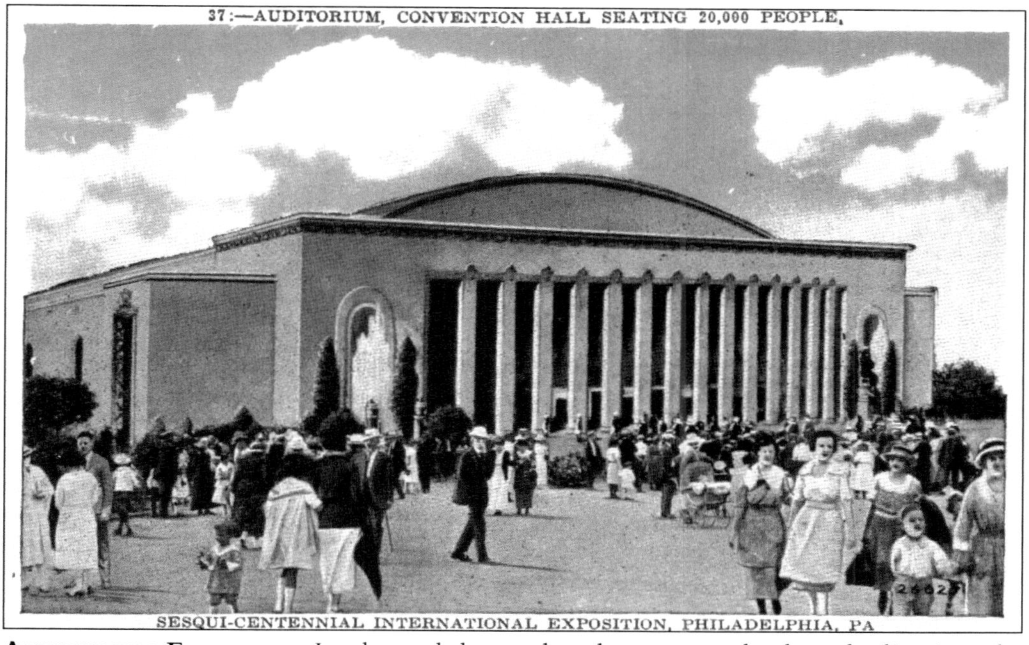

Auditorium Entrance. Just beyond the stately columns were the doors leading into the spacious auditorium. The building was designed so that sections could be curtained off to make room for different-sized events and to help improve acoustic properties. A specially built 164-rank pipe organ, one of the largest in the nation, was installed by the Austin Organ Company of Hartford. (John D. Cardinell.)

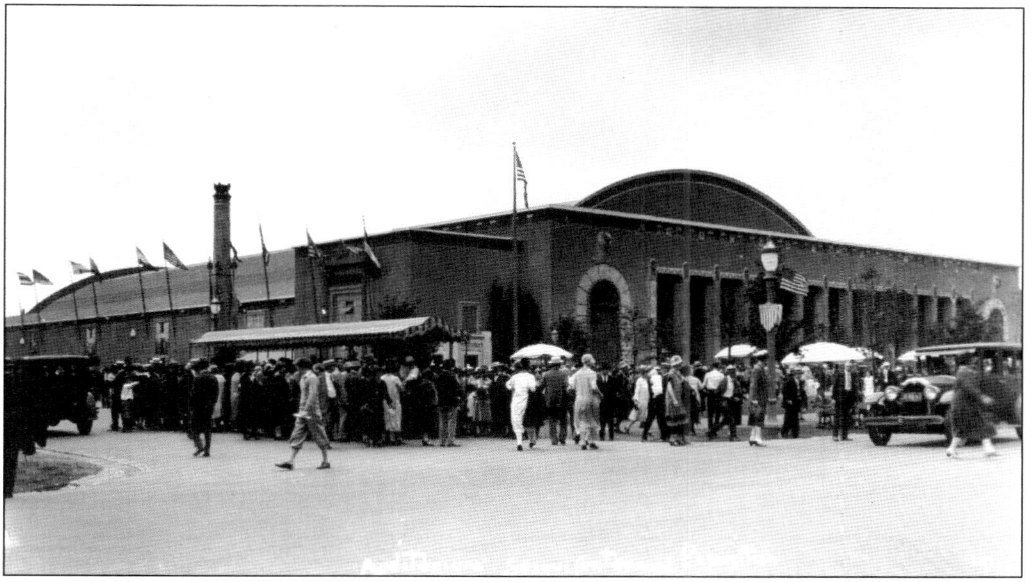

Auditorium Events. Among the many events held here in the auditorium were 32 concerts given by the famed Philadelphia Orchestra, 16 religious meetings, a series of professional tennis matches, an American Kennel Club dog show with over 2,200 entrants, and the public reception held for the queen of Rumania on her visit to the exposition. A number of organizations also used the site to hold their national conventions. (John D. Cardinell.)

MODEL POST OFFICE
SESQUICENTENNIAL EXPOSITION
PHILADELPHIA, PENNSYLVANIA

VIEW FROM GALLERY OPERATIONS OF MODEL POST OFFICE

Early Postal records, reports and guides.
Articles used in mail order medical frauds.
Tools, guns, portraits of notorious criminals.
Chart of Post Office Department organization.
Postal Motor Vehicle Service.
Pneumatic tube for mail transportation.
Alaskan dog sledge mail conveyance.
Air mail plane and operating equipment.
Postage stamps, past and present issues.
Articles lost in the mails.
Properly and improperly prepared parcels.
Undeliverable letters and dead letter facts.
Directory clerks searching for correct addresses.
Machine making Government stamped envelopes.
Postmarking and canceling machine.
Mail boxes, pouches, sacks.
Post route maps of all States.
Model of a Railway Post Office car.
(See full size Railway Postal Car at Transportation Building.)

ALSO OTHER INTERESTING EXHIBITS

THE POST OFFICE SERVICE IS YOUR SERVICE

MODEL POST OFFICE. A United States model post office was conveniently located between the Palaces of Liberal Arts and Agriculture. Inside the nearly 18,000-square-foot building was a functioning post office. A second-floor balcony ran around its four walls allowing visitors to observe the actual handling of mail, while the expansive lobby contained many exhibits. This postcard lists some of the fascinating things that could be seen.

BOSTON POSTAL PNEUMATIC TUBE SYSTEM
DEDICATION AUGUST 6, 1926

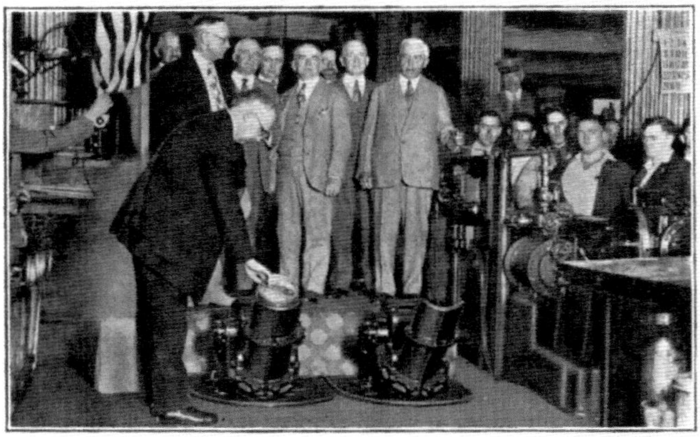

U. S. Senator, Hon. William M. Butler, pressing button to dispatch first container, which carried an American flag and letters addressed to The President, the Postmaster General and other prominent citizens.
Back Row, Hon. Frank E. McMillin, Hon. T. G. Mallalieu, Congressman Dallinger.
Front Row, Assistant Postmaster General Bartlett, Postmaster Baker, Congressman Douglass, Congressman Gallivan, Senator Butler.

BOSTON POSTAL PNEUMATIC TUBE SYSTEM. This souvenir postcard, from the model post office, pictures the dedication of a branch of the Boston pneumatic tube system on August 6, 1926. Such a pneumatic system was first introduced in Philadelphia in 1893. Eventually six major cities would have similar systems to deliver mail at an average speed of 35 miles per hour through tubes buried beneath city streets.

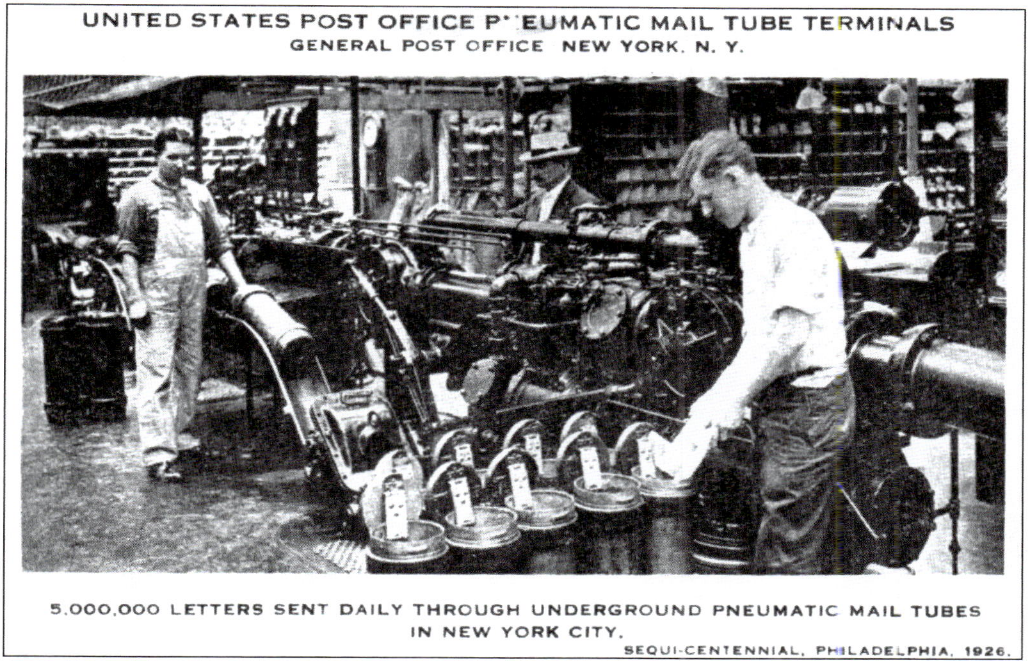

NEW YORK CITY PNEUMATIC TUBE TERMINAL. At the model post office was a demonstration of how the pneumatic postal delivery system worked. This postcard shows a tube terminal in New York City, part of a system that delivered upward of five million letters daily through 27 miles of underground pipes. New York's system, perhaps the nation's most successful, operated until 1953. (James T. Towhill.)

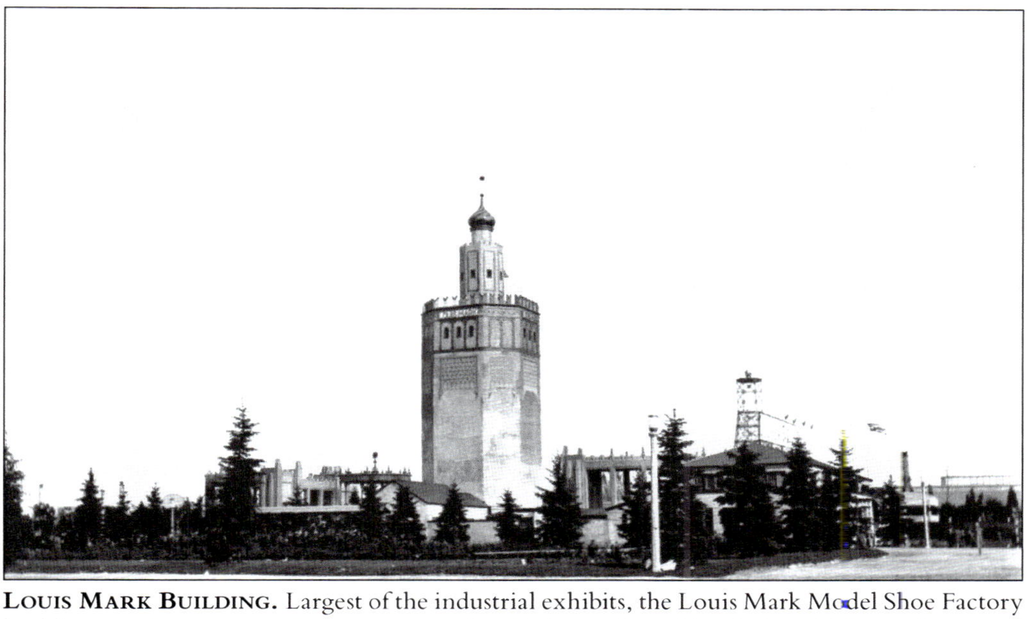

LOUIS MARK BUILDING. Largest of the industrial exhibits, the Louis Mark Model Shoe Factory building was located near the entrance to the Gladway. One of its distinguishing architectural features was the 10-story tower that stood above it. The company hoped that this extensive exhibit would help to promote its products.

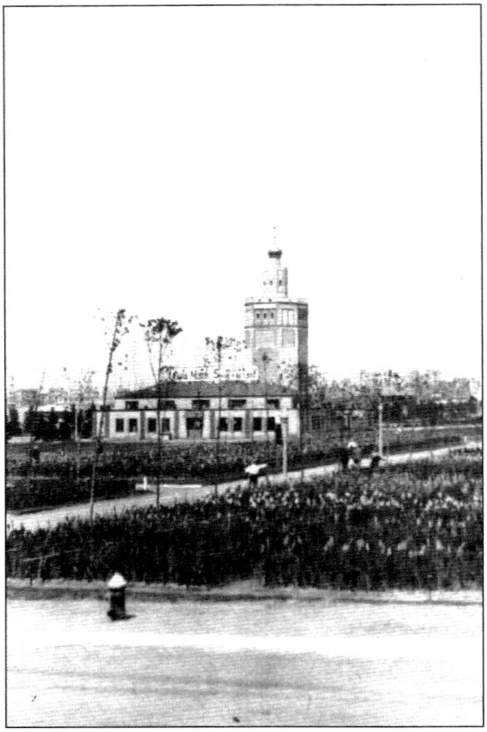

MODEL SHOE FACTORY. The Louis Mark Model Shoe Factory, seen just beyond the gardens, was an actual working facility. Here people were invited to enter and observe the manufacturing of Goodyear welt shoes from start to finish. Several hundred pairs of shoes were produced each day as interested visitors looked on. (W. J. Gambino.)

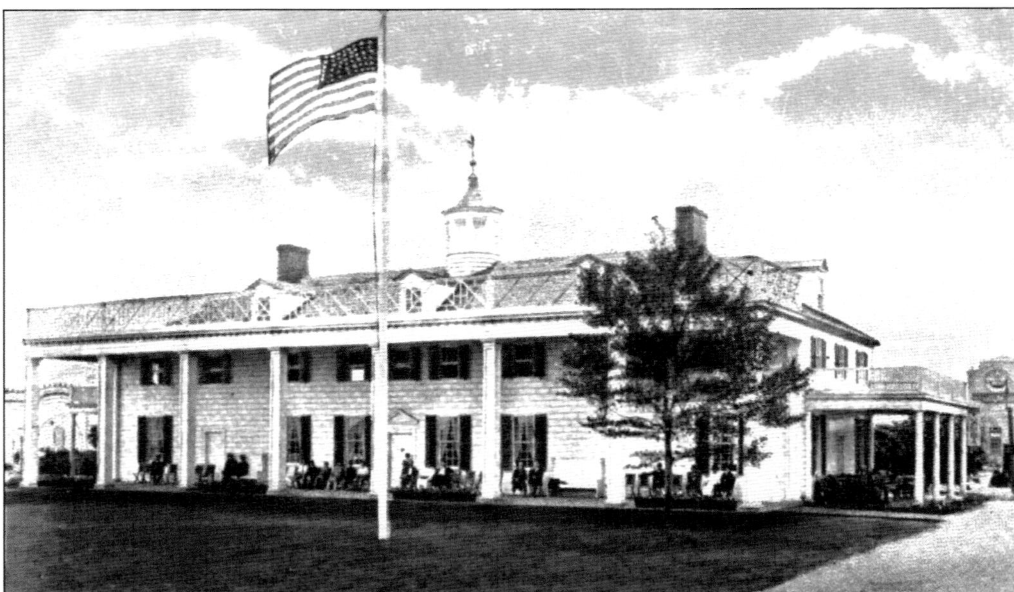

MOUNT VERNON REPLICA. Starting on June 4, this reproduction of George Washington's Mount Vernon home was open to the public. Built by the YWCA of Philadelphia, this handsome wooden replica measured 85 feet by 125 feet. It housed an information desk, a lounge, a second-floor hospitality center for foreign groups, and a cafeteria that served 302,719 people during the course of the exposition. (John D. Cardinell.)

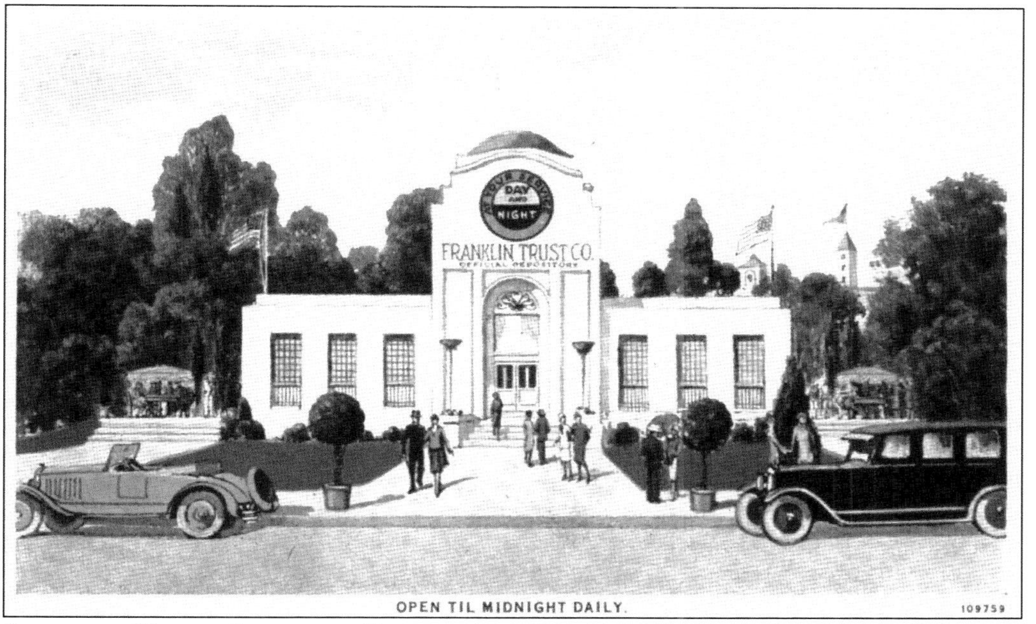

FRANKLIN TRUST COMPANY. Construction of the Franklin Trust Company building was completed in only 24 working days. As the official bank depository for the Sesqui-Centennial International Exposition, the Franklin Trust Company handled all the money collected at the exposition. Also open to the public and offering many services, this bank was open daily until midnight, even on holidays. In the first month of operations, it took in over $1 million. (John D. Cardinell.)

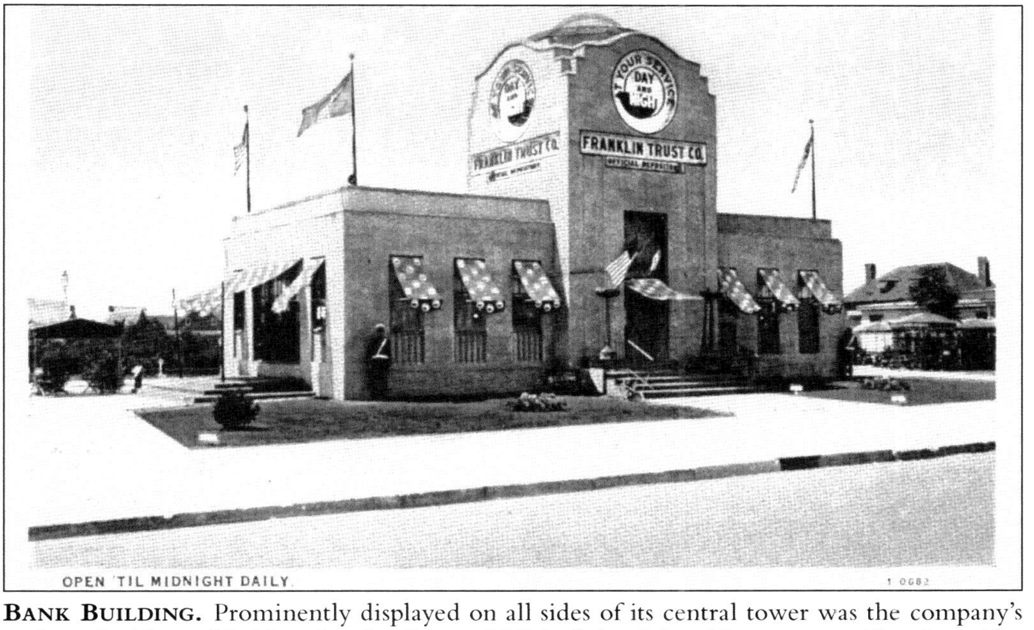

BANK BUILDING. Prominently displayed on all sides of its central tower was the company's trademarked logo, "At Your Service Day and Night." At night, this tower was illuminated by floodlights. The bank was given a medal of honor by the Jury of Awards, the first time in world fair history that a bank received such an honor. (John D. Cardinell.)

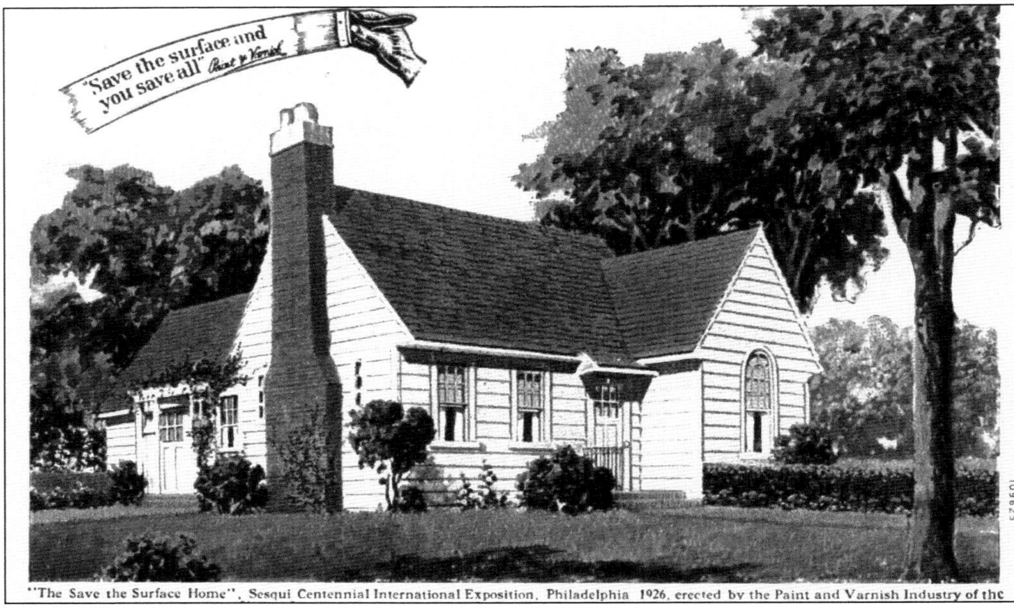

SAVE THE SURFACE HOUSE. Sponsored by the Paint and Varnish Manufacturers Association, this lovely six-room cottage and garage was used to demonstrate the benefits of the proper application of paints and varnish. Visitors were given a free lottery ticket for a drawing to be held at the end of the exposition; the winner would receive $1,000 or the right to dismantle and keep the home. (Curt Teich and Company.)

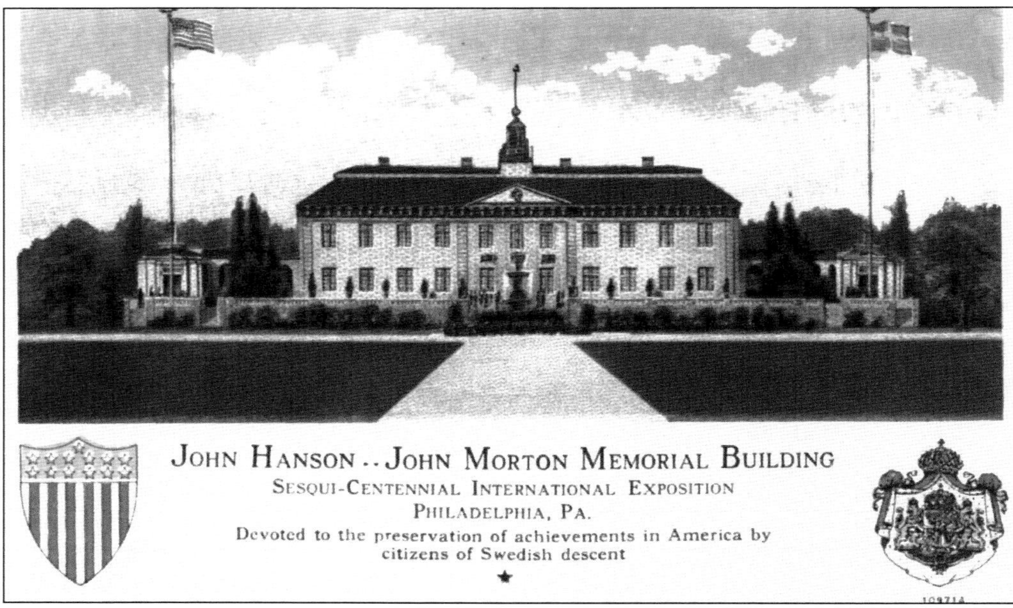

JOHN HANSON-JOHN MORTON MEMORIAL BUILDING. Sponsored by the Swedish-American Society, the cornerstone of this building was laid on June 2, 1926, by Sweden's Crown Prince Gustav Adolf. Constructed at a cost of $234,000, it was not completed until after the close of the exposition. Today it still stands in what is known as Franklin D. Roosevelt Park and serves as the American Swedish Historical Museum. (John D. Cardinell.)

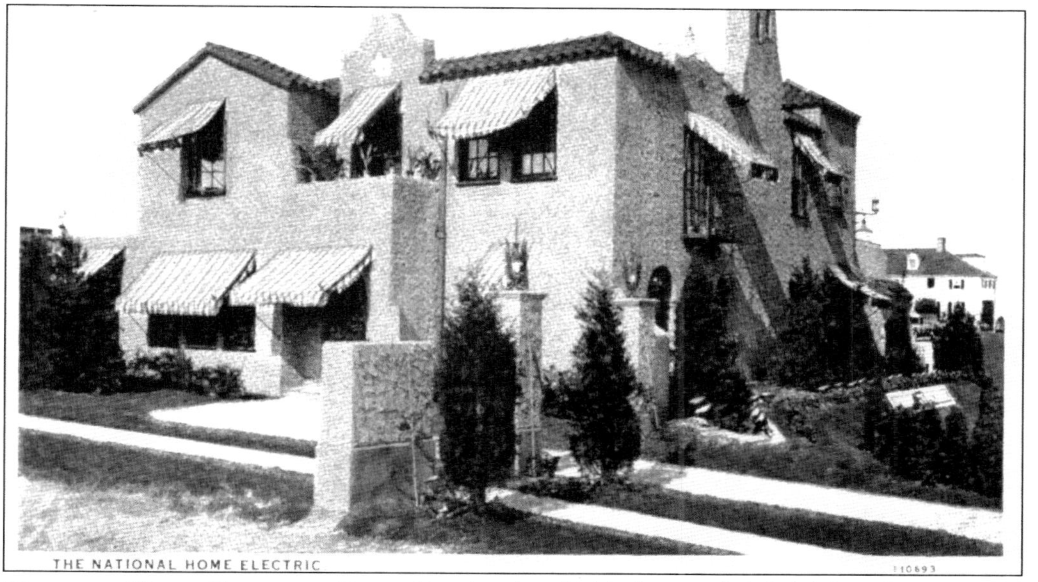

NATIONAL HOME ELECTRIC. Erected by the electrical industry of Philadelphia, this attractive model home served to demonstrate all the "modern" conveniences that electricity could provide the average household. The completely furnished eight-room home was 52 feet wide by 46 feet long and contained all manner of electrical devices from refrigerators and dishwashers to burglar alarms. Also highlighted were electrical heating and lighting systems. (John D. Cardinell.)

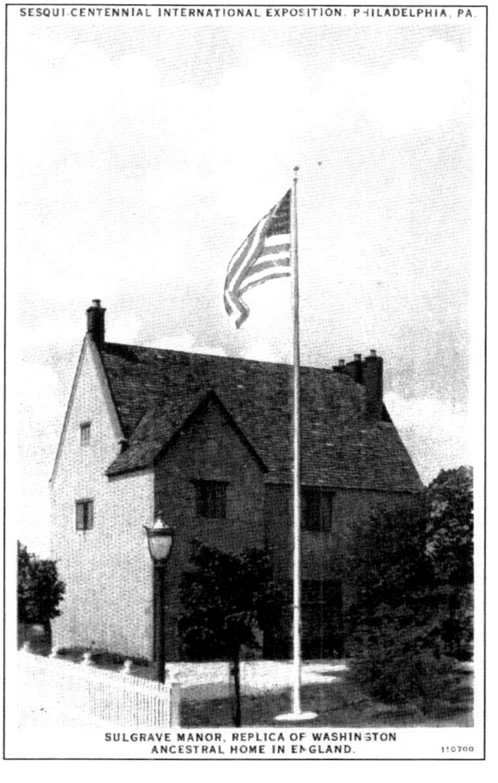

SULGRAVE MANOR. George Washington's ancestral home is located near Banbury, England. Owned by Lawrence Washington in the 1500s, the estate was known as Sulgrave Manor. For the Sesqui-Centennial International Exposition, the National Society of Colonial Dames planned and financed this replica erected from plans of the original home. Open daily to the public from June 1 onward, this reconstruction was architecturally correct both inside and out. (John D. Cardinell.)

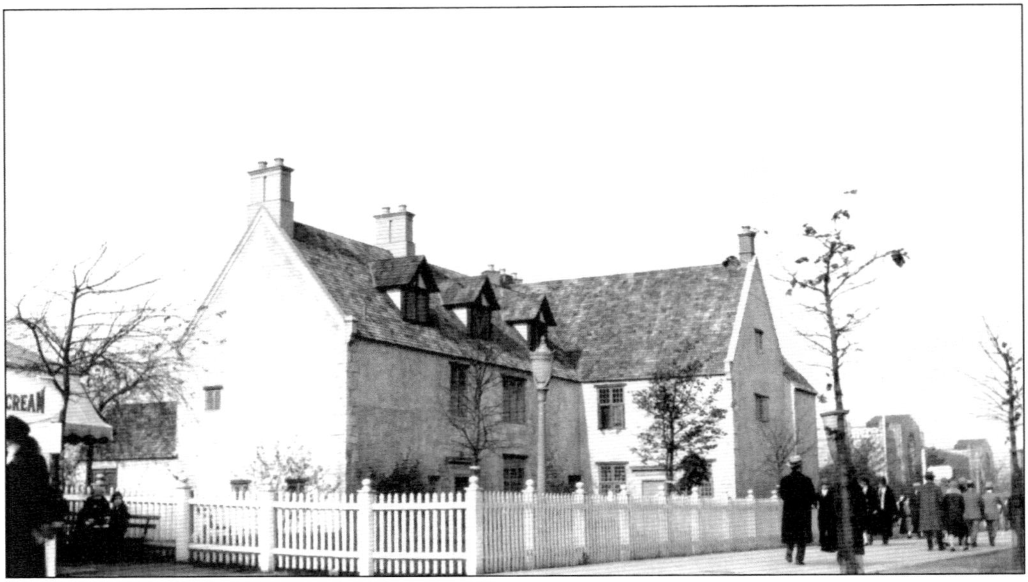

WASHINGTON'S ANCESTRAL HOME. Sited on Broad Street just off Pattison Avenue, this re-creation of Sulgrave Manor occupied a prime location near the center of the exposition. It was hoped that the building would serve as a "stimulus to patriotism in American youth." Members of the National Society of Colonial Dames, who served as hostesses, regaled visitors with stories of this historic home and the Washington family.

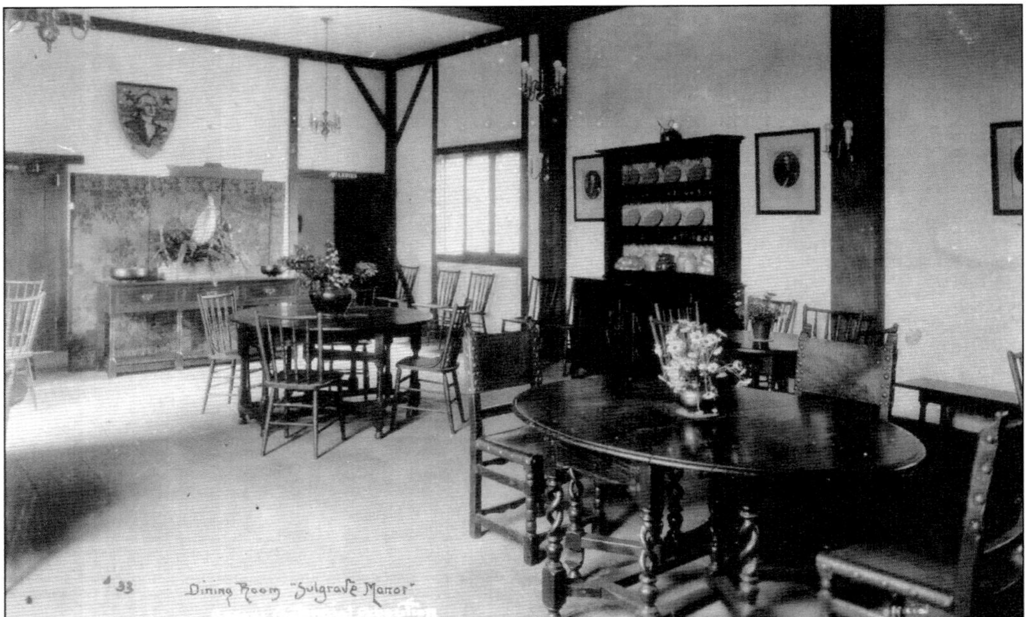

DINING ROOM IN SULGRAVE MANOR. Stained-glass windows helped provide natural light to the long dining room that was a duplicate of that in the original home. A plaque bearing the likeness of George Washington hangs on the far wall. Handcrafted woodwork and wrought-iron finishes added ambiance. An average of 500 people per day toured the house and had the opportunity to view its architectural details. (John D. Cardinell.)

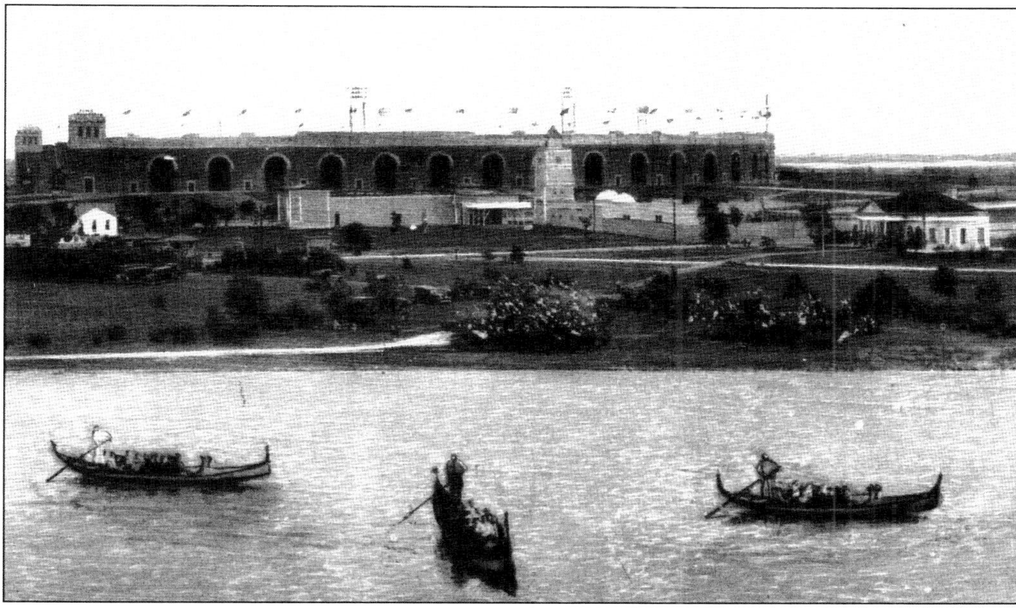

MUNICIPAL STADIUM. The Sesqui-Centennial International Exposition Stadium is seen here from across Edgewater Lake. The stadium was erected by the city at a cost of $2 million and opened on April 15, 1926. Occupying 13.5 acres, the stadium could hold 100,000 people or more depending on the venue. For nighttime events, the field was illuminated by 190 projectors located atop steel towers, each having a 1,500-watt lamp. (John D. Cardinell.)

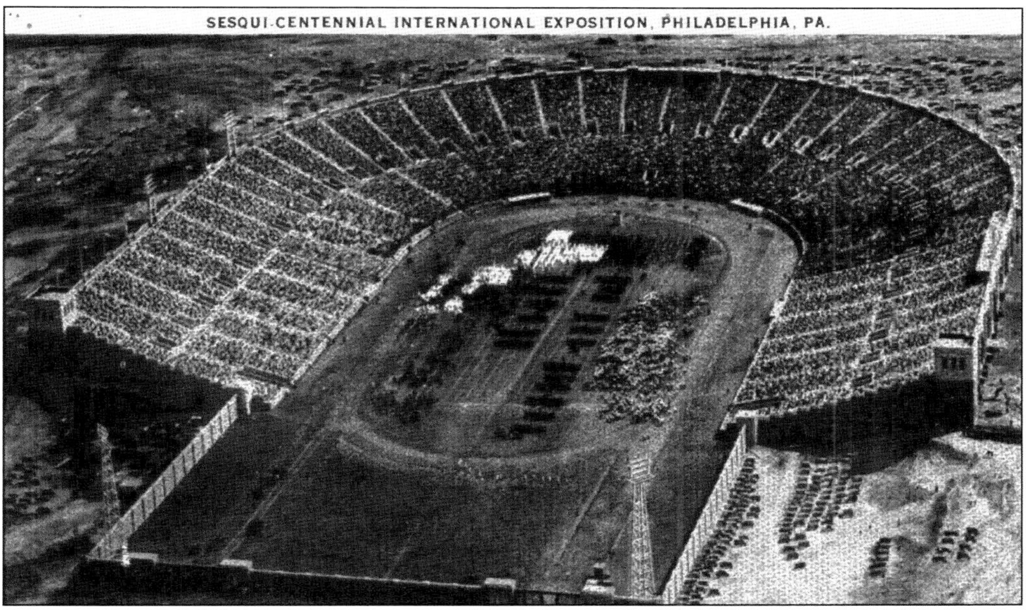

STADIUM. Designed by the architectural firm of Simon and Simon, the stadium stood at Broad Street and Pattison Avenue. Horseshoe shaped, with its open end to the north, the stadium was constructed of reinforced concrete, brick, and stone. Measuring 710 feet in width with an overall length of 1,020 feet, it was built with the intention of remaining after the exposition as a permanent structure. (John D. Cardinell.)

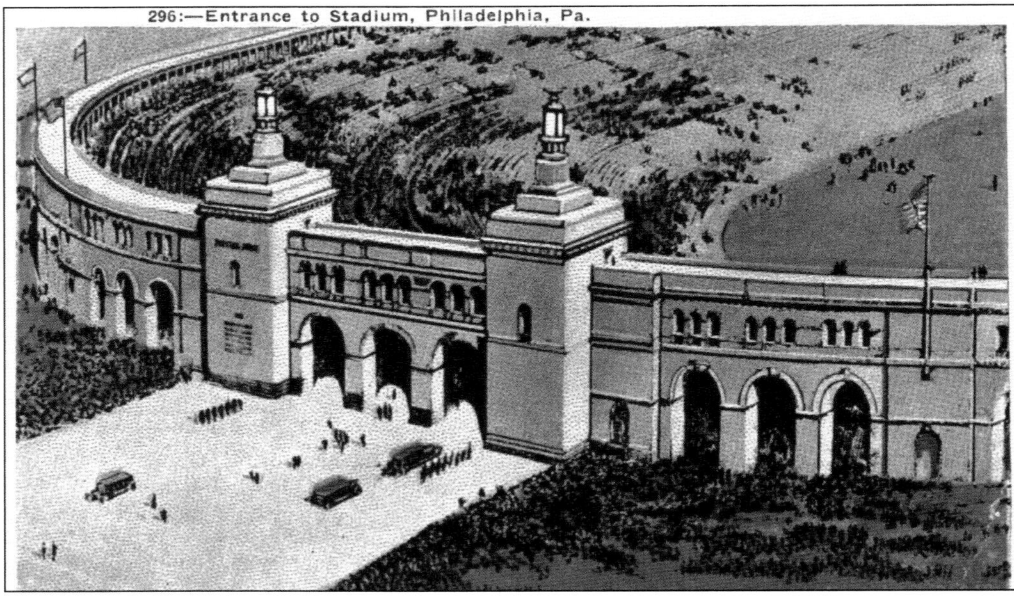

Main Entrance to Stadium. It was possible to enter the stadium by means of 39 entrance gates, while 38 exits hastened departures after an event. During the exposition, events held here included baseball, football, track and field competitions, gymnastics, rodeos, parades, pageants, concerts, dances, a religious field mass celebrated by over 135,000 participants, and much more. Numerous international and national sports championships took place here as well. (John D. Cardinell.)

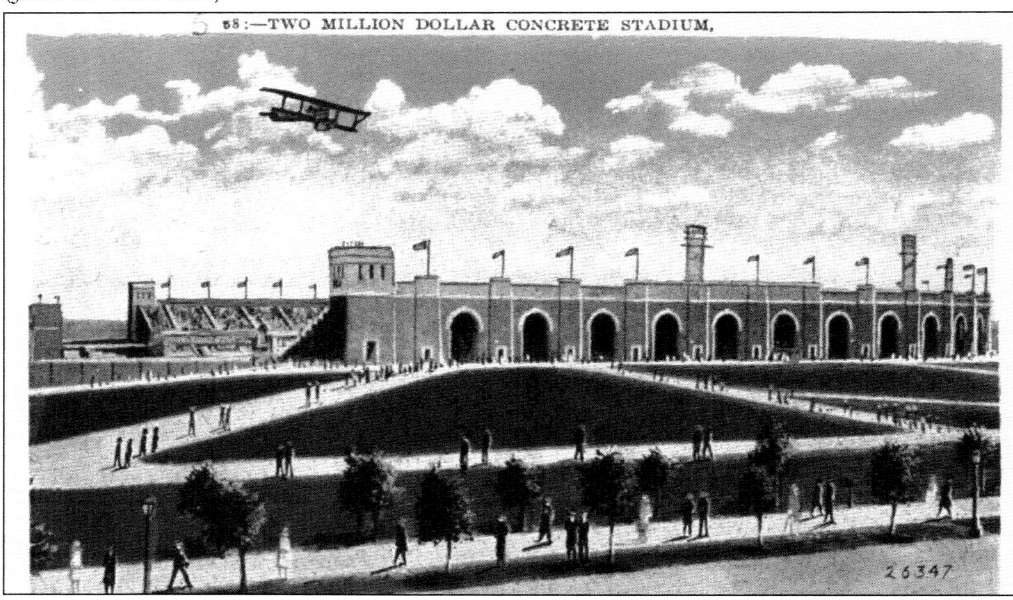

Dempsey-Tunney Fight. Perhaps the most famous event held at the exposition took place on September 23, when one of the largest crowds to ever witness a sporting event in this country packed into the stadium to see Jack Dempsey defend his heavyweight boxing title against Gene Tunney. Over 120,000 spectators sat in the rain to see Tunney win the historic championship bout in a 10-round decision. (John D. Cardinell.)

JACK DEMPSEY. One of the most popular athletes of all time, Jack Dempsey (1895–1983) was nicknamed the "Manassa Mauler." Known for his powerful fighting style, he won 50 of his bouts by knockout. He was the world heavyweight champion from 1919 to 1926. Upon retiring from the ring, Dempsey went on to become a renowned restaurant owner on Broadway in New York City. (Eagle Post Card View Company.)

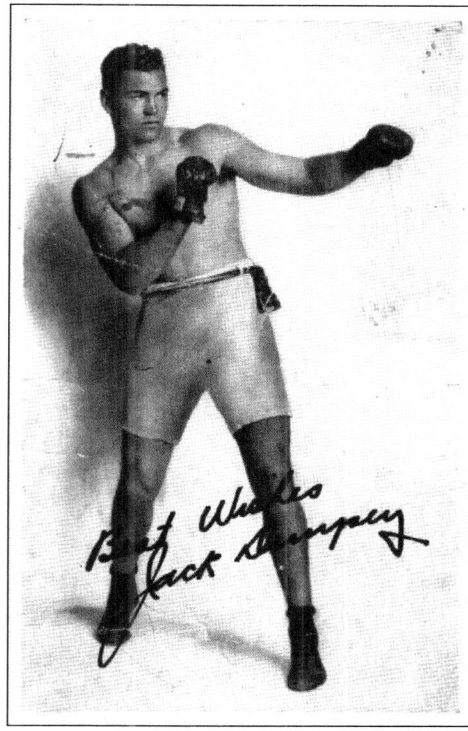

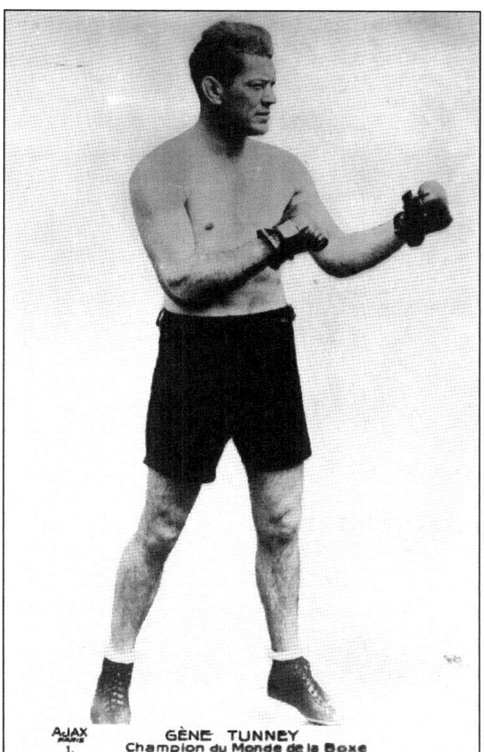

GENE TUNNEY. Seen here after becoming the world heavyweight boxing champion, Gene Tunney (1897–1978) was known as the "Fighting Marine." A highly intelligent boxer, he only lost one fight in his professional career and retired undefeated as a heavyweight in 1928. After leaving the sport, he went on to become a highly successful businessman. (Ajax.)

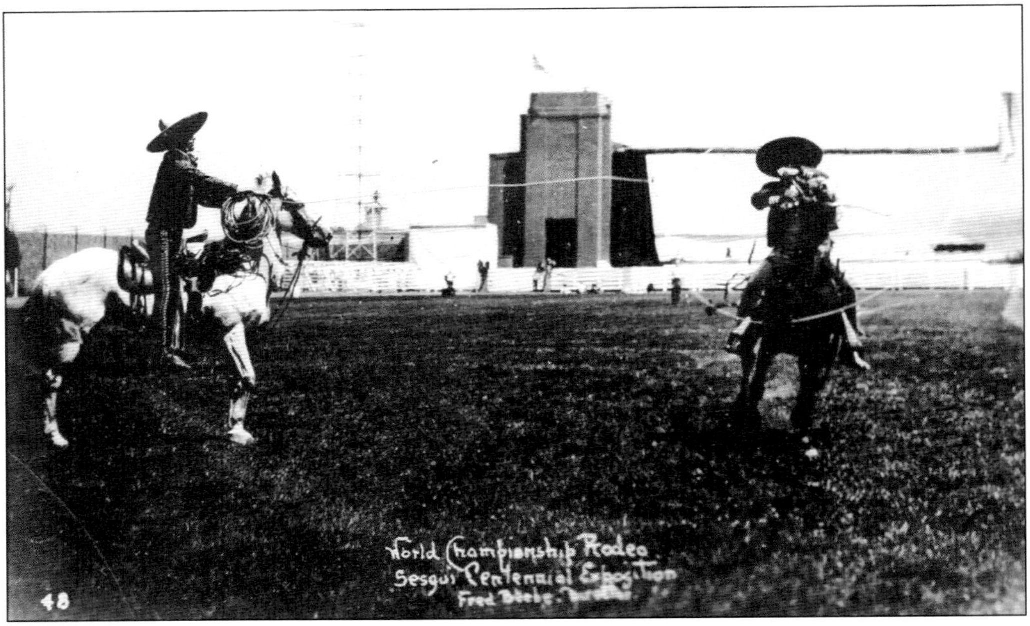

WORLD CHAMPIONSHIP RODEO. Included among the many sports events held in the stadium were track and field, lacrosse, field hockey, baseball, football, and even rodeo competitions. Here two riders dressed in Mexican-style outfits practice a rope trick. What was billed as the "World Championship Rodeo" was held here under the direction of Fred Beebe, a noted promoter of the sport.

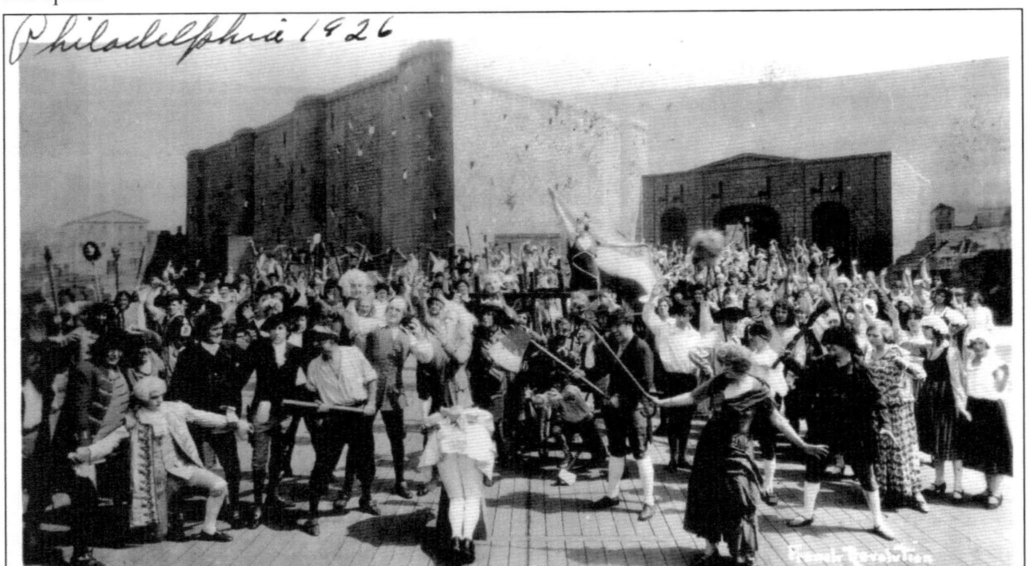

"FREEDOM" PAGEANT. One of the greatest spectacles given in the stadium was the pageant titled "Freedom." Tracing the history of freedom from the Stone Age to the inauguration of America's first president, this lavish production included some 1,500 performers. Unfortunately, due to poor weather, only about half of the three-hour-long performances were given. Here is a scene depicting the French Revolution.

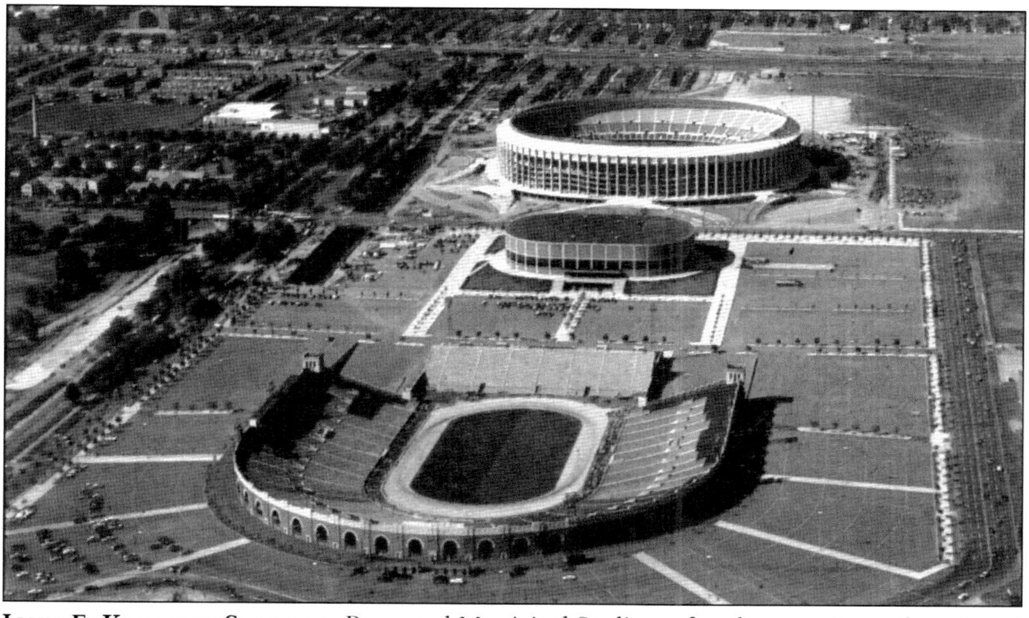

JOHN F. KENNEDY STADIUM. Renamed Municipal Stadium after the exposition, the original Sesqui-Centennial International Exposition Stadium would become known as the John F. Kennedy Stadium in 1964. Site of the annual Army-Navy football games, and countless other sporting events and music concerts over the years, it was razed in 1992. Also seen here are the Spectrum (scheduled for demolition in 2009) and the old Veterans Stadium, which came down in 2004. (Art Color Card Distributors.)

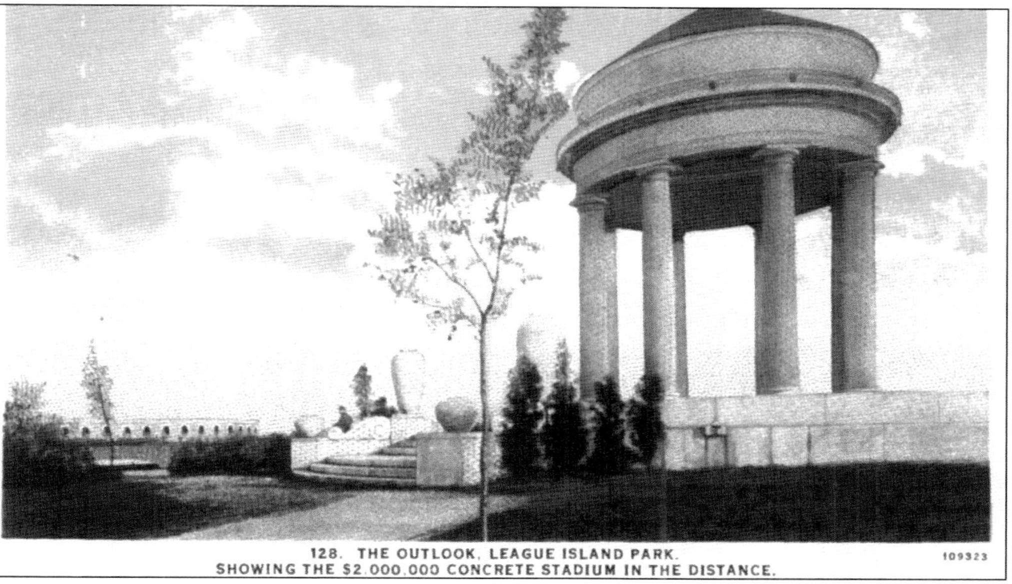

128. THE OUTLOOK, LEAGUE ISLAND PARK. 109323
SHOWING THE $2,000,000 CONCRETE STADIUM IN THE DISTANCE.

GRAND GAZEBO. Perched on a point of land overlooking Edgewater Lake, this wonderful gazebo offered a lovely place to sit, relax, and enjoy the views. Originally a part of League Island Park and designed by the landscape architectural firm the Olmsted Brothers, it existed prior to the Sesqui-Centennial International Exposition, having been erected back in 1914. It still stands today. Noticeable off in the distance is the great stadium. (John D. Cardinell.)

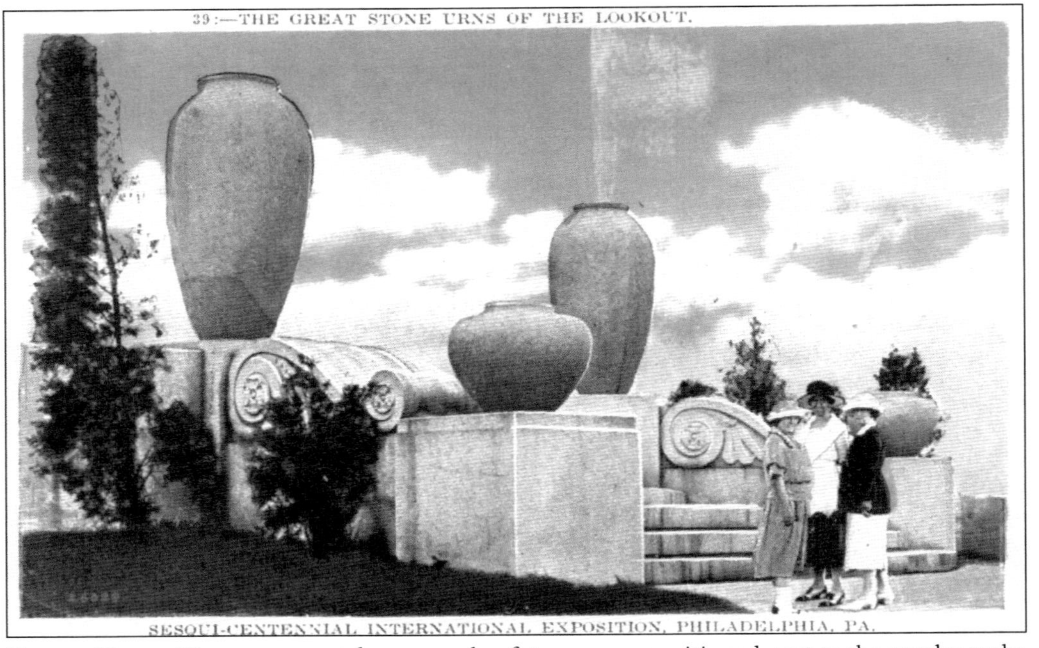

GREAT URNS. Giant ornamental urns, made of stone, were positioned next to the gazebo at the outlook on Edgewater Lake. Three ladies are seen here posing for the postcard photographer near these decorative features. It was not unusual for people to want to stop and have their photograph taken at this picturesque setting. (John D. Cardinell.)

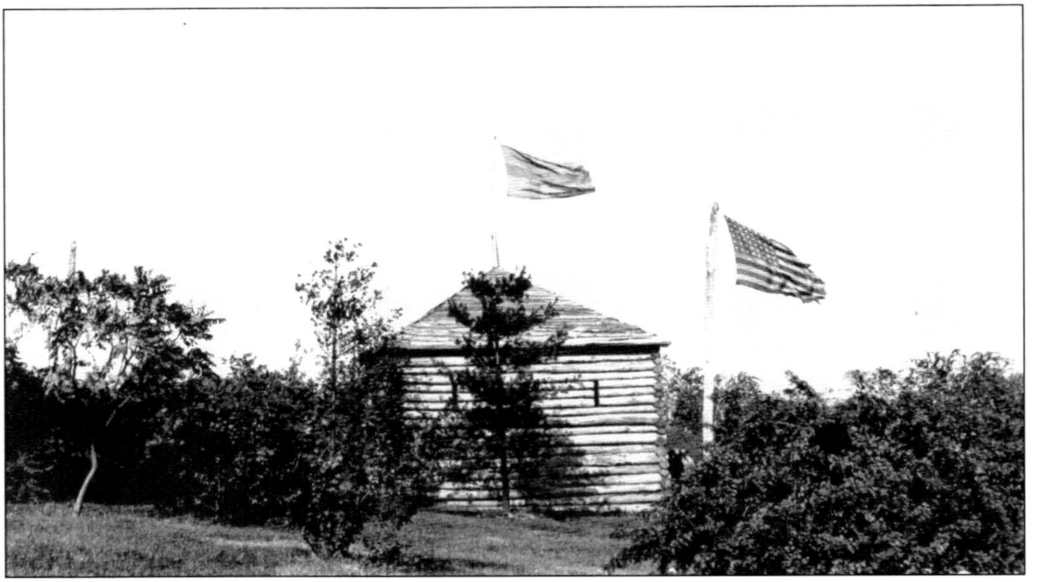

WICACO BLOCK HOUSE. A reproduction of an early Philadelphia fort, a type originally erected by Swedish settlers, was built by the Swedish Colonial Society. It was officially dedicated on June 2 in the presence of the crown prince and princess of Sweden. Some 36 historical talks describing the Swedish colonization of America were given each day to visitors with daily attendance averaging 1,000.

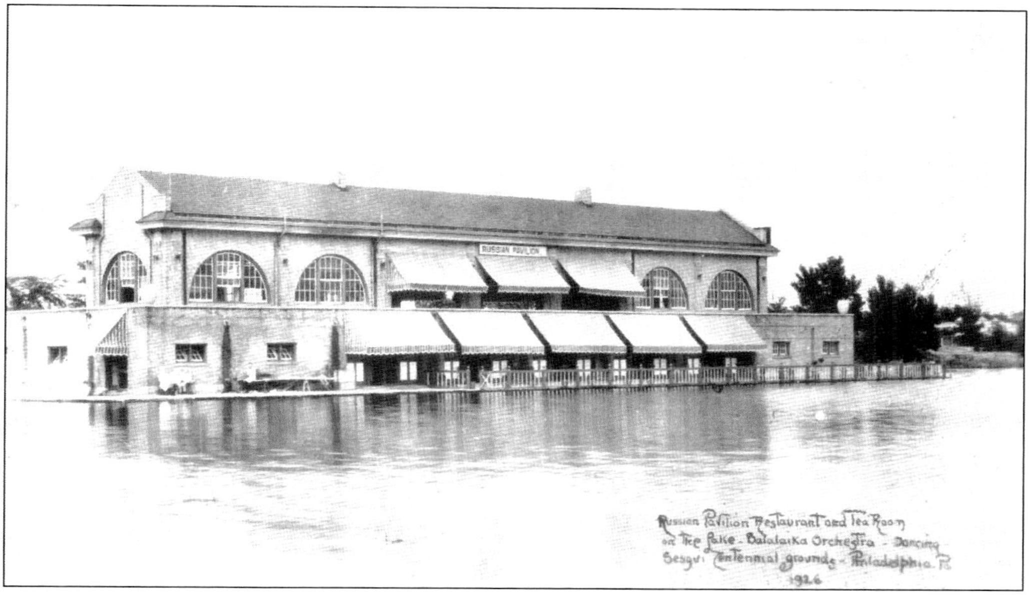

RUSSIAN PAVILION RESTAURANT. Situated directly on the shores of Edgewater Lake, this building was originally built in 1914. During the Sesqui-Centennial International Exposition, it housed a restaurant and tearoom, in what was referred to as the Russian Pavilion. It also featured dancing to the Balalaika Orchestra. After the exposition, it became a boat rental facility and recreation pavilion and still stands today in what is now known as FDR Park.

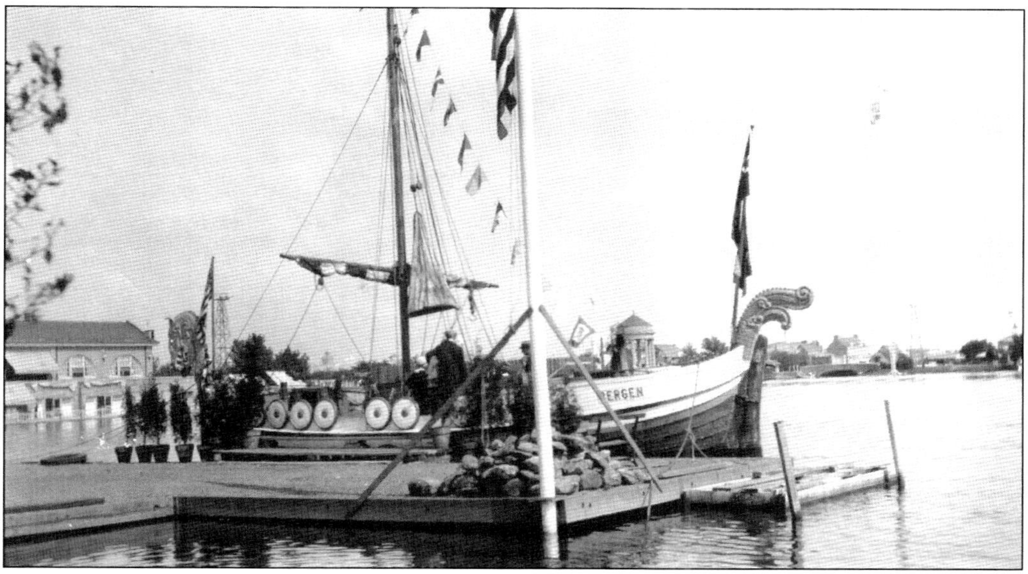

VIKING SHIP. Tied up to a wharf on Edgewater Lake was a 42-foot-long replica of a Viking ship named the *Leif Erikson*. Sailing from Bergen, Norway, on May 23, 1926, the ship arrived in Boston on August 12 after a 6,700-mile voyage, bound for Philadelphia. While on display at the Sesqui-Centennial International Exposition, the unusual craft drew plenty of attention. (W. J. Gambino.)

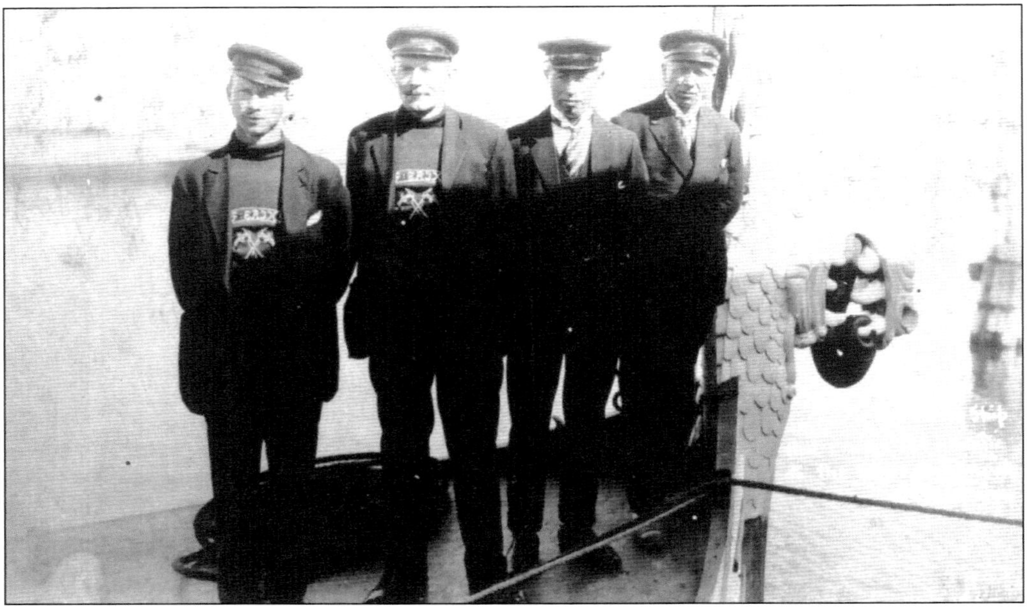

CREW OF THE *LEIF ERICKSON*. Posing for the camera aboard the *Leif Erikson* are Capt. Gerhard Folgaro and his three-man crew. These men, accompanied by a small dog, made the treacherous journey following the same route taken by Leif Erikson back in AD 997. The Atlantic crossing was made entirely under sail, except when the crew had to resort to rowing when becalmed.

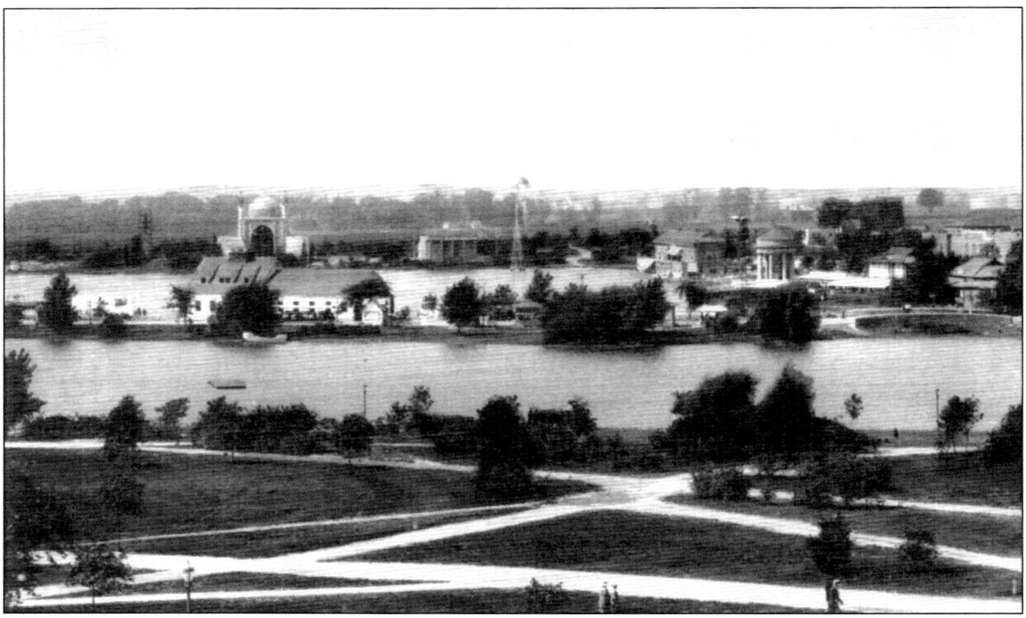

COAST GUARD STATION. Erected on the shores of Edgewater Lake was a typical U.S. Coast Guard station, which was manned by 3 officers and 21 enlisted men. Daily lifesaving and boat drills were held for the public to witness. Inside the 4,880-square-foot building were numerous displays related to the duties of this branch of service. (John D. Cardinell.)

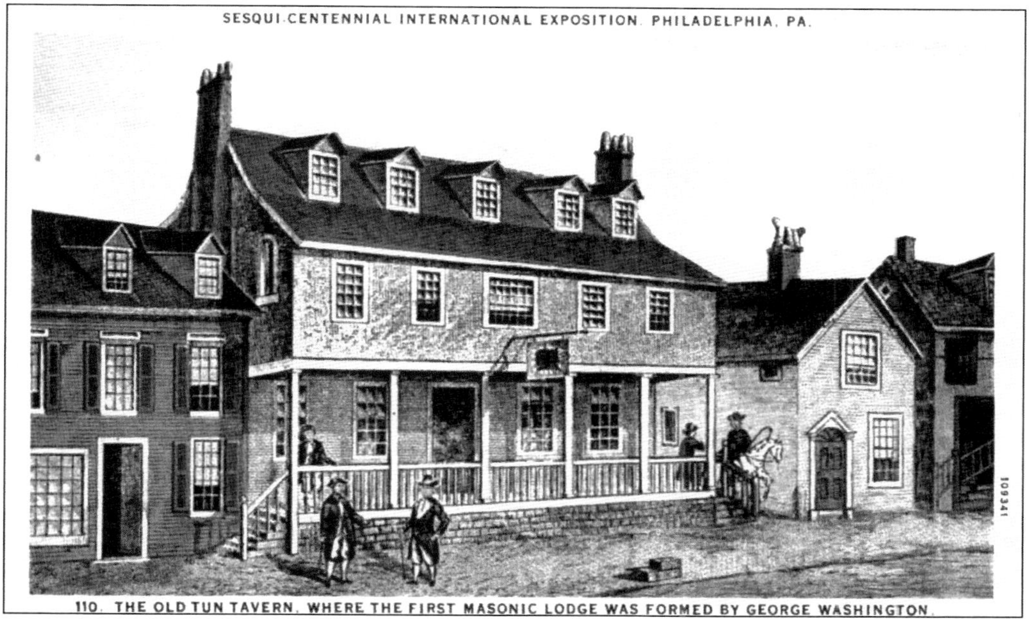

ORIGINAL TUN TAVERN. This artistic drawing portrays the famous Tun Tavern that once stood along Water Street in Philadelphia. Built by Samuel Carpenter in 1685, the tavern was home to America's first Masonic Lodge, which met here as early as 1730. This building is probably best known, however, as the birthplace of the U.S. Marine Corps. It was here in 1775 that the first marines were recruited. (John D. Cardinell.)

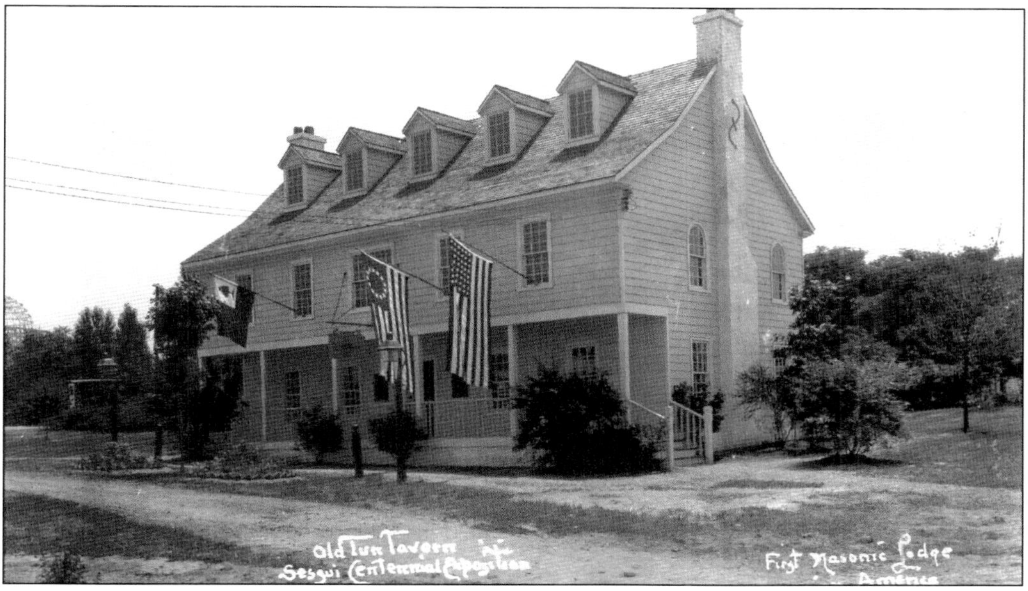

TUN TAVERN. As part of the U.S. Marine Corps exhibition, this replica of the Tun Tavern was located adjacent to a model military camp named Camp Samuel Nicholas. The camp was manned by men of the 43rd Company of the 5th Marines. The building was open daily between the hours of 10:00 a.m. and 10:00 p.m. and housed 11 large oil paintings depicting events in the history of the U.S. Marines.

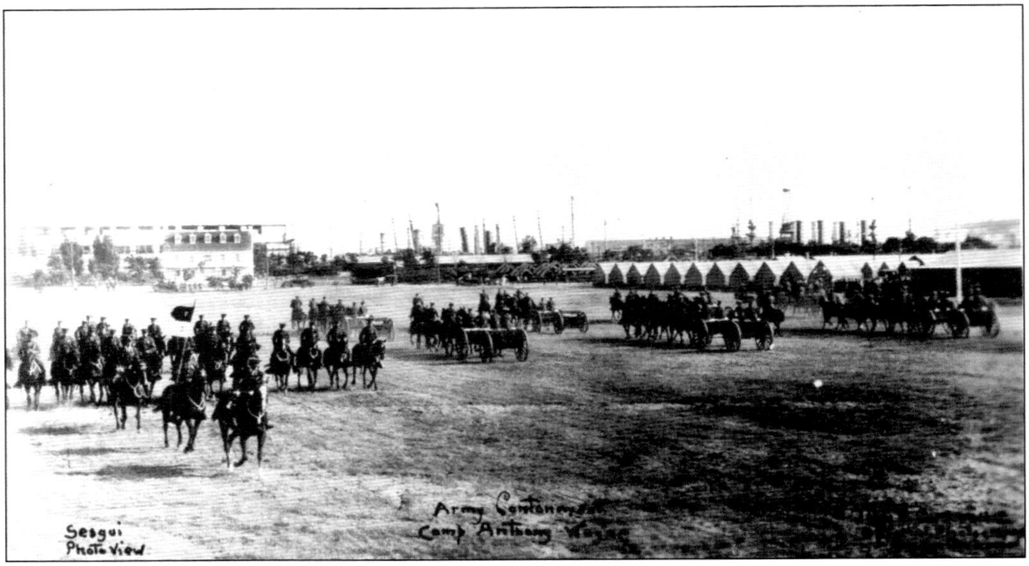

Camp Anthony Wayne. Just south of Edgewater Lake, the U.S. Army maintained a model army camp where 1,000 soldiers were stationed. These men represented units of the infantry, artillery, air service, and cavalry. Here members of Troop G, 3rd Cavalry, are seen performing maneuvers on the parade ground. Daily drills such as this were put on for public viewing. (John D. Cardinell.)

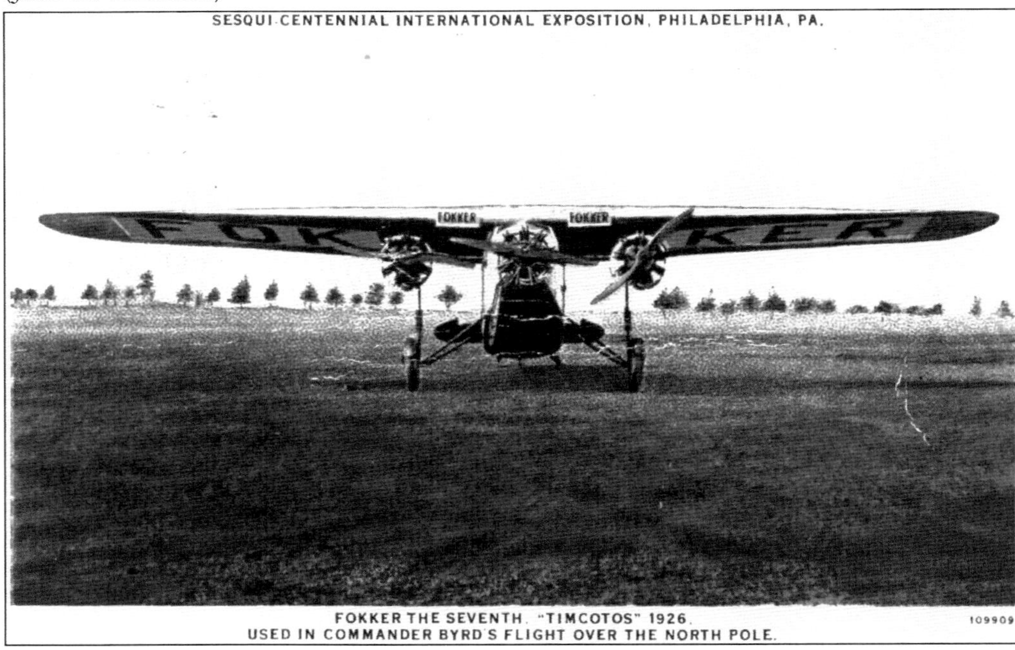

Commander Byrd's Plane. Attracting the interest of many people was the Fokker F. VII that was on display. This was the same airplane that was navigated by naval commander (later admiral) Richard E. Byrd and piloted by Floyd Bennett over the North Pole on May 9, 1926. The 49-foot-long, trimotor monoplane had a wingspan of 63 feet and a top speed of 118 miles per hour. (John D. Cardinell.)

Six

High Street

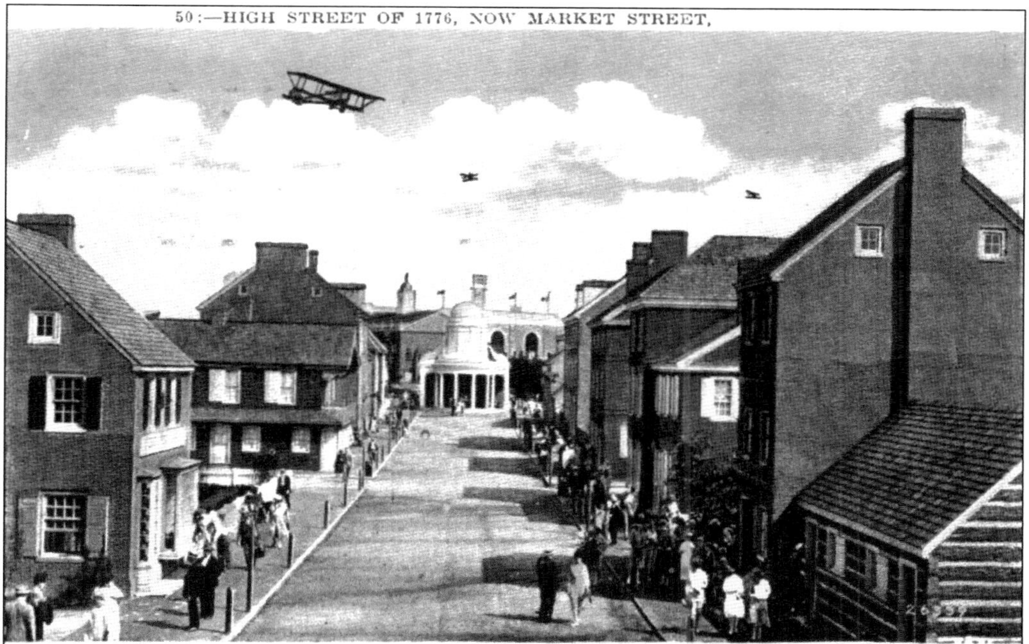

High Street. This reproduction of Philadelphia's Market Street of 1776 included replicas of 20 historic houses as well as the marketplace and town hall. Officially opened on June 5, 1926, millions of visitors would eventually walk the street and visit the homes before the exposition closed. During its all-too-brief existence, 22 state governors, 10 foreign notables, and Pres. Calvin Coolidge and his wife would be received here. (John D. Cardinell.)

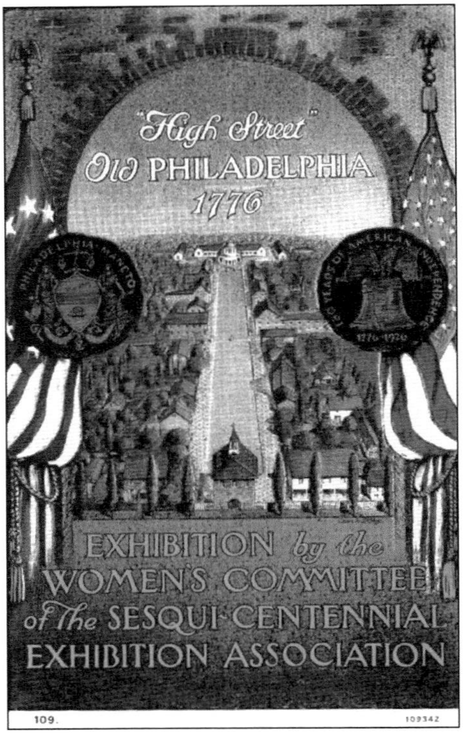

WOMEN'S COMMITTEE. Formed on October 16, 1925, with 100 women appointed by Mayor W. Freeland Kendrick, this group was later greatly expanded. It was through their efforts that High Street came about and was such a success. This women's group not only helped to establish High Street but also arranged patriotic programs, published booklets, acquired antique furnishings for exhibits, established information booths throughout the city, and did much more. (John D. Cardinell.)

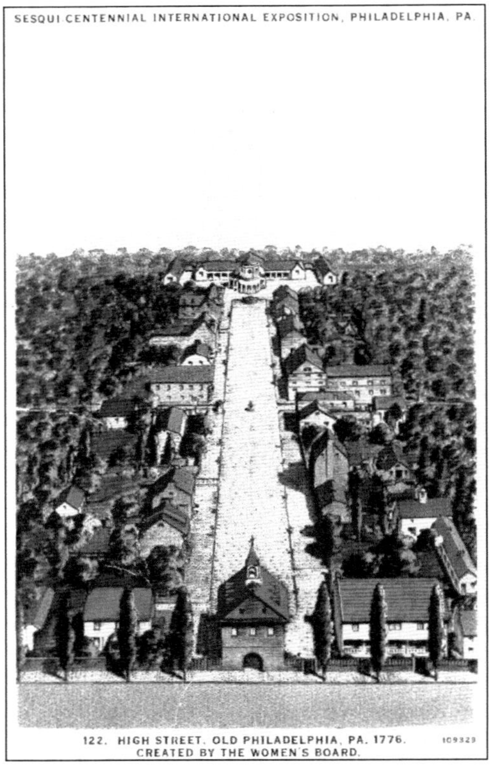

ARTISTIC VIEW OF HIGH STREET. An artist's conception of High Street shows its general layout and design. As it was planned, there was just one main street with replicated historic homes and buildings lining both sides. Anchoring opposite ends of this boulevard were representations of the town hall and a marketplace. (John D. Cardinell.)

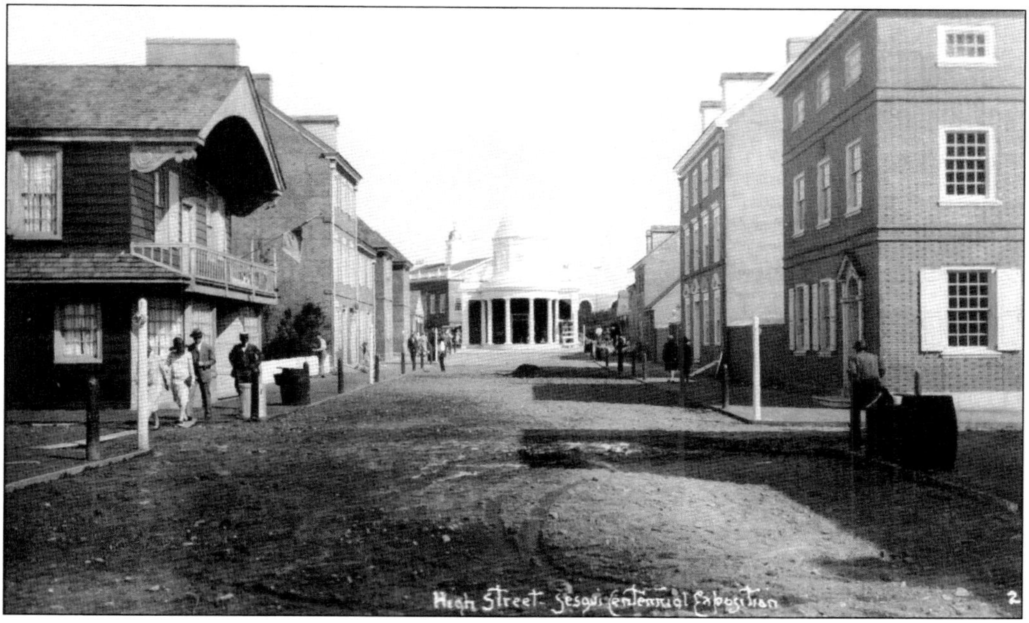

HISTORIC HIGH STREET. Great care to detail and historic accuracy was taken by the architects R. Brognard Okie and Bissel, Sinkler and Wadsworth, who helped to create the atmosphere of Colonial Philadelphia. Visitors were encouraged to enter and inspect the homes, with admission to each being free of charge. To assist visitors, there were costumed guides, stationed along the street, who provided directions and information to those in need. (W. J. Gambino.)

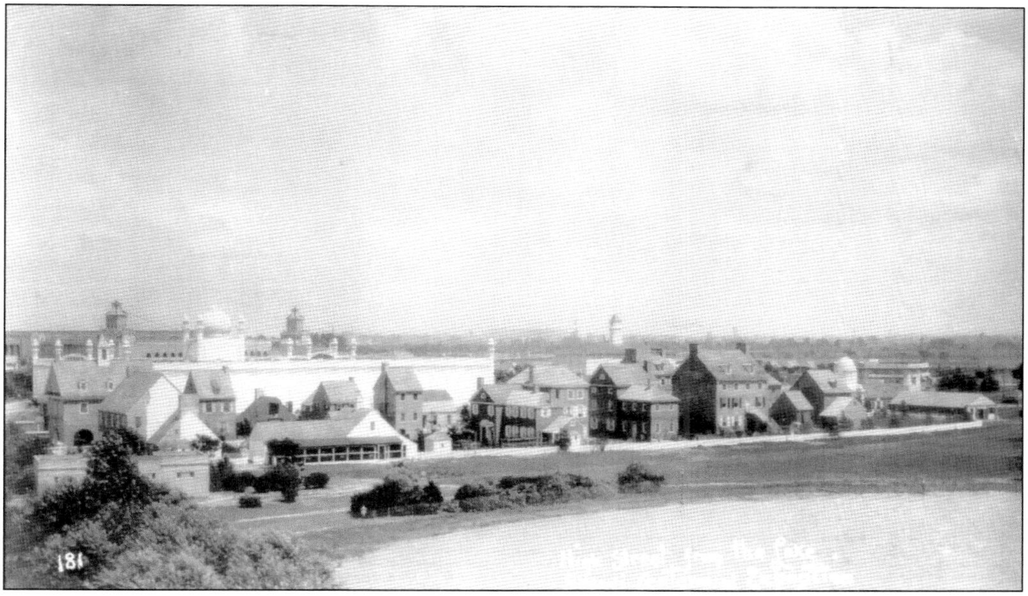

HIGH STREET AT A DISTANCE. Viewed from across the lake, High Street looked like a true pre–Revolutionary War street brought back to life. It was quite amazing, with a limited budget and just a few months allowed for construction, that such a marvelous recreation could be accomplished. Ultimately millions of people would have the opportunity to stroll along its sidewalks and inspect its buildings.

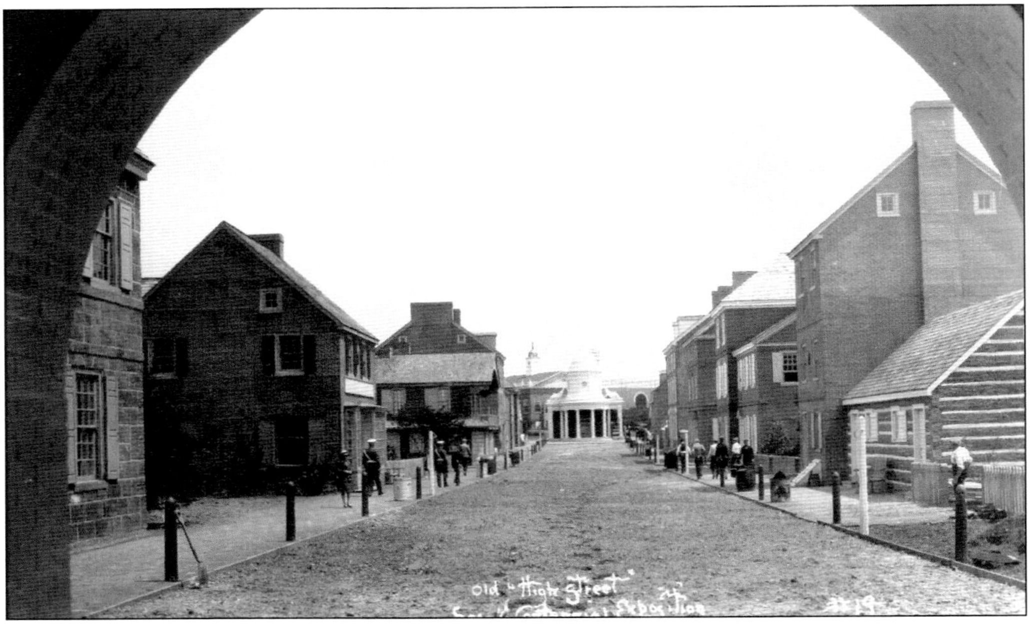

View from Town Hall. From town hall, a view along High Street shows the marketplace in the distance. Within the marketplace was an exhibit of dolls from around the world, as well as a doll representing an outstanding historic figure associated with each of the 48 states. On either side of the marketplace were stalls where commercial goods of all kinds were sold under the supervision of the Junior League of Philadelphia.

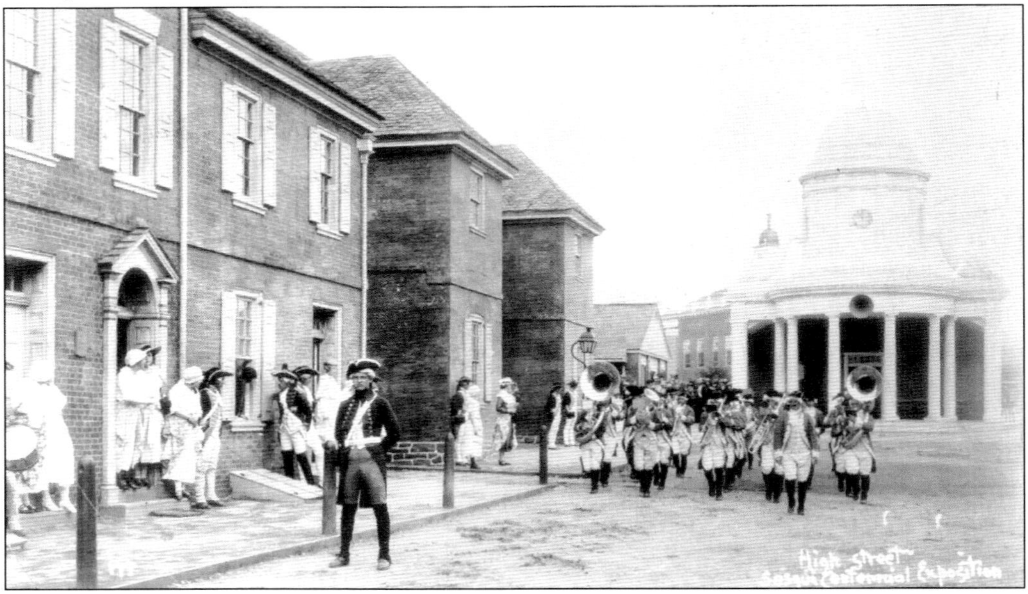

Parade on High Street. A band, dressed in Colonial military attire, marches down the center of High Street. Every Wednesday afternoon, pageants were held on the street, and an appropriately attired town crier daily walked the streets, calling attention to the various activities that were to take place. Highlights such as these helped to make High Street one of the more popular areas to visit. (John D. Cardinell.)

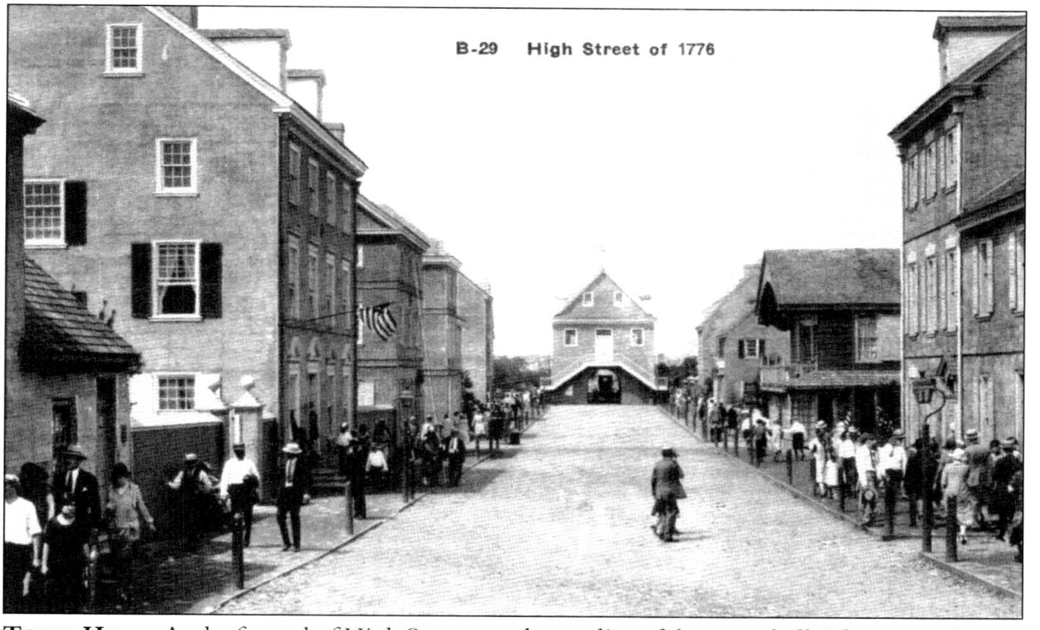

Town Hall. At the far end of High Street stands a replica of the town hall. The original town hall built in 1709 existed for 128 years, not being taken down until 1837. It was customary for new governors to give their inaugural speeches from its balcony. During Colonial times, the town hall was considered the very center of the city, and all distances where measured from that point.

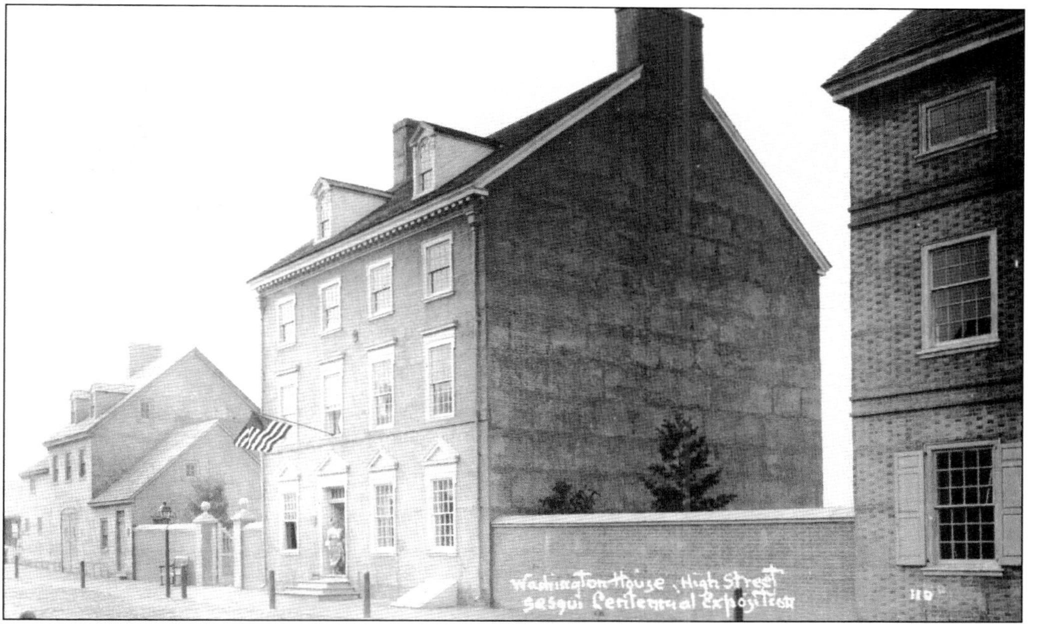

The Washington House. An imposing replica of the Philadelphia home occupied by George Washington as the nation's first president, this building was under the supervision of the Daughters of the American Revolution. Marvelously furnished and decorated, the house was perhaps the most frequented on the street, with some 75,000 registered visitors.

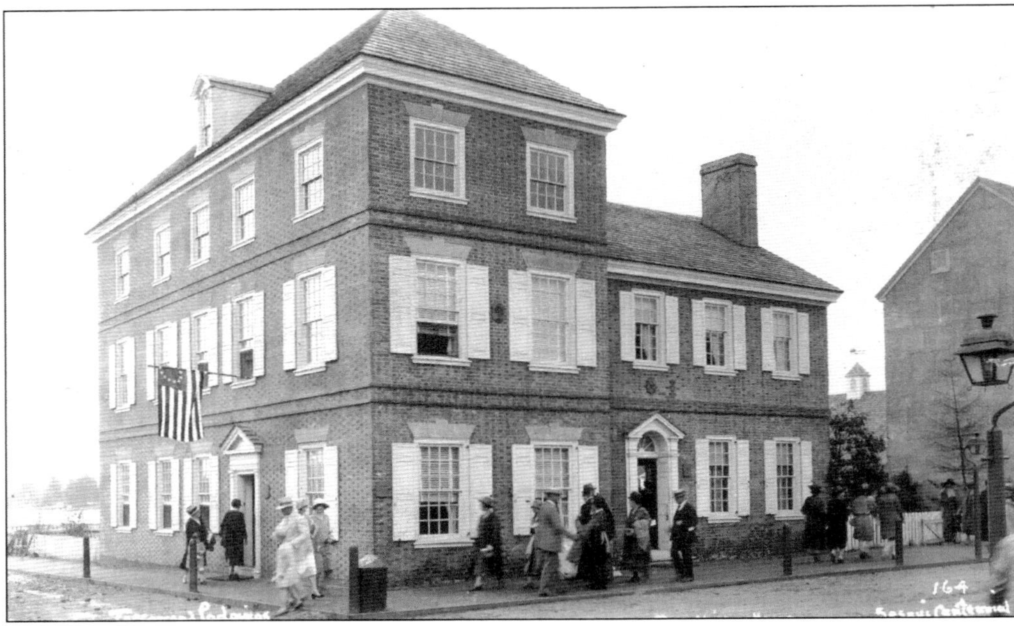

SHIPPEN HOUSE. A reconstruction of the two-story home of Dr. William Shippen was constructed along High Street. Shippen had been director general of all military hospitals during the Revolutionary War and was cofounder of the nation's first medical school, which was named University Medical School. Adjoining the house, on the corner, was a replica of the three-story lodging house where Thomas Jefferson wrote the Declaration of Independence. (John D. Cardinell.)

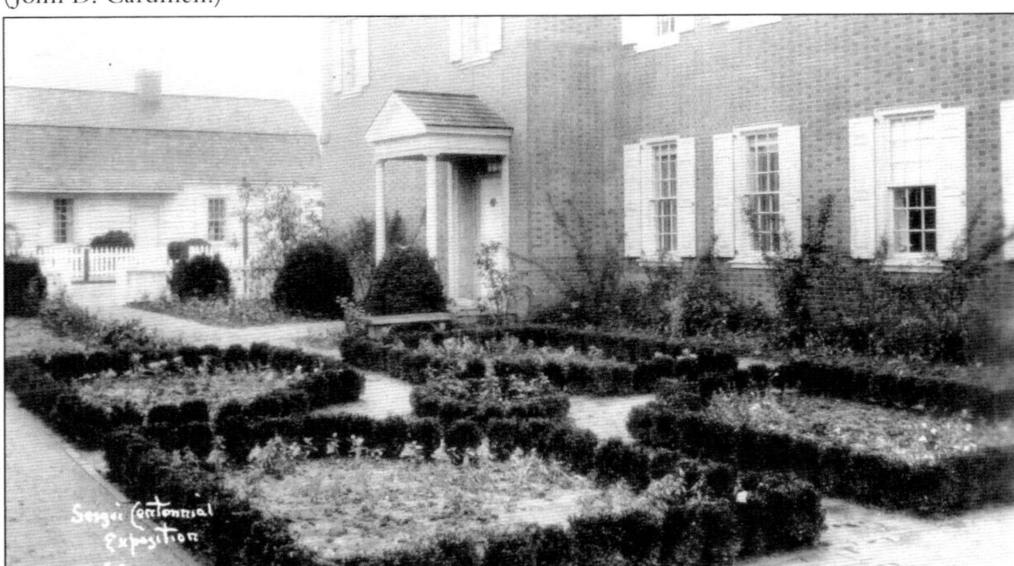

GARDENS OF SHIPPEN HOUSE. Many flower gardens were laid out to complement the houses along High Street. One of the nicer examples was that of the Shippen House. Planted by the Weeders Garden Club, this garden with its evergreen box-edged borders was a more formal example and contained such flower species as zinnias, marigolds, and snapdragons.

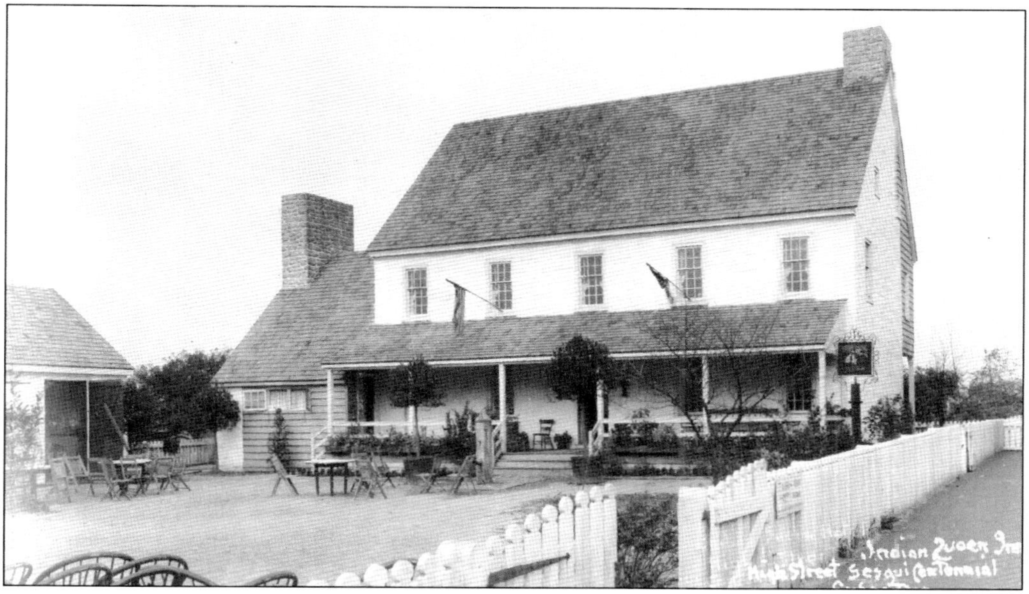

INDIAN QUEEN INN. Surrounded by a white picket fence was the Indian Queen Inn. Here visitors could enjoy a meal or refreshments and imagine themselves back in historic times. Decorated with authentic early-American furniture, it provided the atmosphere typical of early-day taverns. This was all under the supervision of the Emergency Aid Committee of Pennsylvania.

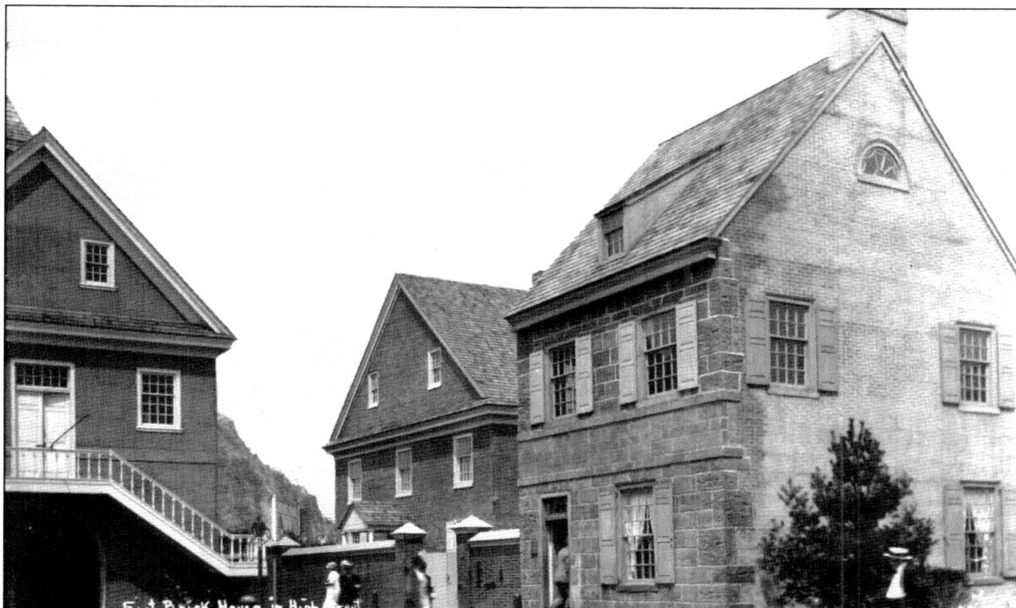

FIRST BRICK HOUSE. This building, often referred to as the Dame School, represented the first brick home in Philadelphia. Erected by Andrew Griscom in 1683, it was here that the Quakers set up a school in 1689. So under direction of the Philadelphia Teacher's Association, a classroom complete with lifelike wax figures of students was on display and thousands of copies of the *New England Primer* were handed out to visitors. (JMC Publishing.)

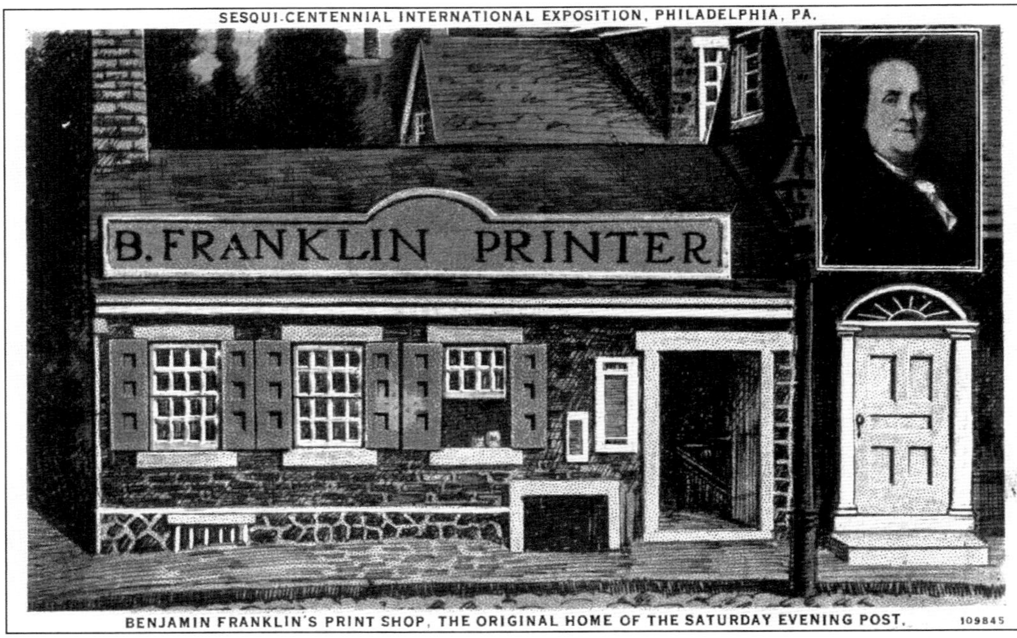

BENJAMIN FRANKLIN PRINTER. An artistic rendition shows how Benjamin Franklin's print shop may have looked in the 1700s. Franklin, the famous scientist, statesman, and writer, first came to Philadelphia in 1723. By 1728, at the age of 22, he had opened his own print shop where he put out such well-known works as the *Pennsylvania Gazette* and his annual *Poor Richard's Almanack*. (John D. Cardinell.)

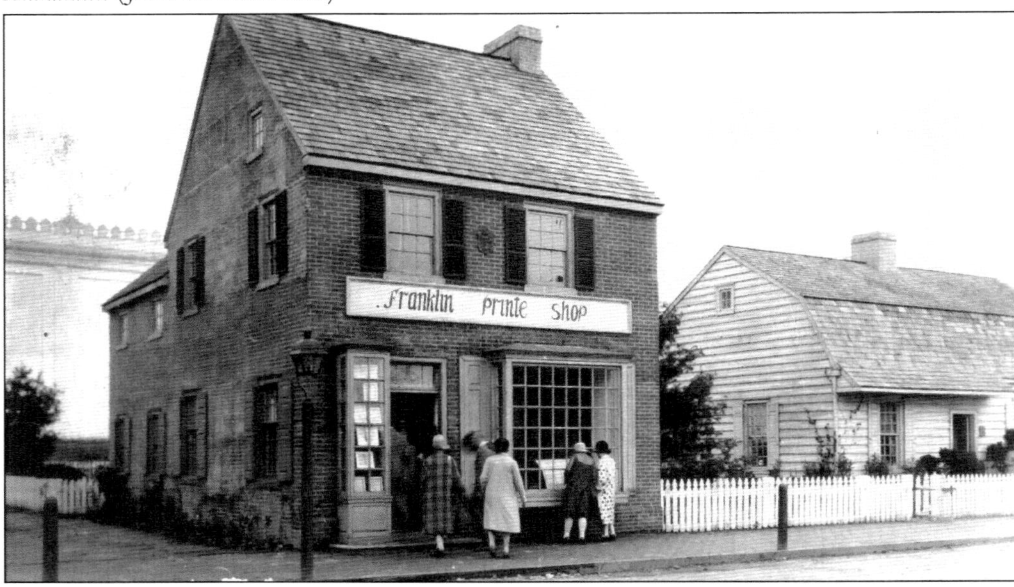

FRANKLIN PRINTE SHOP. For the Sesqui-Centennial International Exposition, the *Philadelphia Ledger* newspaper fittingly sponsored the replica of Franklin's print shop. Furnished with equipment loaned by the American Type Founders, the shop was staffed by people dressed as Colonial-day printers and apprentices. Here visitors could learn about the operation of the early presses and see how the type was laboriously handset.

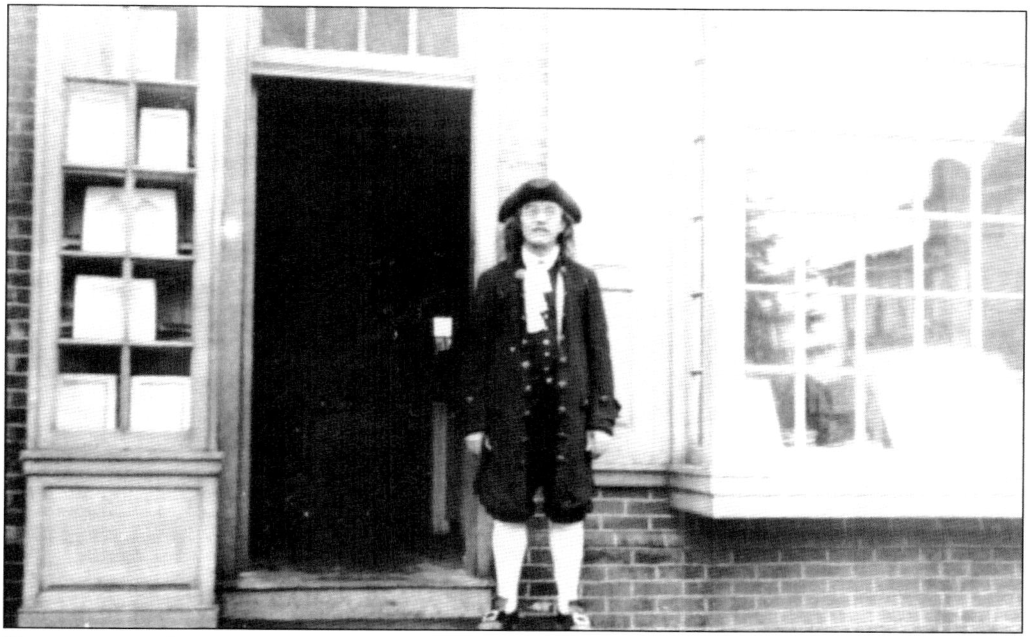

DOORWAY TO PRINT SHOP. Standing in the doorway to this reproduction of the Franklin Printe Shop, ready to greet visitors, is a reenactor dressed as the great man himself. In the window of the shop are copies of books that had been printed by Franklin. (W. J. Gambino.)

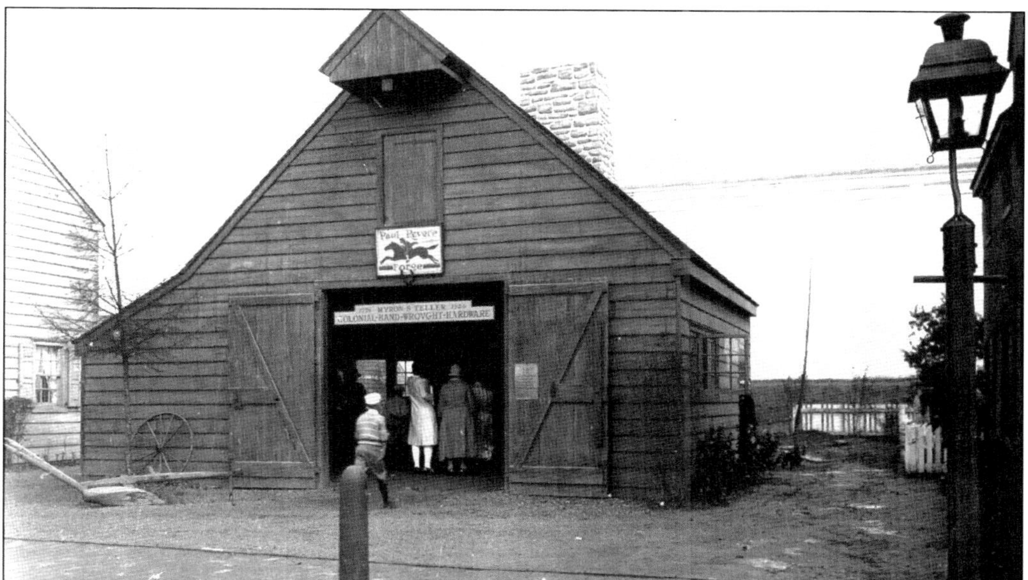

BLACKSMITH SHOPPE. Also known as Paul Revere's Forge, this exhibit was sponsored by the Pennsylvania Society of New England Women. Inside a blacksmith demonstrated the art of working metal as he described how Paul Revere had created the ironwork used in the construction of the U.S. frigate *Constitution*. It was also in this building that all the wrought-iron work for the High Street houses was produced.

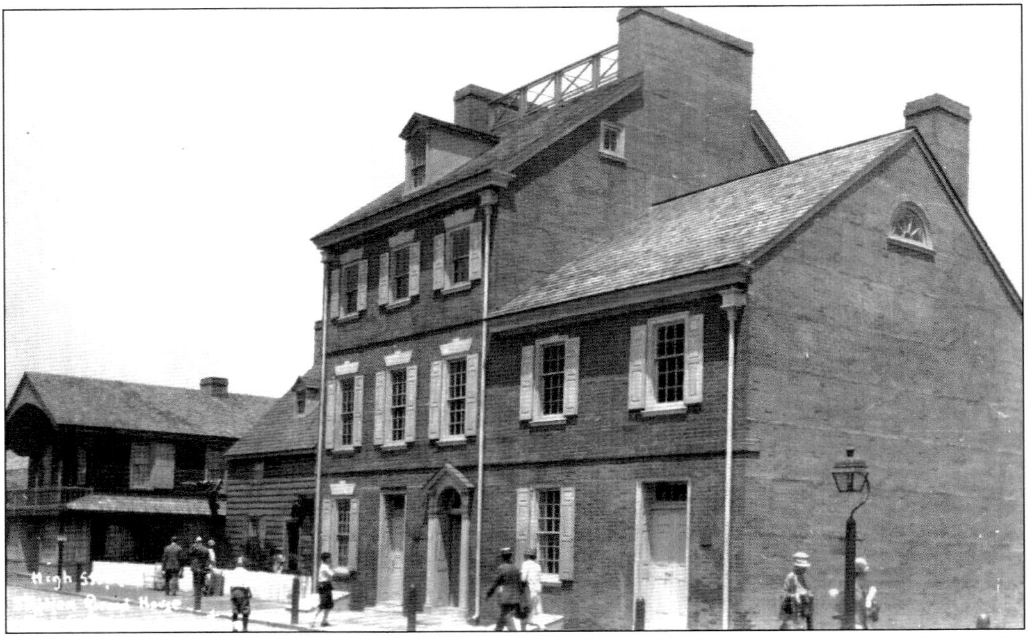

STEPHEN GIRARD HOUSE. Under the auspices of the Foreign Committee was a replica of the home and counting house of famous banker and philanthropist Stephen Girard. In the counting house was his actual desk, money chests, keys, and the like, while the home was decorated in the French Empire style. As the headquarters for foreign visitors, the home was the site of 16 teas held to honor various ambassadors and foreign dignitaries.

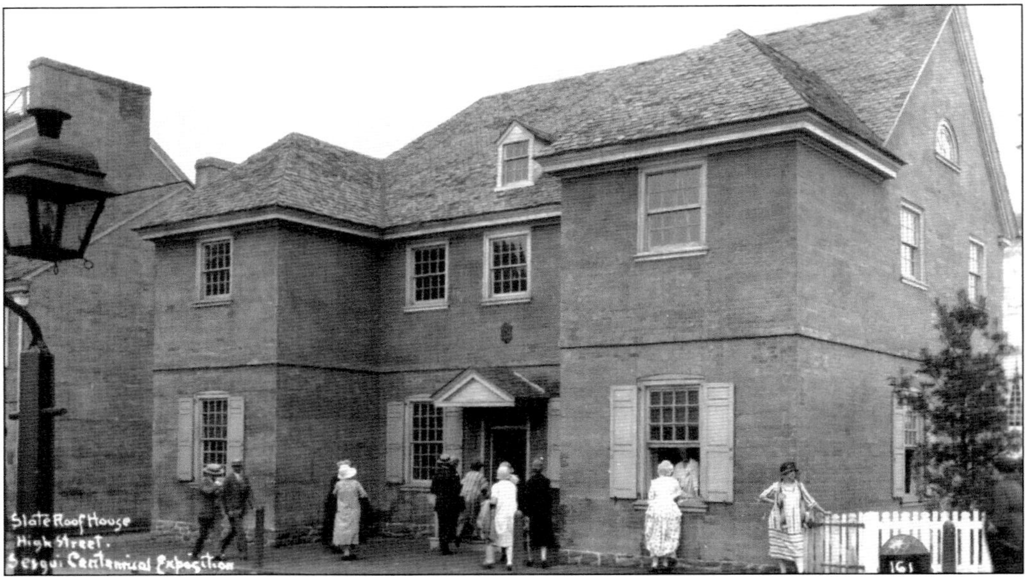

SLATE ROOF HOUSE. One of the most frequented buildings was this replica of William Penn's home originally located at Second and Sansom Streets. It was decorated with antiques dating back to 1660. Sponsored by the States' Committee, it served as the center for women visiting the exposition and as the location for the presentation of state flags by representatives of the governors. A total of 22 state governors were greeted here.

Seven

The Gladway and Treasure Island

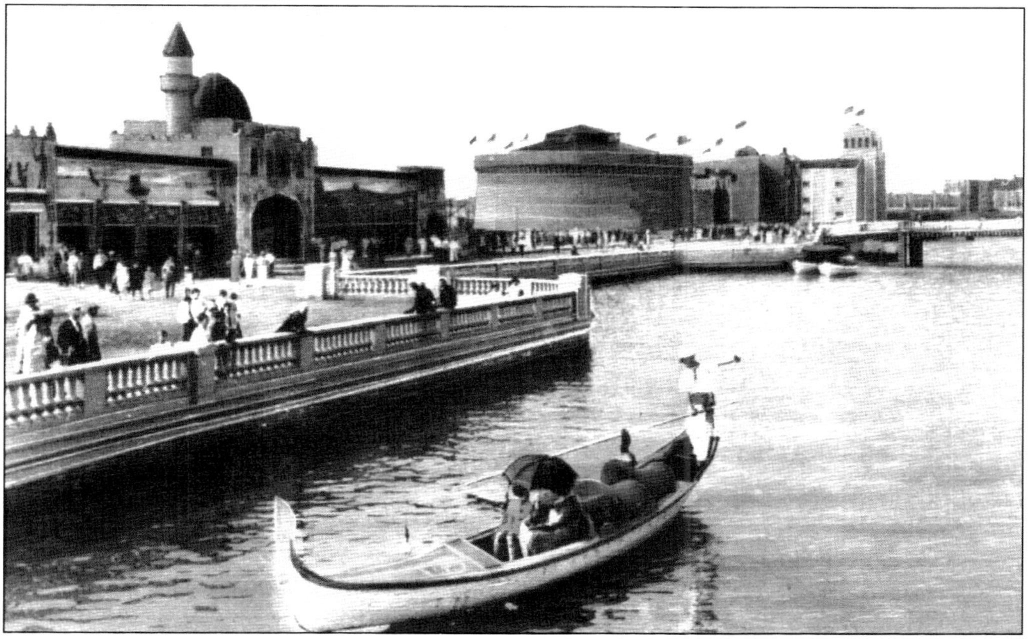

The Gladway. Just west of Broad Street and between Packer and Pattison Avenues was a large section of the exposition grounds known as the Gladway. Consisting of approximately 80 acres, this area was set aside for general amusement and entertainment venues. Found here were man-made lagoons, small lakes, various concessions, restaurants, numerous major attractions, rides, and other features designed to thrill and delight. (John D. Cardinell.)

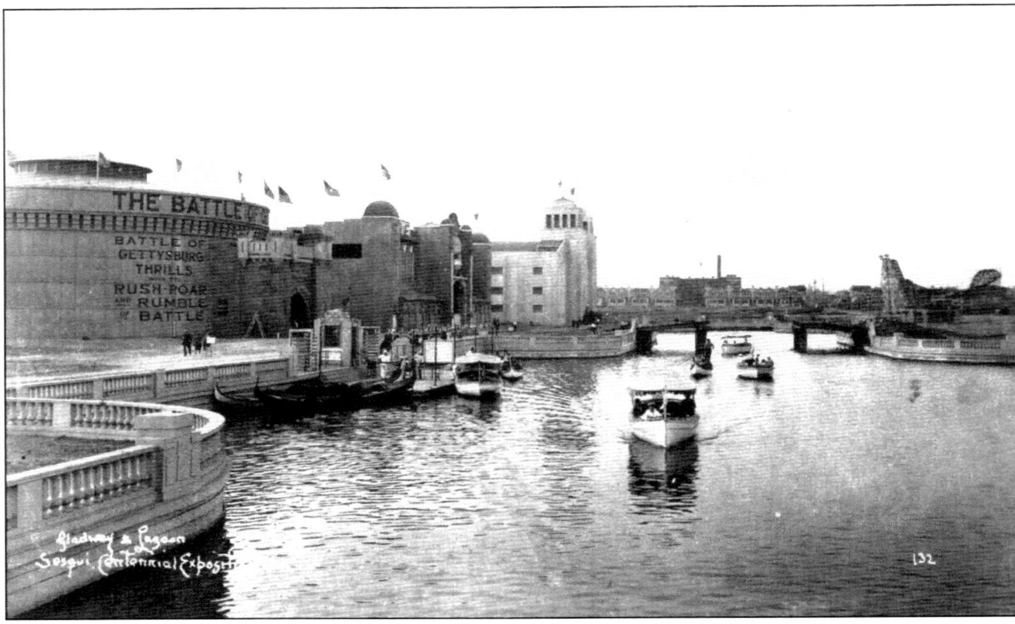

GLADWAY LAGOON. Spacious man-made lagoons in the area of the Gladway offered not only aesthetically pleasing views but also allowed exposition-goers the opportunity to enjoy boating excursions. Numerous motor launches and gondolas were among the craft that provided transport on the calm waters. (John D. Cardinell.)

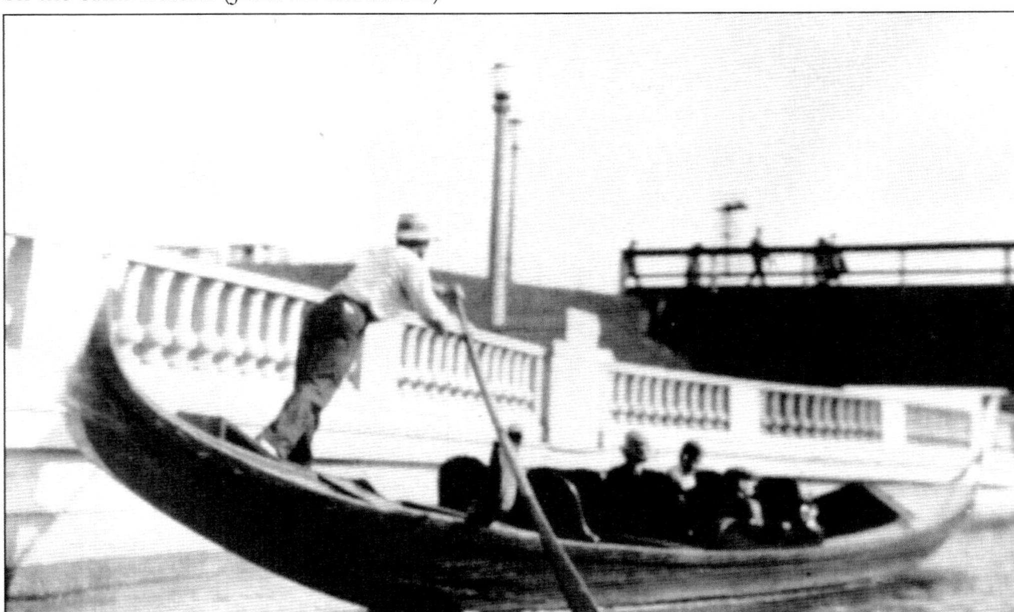

GONDOLA RIDE. Visitors could experience a comfortable boat ride as they glided along the water in an Italian gondola handled by a true Venetian gondolier. As the boat handler maneuvered his craft, he would often serenade his passengers with traditional songs. This form of transport provided passengers a unique and charming means of viewing this portion of the fairgrounds. (W. J. Gambino.)

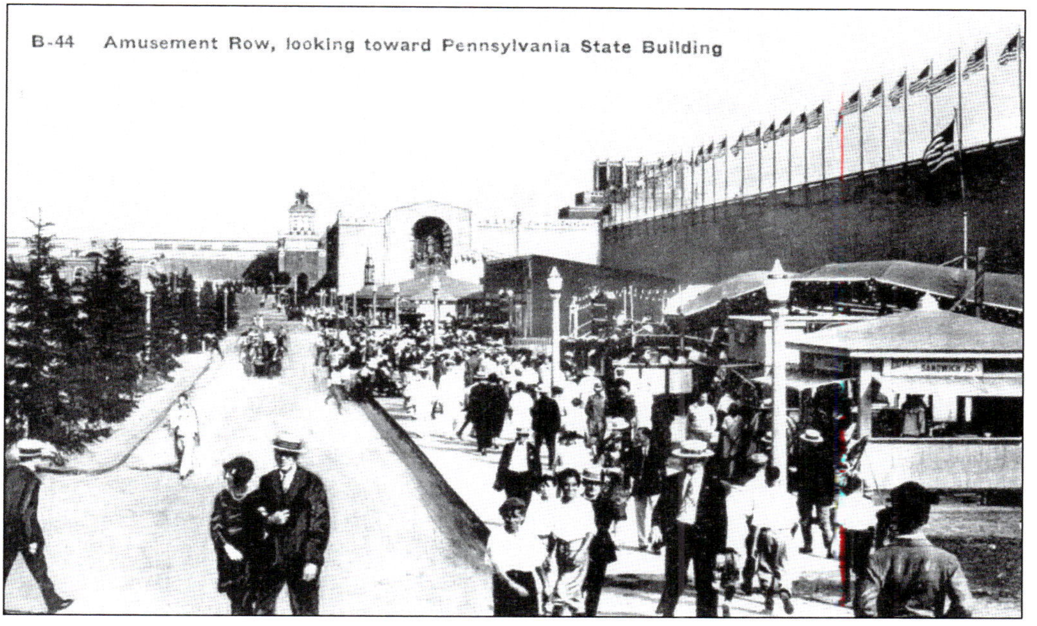

AMUSEMENT ROW. Looking toward the Pennsylvania State Building, with the Palace of Education on the right, a row of small amusement concessions can be seen lining the promenade. These varied diversions, designed not to "possibly offend the most refined tastes," attracted many to participate in the fun and games. (John D. Cardinell.)

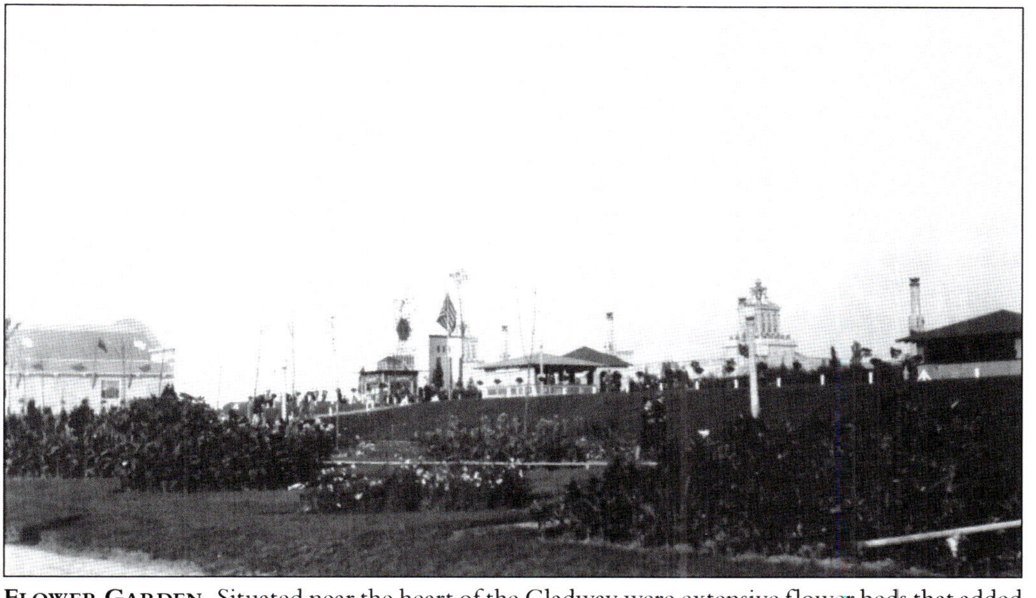

FLOWER GARDEN. Situated near the heart of the Gladway were extensive flower beds that added eye-catching color to the area. Numerous carefully cultivated plots of land were devoted to a wide assortment of flower species, some of which are seen here in bloom. Many people enjoyed strolling along the pathways to behold nature's beauty.

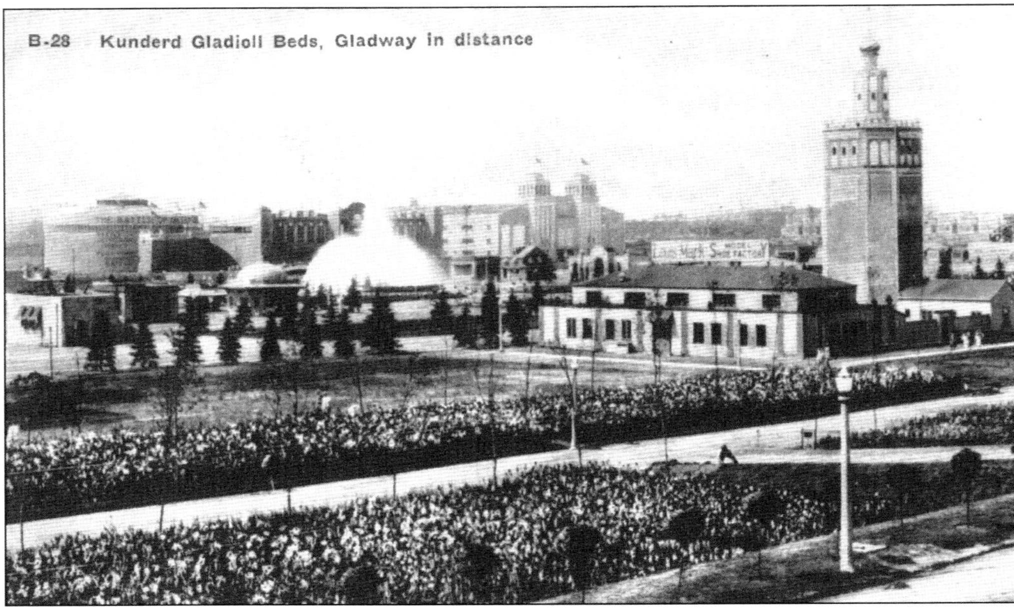

GLADIOLI BEDS. A large portion of the Gladway flower bed was especially devoted to gladioli. Here beds containing thousands of these flowers, representing many varieties, were on display. These particular flowers had been hybridized by Amos E. Kunderd (1866–1965), a nationally recognized gladiolus grower. To the right stands the Louis Mark Shoe Factory building. (John D. Cardinell.)

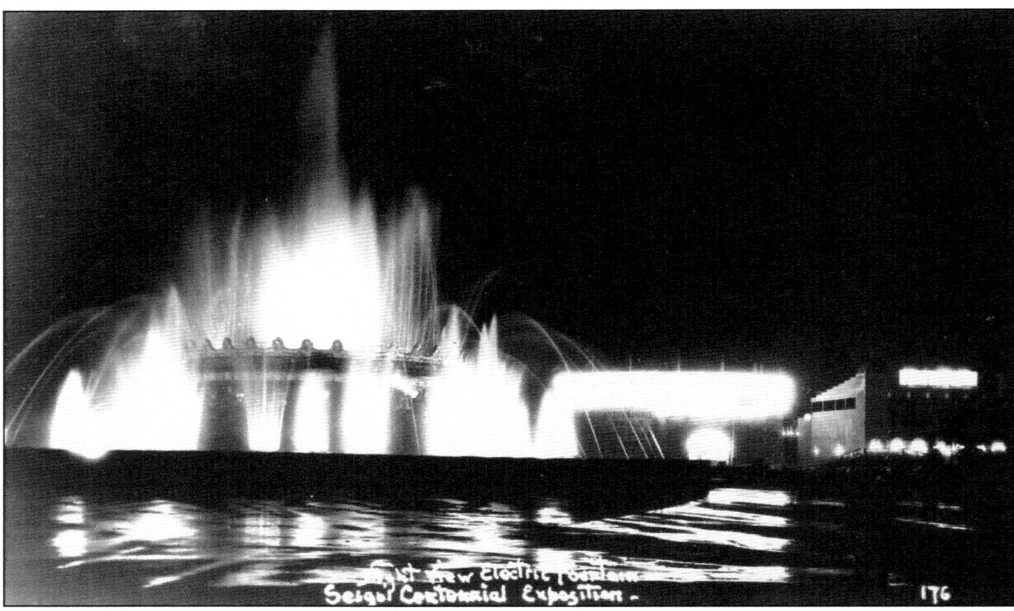

ELECTRIC FOUNTAIN. Placed at the center of the Gladway flower beds was a magnificent fountain. At night, its spraying waters were a display of dazzling colors, the result of being illuminated by a multitude of electric lamps. Known as the Electric Fountain, it was sure to capture the attention of anyone in its vicinity.

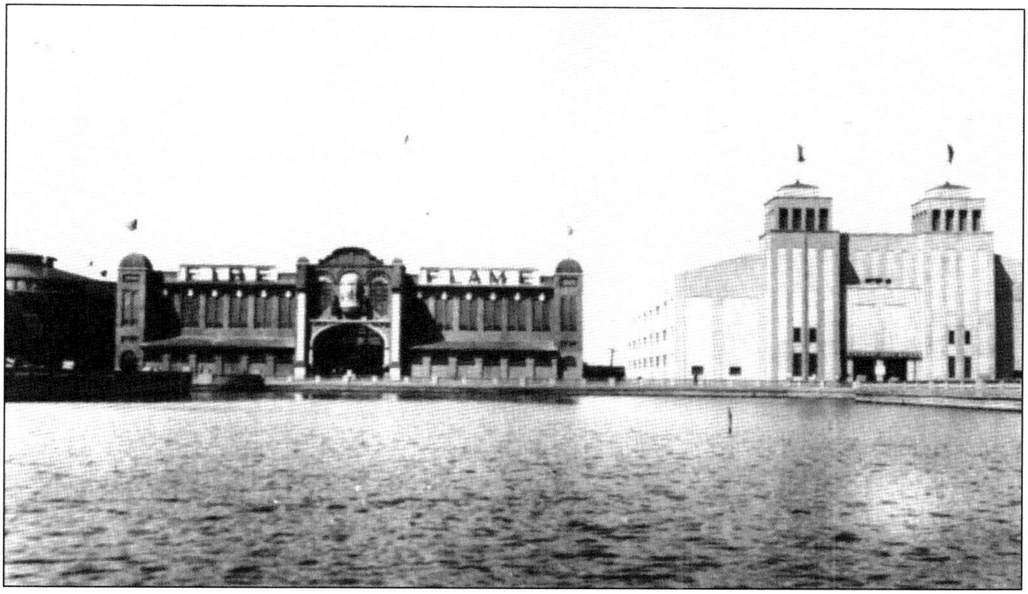

LAGOON VIEW. Viewed from across one of the lagoons are three of the larger buildings on the Gladway. In the center is the Fire and Flame building with the Battle of Gettysburg attraction to its left, while the Alpine Haus restaurant is seen on the right. The Fire and Flame attraction provided visitors a unique and thrilling experience. (W. J. Gambino.)

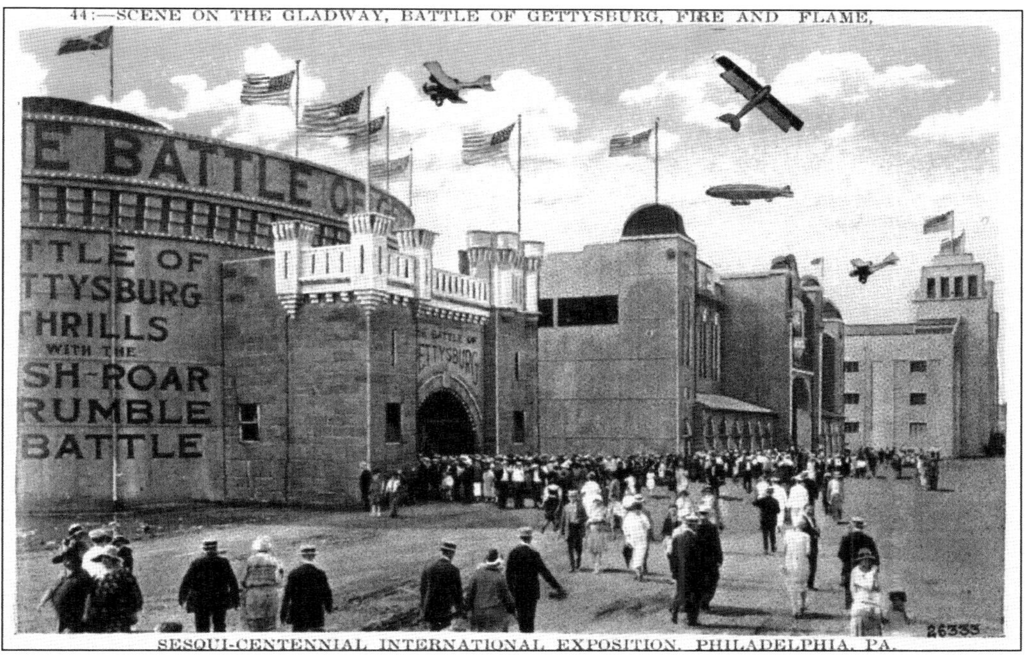

BATTLE OF GETTYSBURG. People line up to enter one of the more popular attractions on the Gladway. The Battle of Gettysburg was a large theater displaying panoramic scenes of the famous battle accompanied by sound effects. It provided both an entertaining and educational experience that was enjoyed by young and old. (John D. Cardinell.)

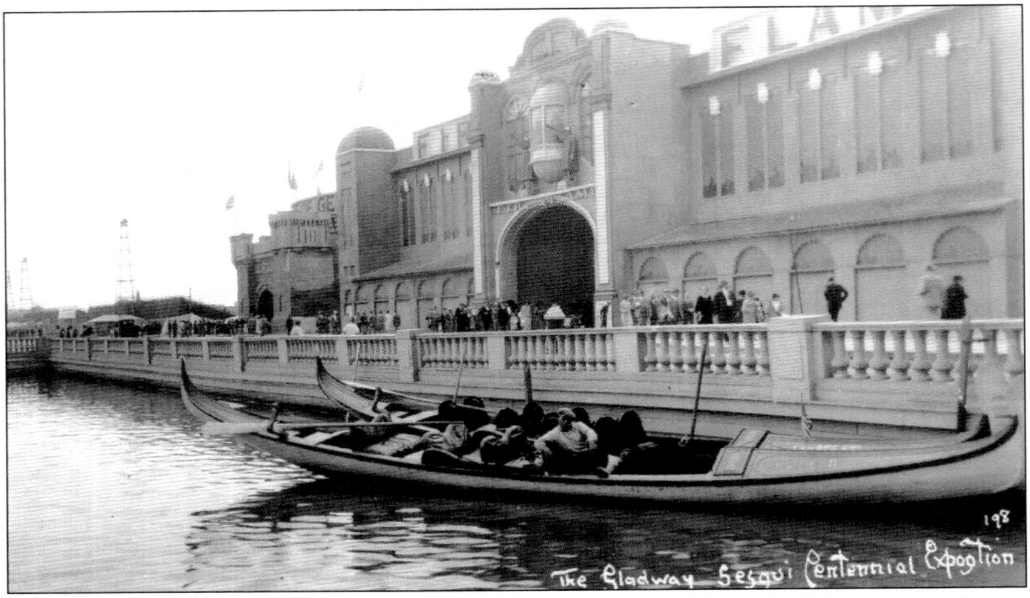

FIRE AND FLAME. The program presented in the Fire and Flame building centered on a reconstruction of a typical eastside New York City street. A peaceful city setting was broken when a raging fire and rescue was enacted. More than 150 actors, some veteran firefighters, put on a thrilling and dramatic show as galloping horses pulled fire equipment to the re-created scene where men scaled ladders and manned the hoses. (W. J. Gambino.)

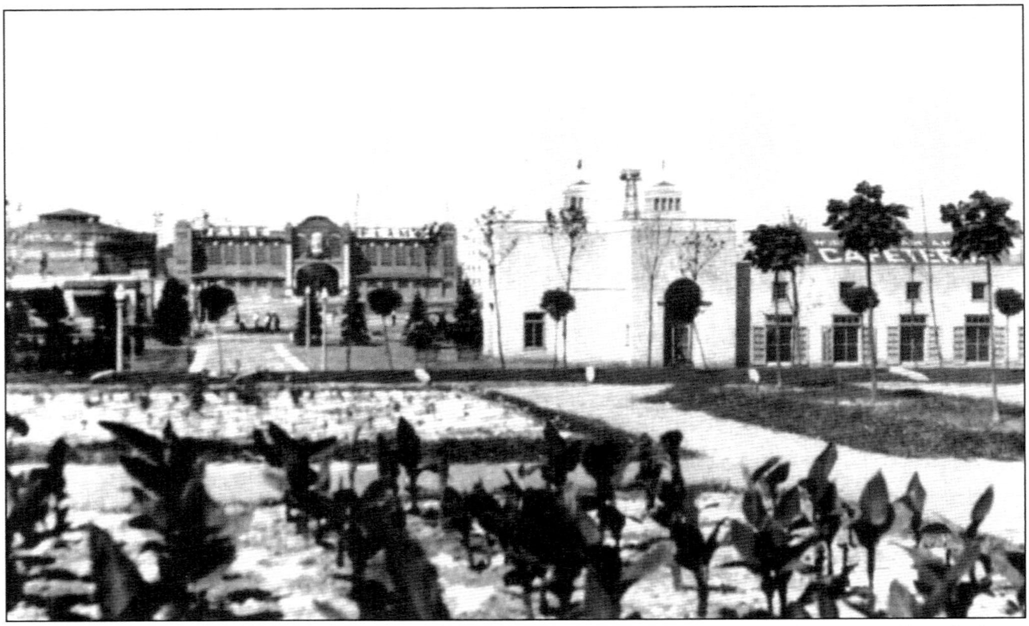

GLADWAY CAFETERIA. Standing just beyond a portion of the flower gardens was the Gladway Cafeteria. This large structure provided yet another place where visitors to the exposition could find a meal or quick refreshment. Off in the distance, the Battle of Gettysburg and Fire and Flame attractions are visible. (W. J. Gambino.)

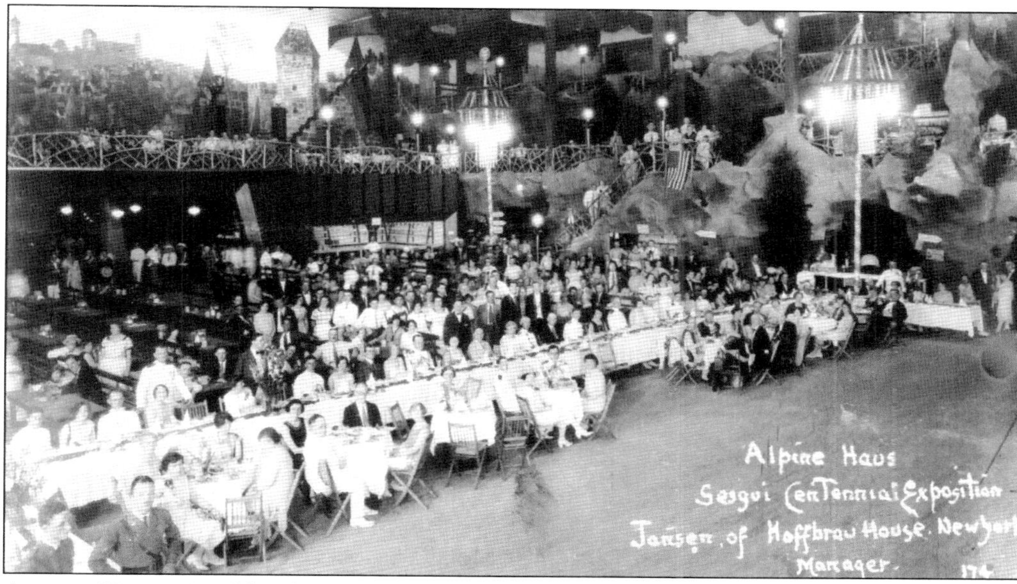

ALPINE HAUS. Capable of seating 5,000 patrons, the Alpine Haus was a replica of the famous Restaurant Oberbayern in Bavaria, Germany. Situated just next door to the Fire and Flame attraction, it was in a good location to draw in customers. Here a good-sized crowd can be seen enjoying the beer hall–style atmosphere.

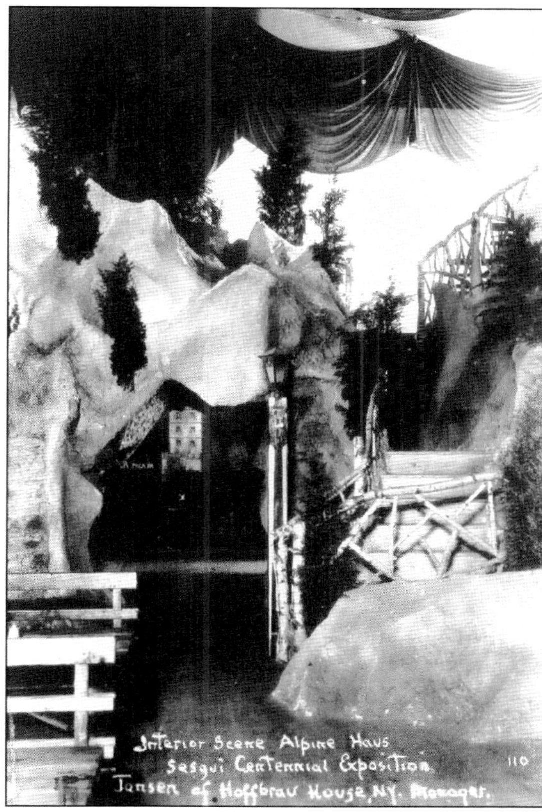

INTERIOR VIEW OF ALPINE HAUS. Decorated to give patrons the impression of being in the Alps, the Alpine Haus tried to give the illusion that it was truly located in the heart of Tyrolea. To further enhance its ambiance, the eatery was staffed with men and women brought over from Bavaria to act as servers.

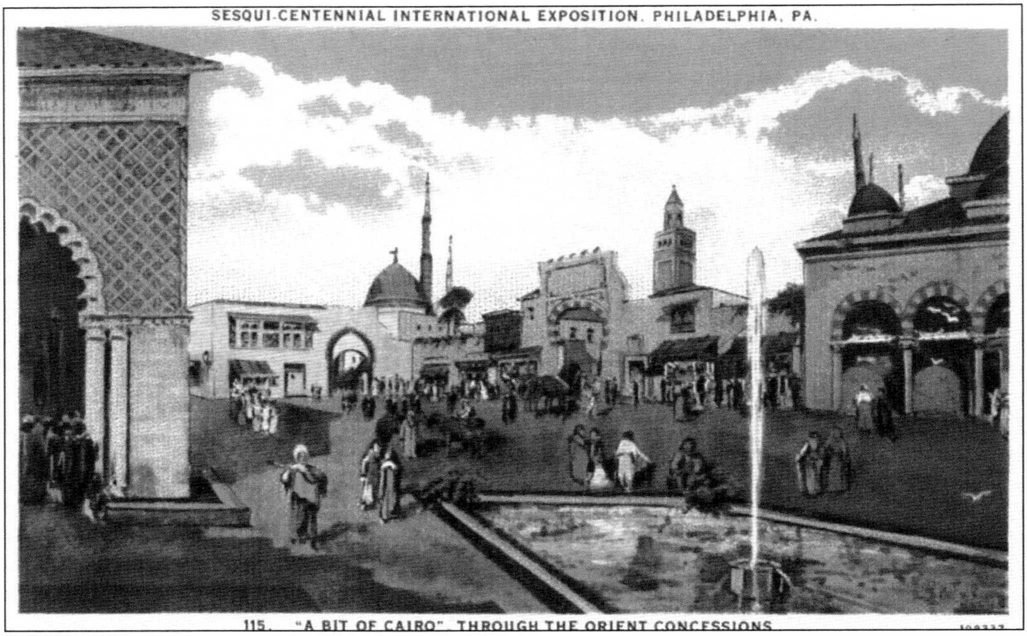

A BIT OF CAIRO. An exhibit known as the Streets of Cairo presented a chance to experience an exotic bazaar such as that found in Egypt. Besides the stalls selling merchandise, there was a theater, a Temple of Mystery, the Mosque of Omar, and even dancing girls and magicians to entertain. For those wishing to experience new culinary delights, there was even a restaurant serving native foods. (John D. Cardinell.)

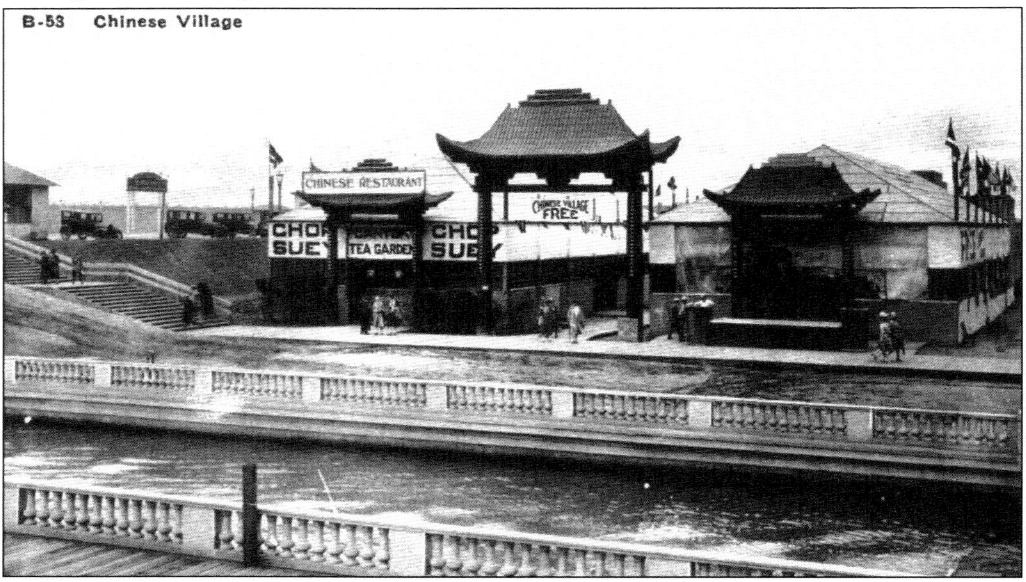

CHINESE VILLAGE. Pagodas marked the entrance to the Chinese Village, located on the southern end of the Gladway. Here a theater, operated by a Chinese theatrical group from New York City, offered entertainment while a restaurant and teahouse provided a place to dine. Those touring the area also found a number of small stores selling a wide variety of goods from the orient. (John D. Cardinell.)

TREASURE ISLAND. An artist's representation of Treasure Island shows the general layout of the attraction. This was designed as a wonderland for children of all ages. It was created in the shape of the famous storybook island and surrounded by a large lagoon. This was a larger version of a similar attraction that proved to be very successful at the British Empire Exhibition held in Wembley, England, in 1924. (Tichnor.)

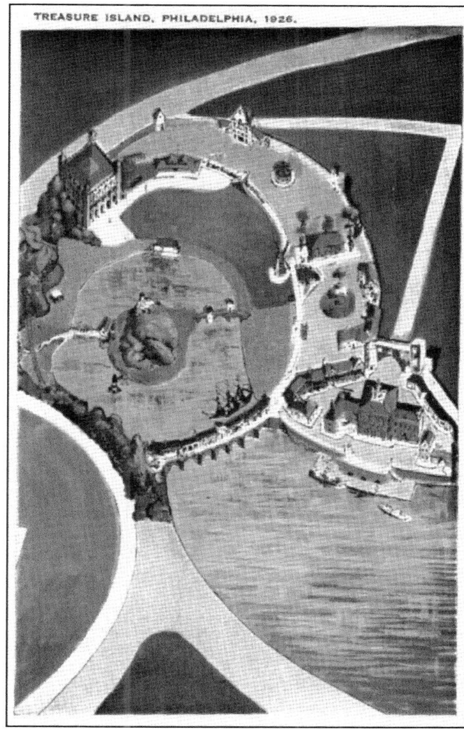

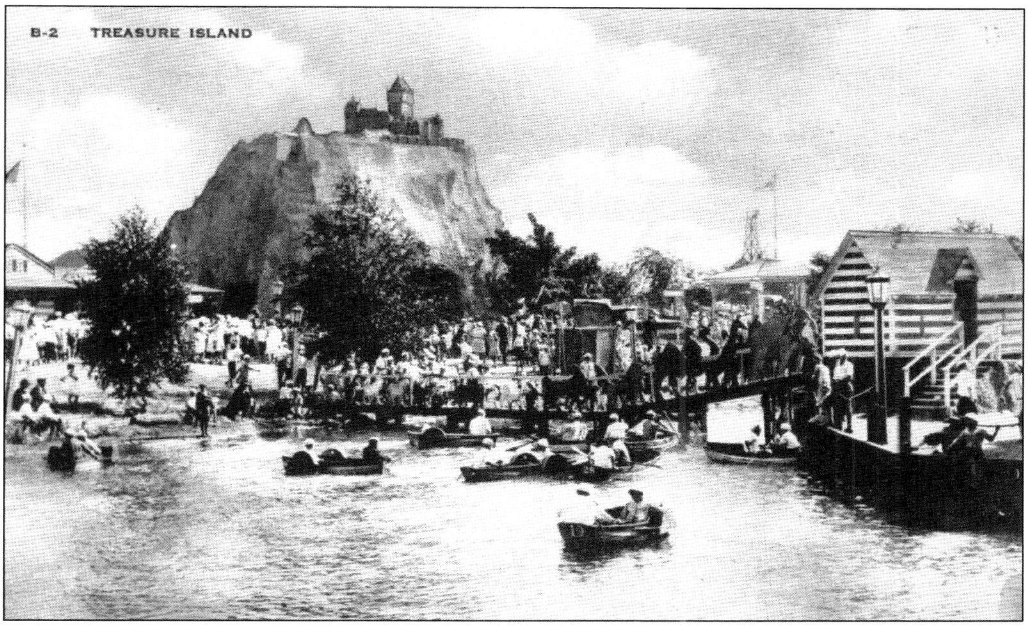

VIEW OF TREASURE ISLAND. Occupying five and a half acres, Treasure Island was referred to as a children's paradise. A variety of amusements and entertainment awaited both young and old. Included were a replica of the Canadian Rockies, a miniature railroad, mountain slide, Robinson Crusoe's beach, a pirate's lair, Noah's Ark complete with animals and boats, and other interesting diversions. (John D. Cardinell.)

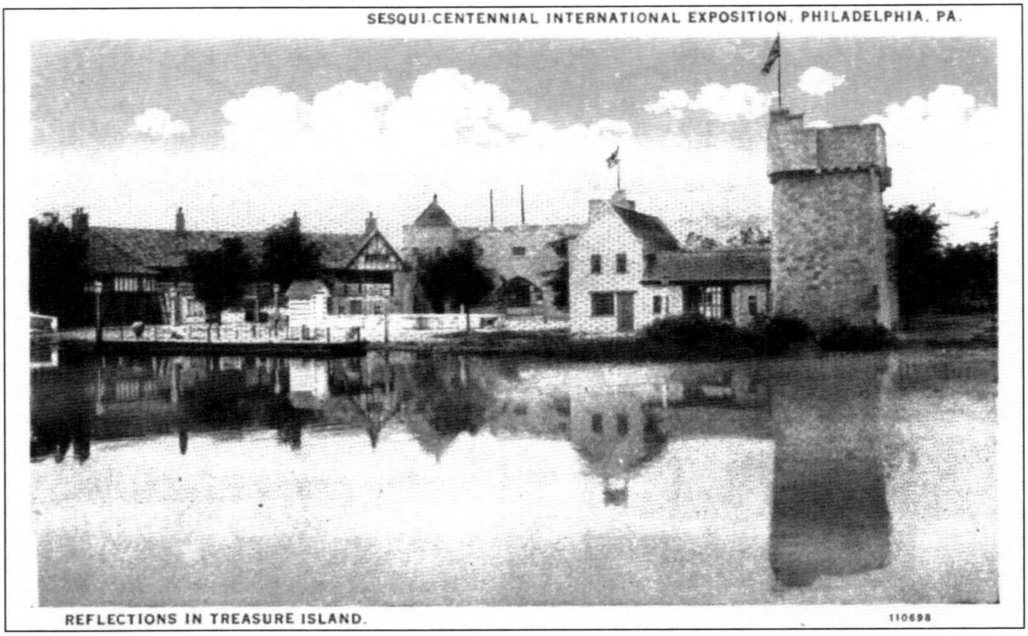

WATER VIEW. Some of the buildings that comprised Treasure Island are seen reflected in the calm of a lagoon that was created from the waters of Edgewater Lake. This fairytale-like attraction was the largest amusement concession at the exposition and was undoubtedly the most popular with children. (John D. Cardinell.)

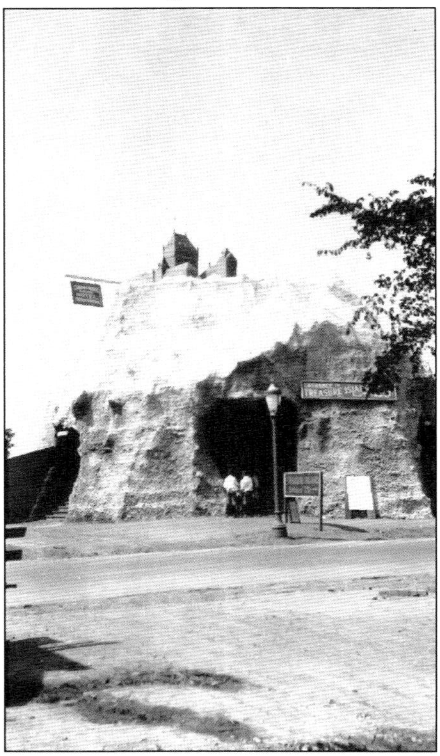

ENTRANCE TO TREASURE ISLAND. A few people stand near one of the entryways to Treasure Island. This particular access passed through a tunnel carved into a man-made mountain. A sign posted outside states that the entrance fee to this wonderland for children of all ages was 25¢.

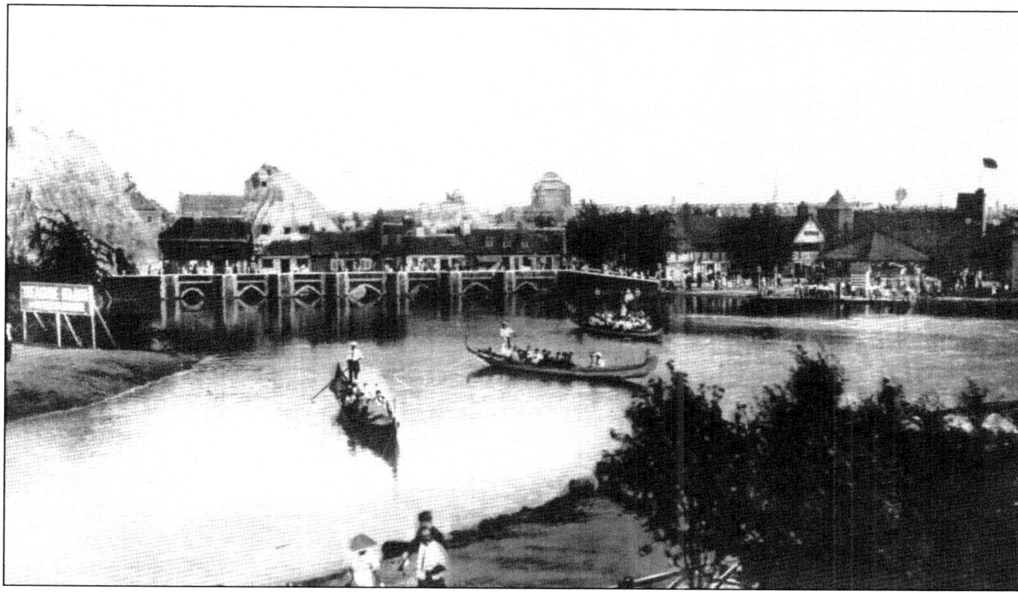

VANCOUVER ENTRANCE. Gondolas peacefully glide along the lagoon with Treasure Island in the distance. A sign on the left points the direction to the Vancouver entrance of the attraction. The island could also be reached by means of Noah's Bridge and the Bridge of Delight. By whatever means of entry, those who decided to visit were assured of a wonderful and unforgettable experience. (John D. Cardinell.)

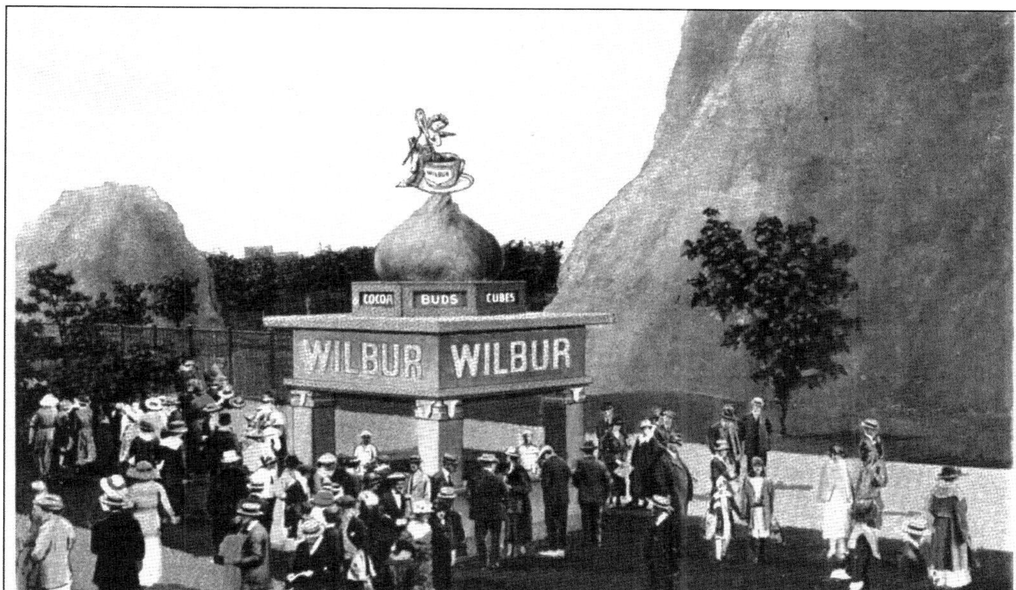

WILBUR CHOCOLATES. People surround a booth selling candy produced by the Wilbur Chocolate Company. Founded in Philadelphia in 1865 by Henry Oscar Wilbur, this company was a rival of the Hershey Chocolate Company. Atop the kiosk is a large facsimile of a Wilbur Bud, similar to the famous Hershey Kiss. This candy was introduced in 1893, 14 years before Hershey's confection. (John D. Cardinell.)

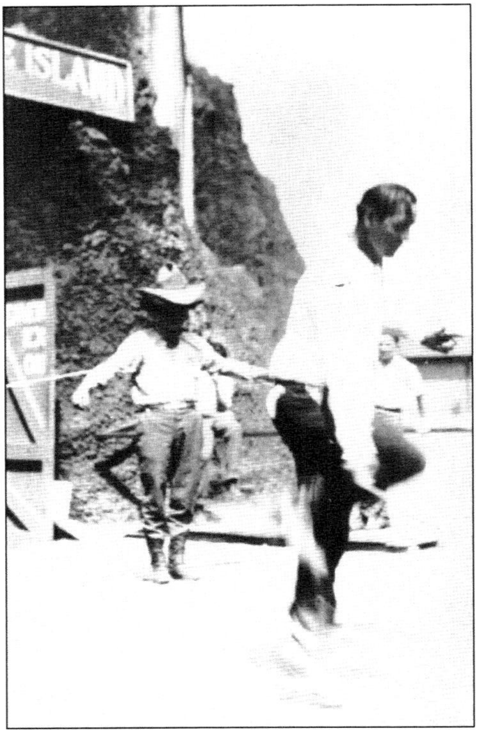

Roping Cowboy. Roaming around the grounds of Treasure Island greeting and speaking to the children were a host of people dressed in the costumes of such popular storybook characters as Long John Silver and Jim Hawkins. Here near one of the entrances a cowboy entertains visitors with some of his rope tricks. (W. J. Gambino.)

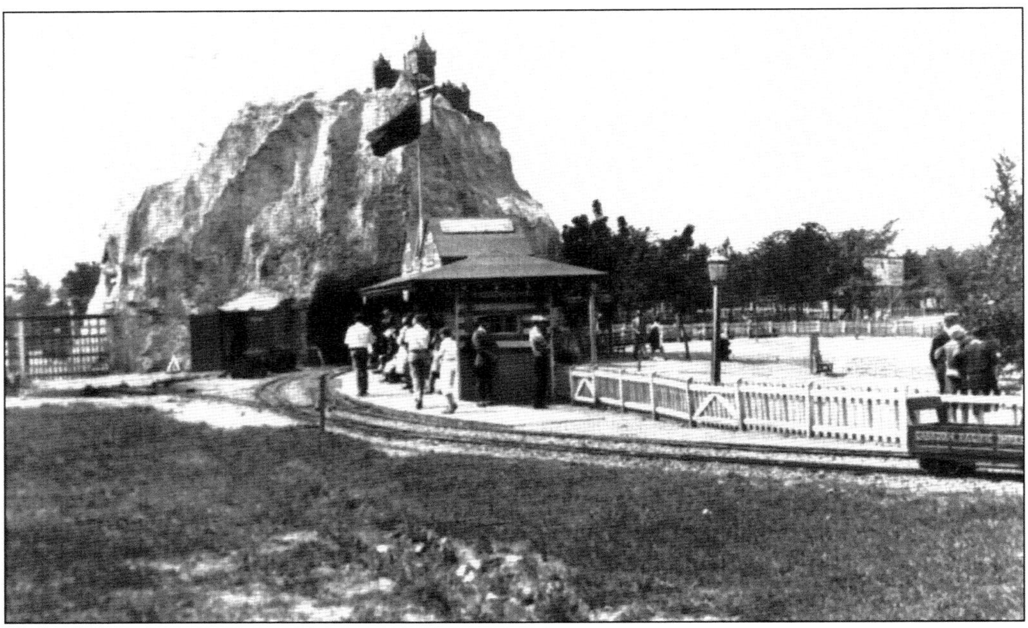

Miniature Railroad. Operating at Treasure Island was a miniature 12-inch gauge railroad that traveled through a mock-up of the Canadian Rockies. Two trains, copied from the Canadian Pacific Railway, were pulled by locomotives specially built in England. Riding in six-foot-long wooden coaches, passengers traveled at speeds up to 20 miles per hour. At the end of the exposition, the railroad equipment was auctioned off. (W. J. Gambino.)

Eight

THE LEAGUE ISLAND NAVY YARD

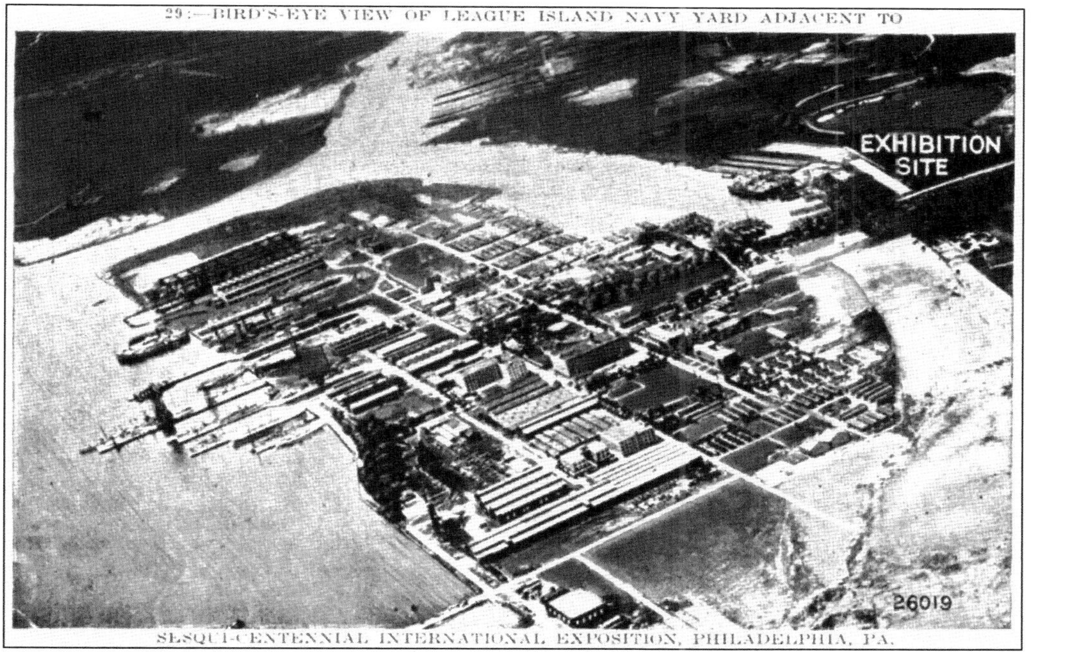

BIRD'S-EYE VIEW OF NAVY YARD. At the very southern end of Broad Street was the entrance to the League Island Navy Yard. As part of the Sesqui-Centennial International Exposition, the U.S. Navy opened its gates to visitors to freely explore the grounds and many exhibits and ships on display. This 923-acre naval facility, which opened in 1876, served the nation proudly until its ultimate closing on September 27, 1996. (John D. Cardinell.)

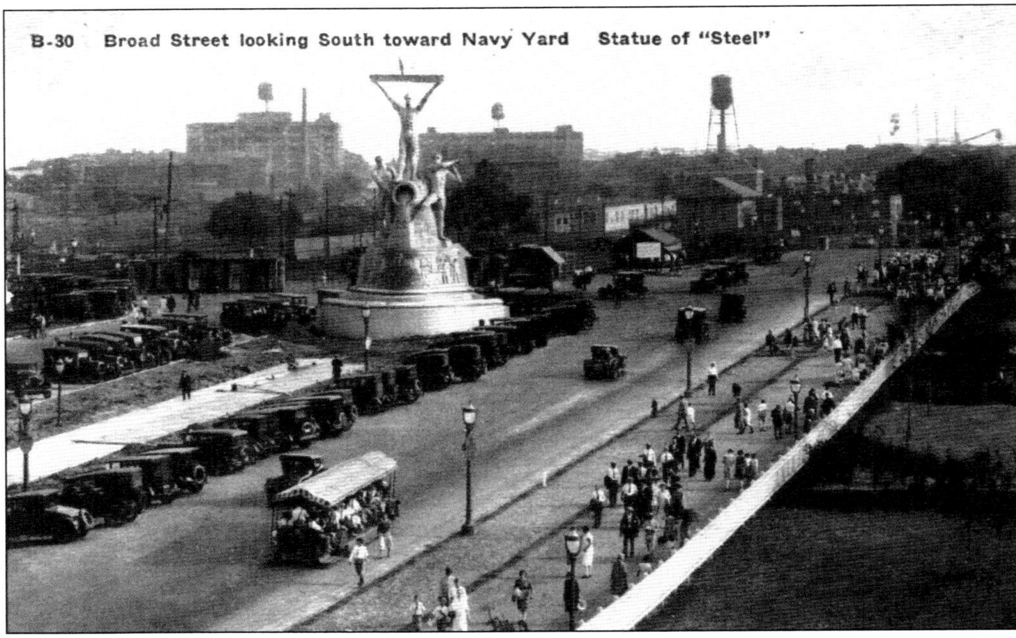

Looking Toward the Navy Yard. This is a view looking south down Broad Street toward the gates and main entrance to the navy yard. In the foreground stands the large statue titled *Steel.* The work of noted sculptor Frank Vittor (1888–1968), this impressive creation sponsored by the Jones and Laughlin Steel Corporation was dedicated on August 4, 1926. (John D. Cardinell.)

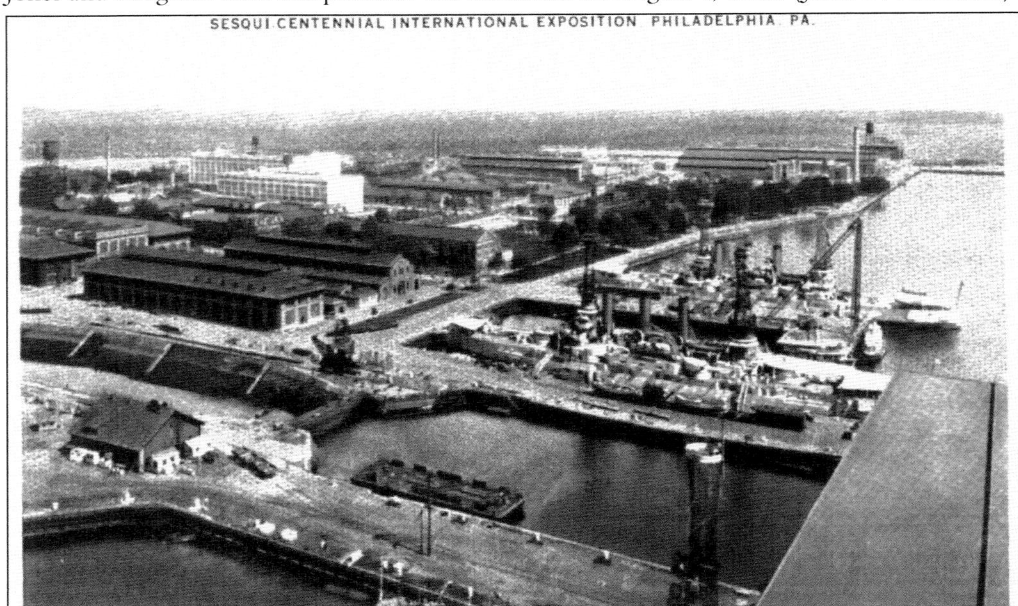

League Island Navy Yard. This view shows only a portion of the vast naval facility with its dry docks, storehouses, machine shops, barracks, and many other buildings. Opened in 1876, this shipyard played a vital role in the navy's shipbuilding and retrofitting programs for 120 years. (John D. Cardinell.)

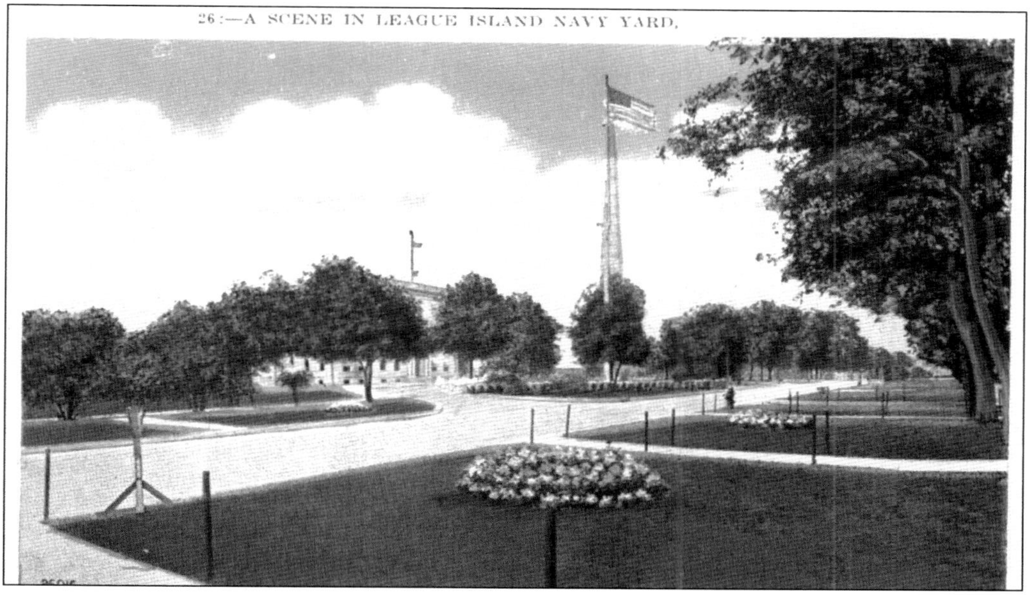

A SCENE IN THE NAVY YARD. In preparation for its participation in the exposition, the U.S. Navy spruced up its grounds and buildings and also constructed a new gatehouse and entrance. Beautifully manicured lawns and flower beds, similar those seen here, greeted visitors as they made their way to see the many exhibits and displays. Seen in the distance is the administration building. (John D. Cardinell.)

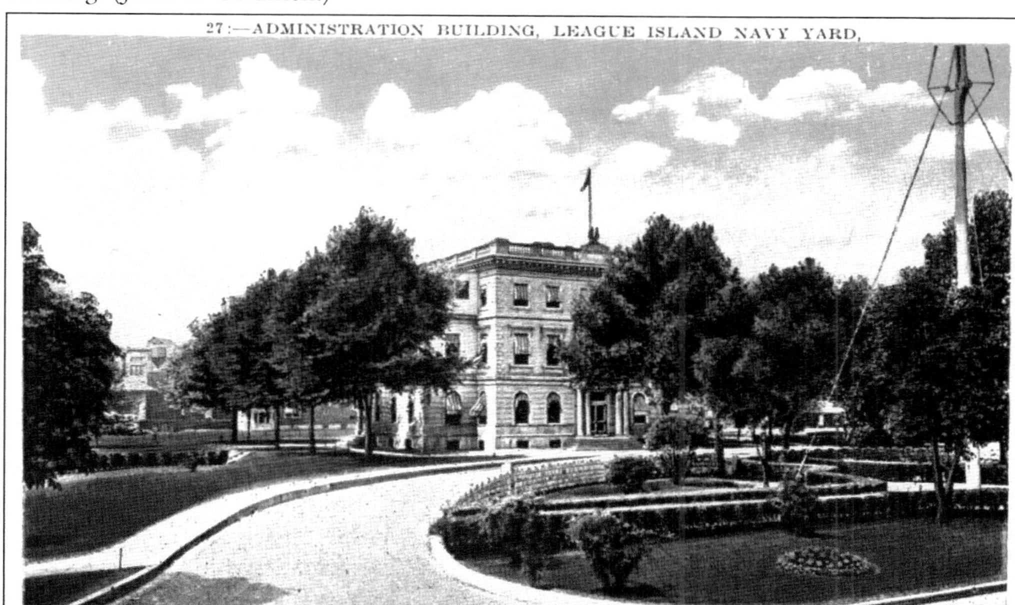

ADMINISTRATION BUILDING. A tall flagpole stood in front of the naval yard's administration building, whose driveway curved around an attractively landscaped plot of ground. This three-story building housed the offices that ran the day-to-day operations of this large shipbuilding and repair facility. (John D. Cardinell.)

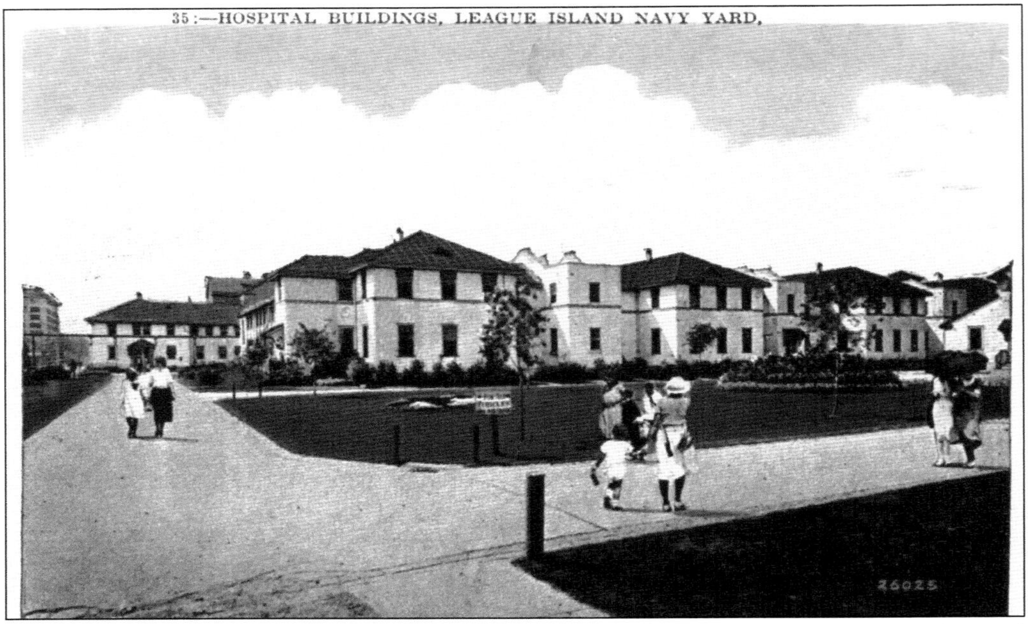

HOSPITAL BUILDINGS. Visitors stroll along the roads near a complex of two-story hospital buildings. These structures were built during World War I to accommodate the large number of wounded military personnel returning from the war zone. After the war, they provided medical care to those stationed at the navy yard and other military personnel in the area. (John D. Cardinell.)

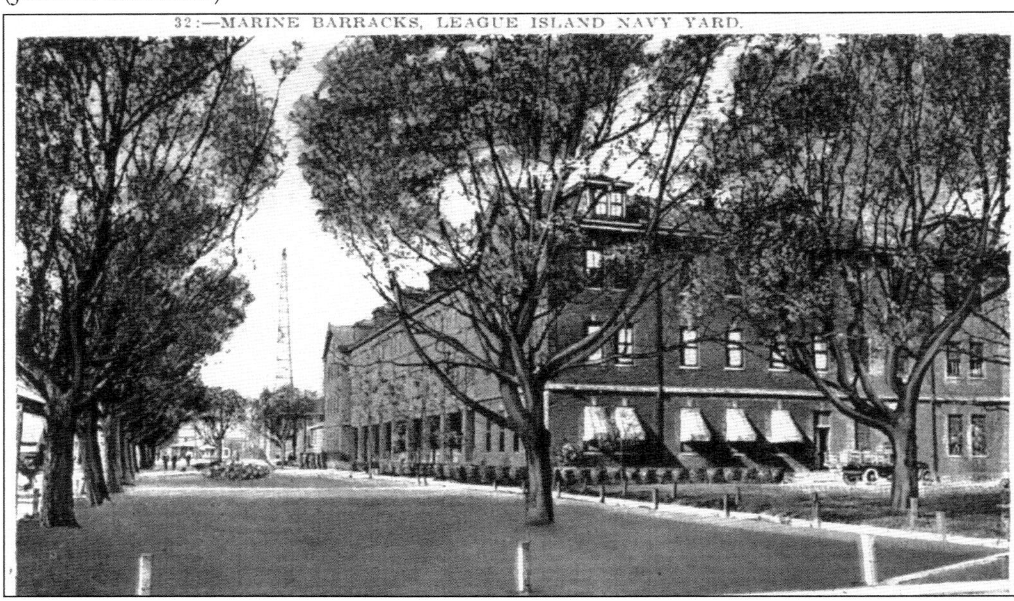

MARINE BARRACKS. Built in 1901, this barracks building, also known as Building No. 100, was used to house U.S. Marines stationed at the naval yard. Constructed of brick, it was an example of Georgian Revival design. In front of the structure was an open parade ground where the men would often be drilled. Since the closing of the navy yard, this building has been renovated and is now a technology and innovation center. (John D. Cardinell.)

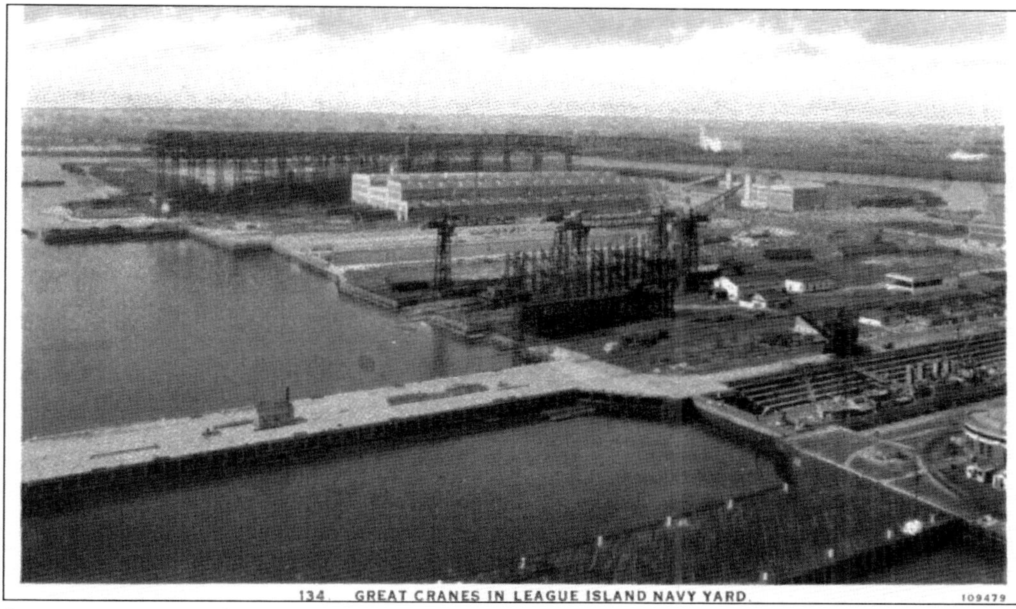

SHIP YARD. One of the roles of the naval yard over the years was to help in the production of ships for the fleet. Seen here is an aerial view of a section of the yard where ship construction took place. In the center with its large cranes is Ship Building Ways No. 1. (John D. Cardinell.)

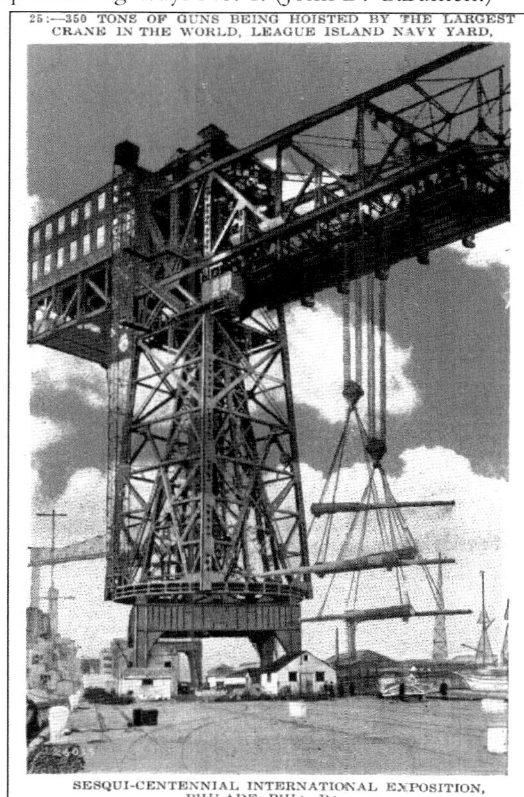

GIANT CRANE. Capable of lifting 350 tons, this immense hammerhead crane was erected in 1917 and was once considered the largest of its kind in the world. Located on pier No. 4, it was used extensively in refitting large vessels such as battleships. Last used in the late 1970s, this visible symbol of the navy yard was demolished and sold for scrap when the shipyard was closed in 1996. (John D. Cardinell.)

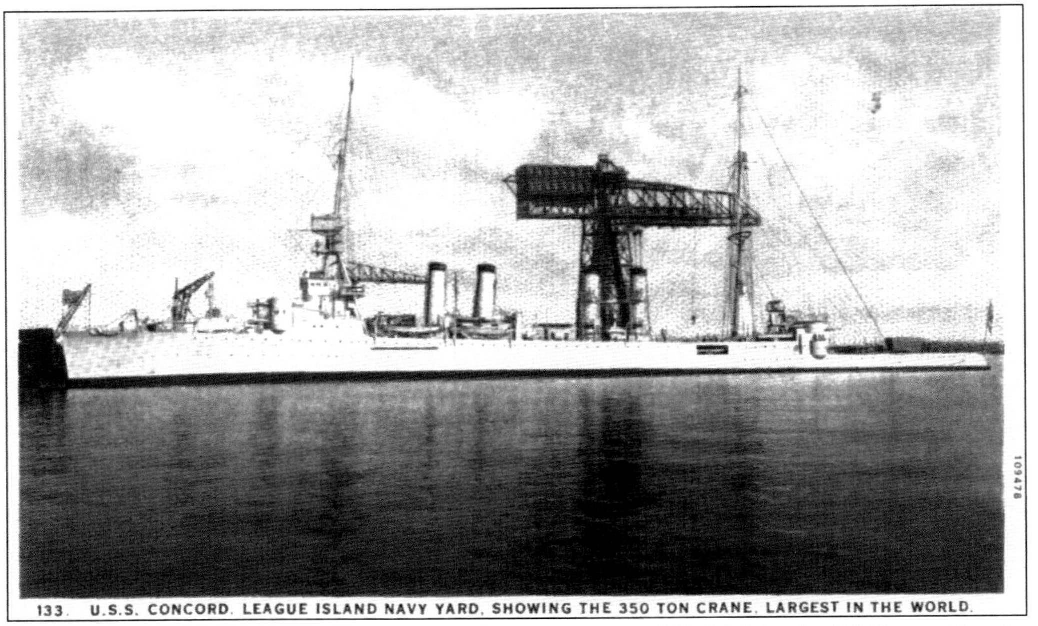

USS *Concord*. Commissioned on November 3, 1923, in Philadelphia, the 7,060-ton Omaha Class light cruiser USS *Concord* is seen berthed near the huge navy yard crane. This vessel would later serve in the Pacific Ocean during World War II and was ultimately decommissioned on December 12, 1945, and subsequently sold for scrap in 1947. (John D. Cardinell.)

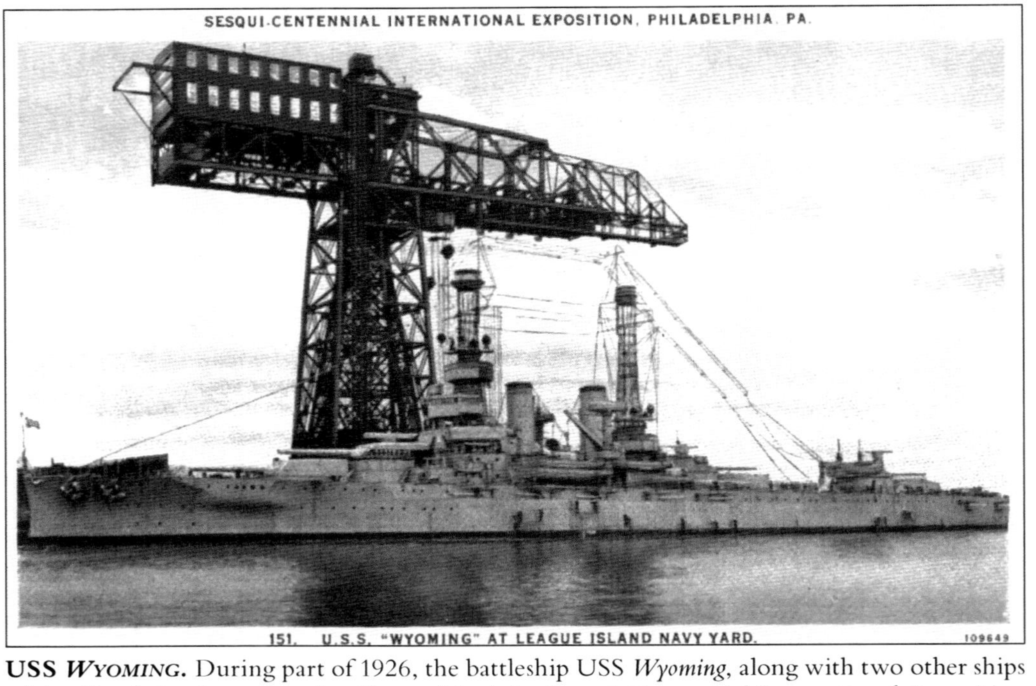

USS *Wyoming*. During part of 1926, the battleship USS *Wyoming*, along with two other ships of the Naval Academy Practice Fleet, visited the Sesqui-Centennial International Exposition for 10 days. Commissioned here at the navy yard on September 25, 1912, it continued to serve until 1947 and was then sent to the scrap yard. (John D. Cardinell.)

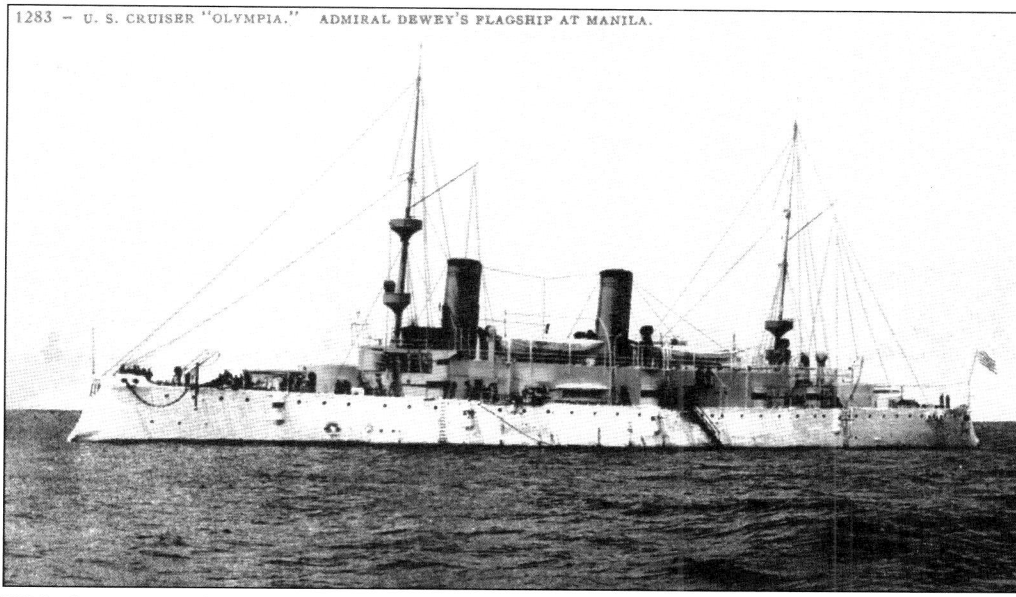

USS *Olympia*. The flagship of Adm. George Dewey at the Battle of Manila Bay during the Spanish-American War in 1898, the cruiser USS *Olympia* was placed on display at the reserve basin near the main gate entrance to the navy yard. The only remaining American naval vessel from that war, she is now on permanent exhibit at Philadelphia's Penn's Landing. This postcard view shows the ship at sea. (Edward H. Mitchell.)

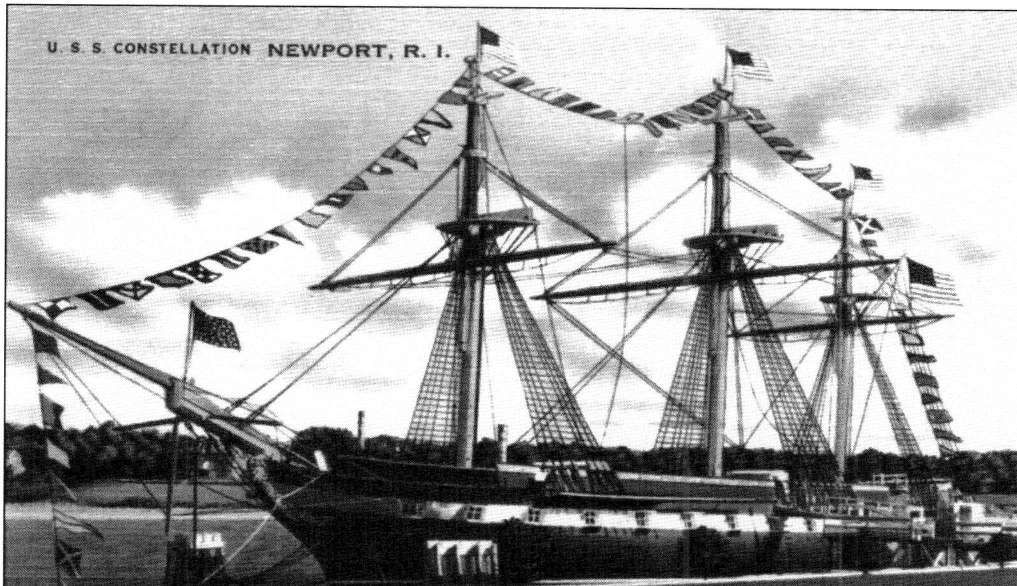

USS *Constellation*. The USS *Constellation*, seen here in Newport, Rhode Island, was one of the historic vessels placed on display at the exposition. Originally launched in 1797, it was rebuilt and relaunched in 1854. In May 1926, it was towed to Philadelphia and moored near the USS *Olympia*, where visitors had the opportunity to walk its wooden decks. Today the USS *Constellation* is berthed in Baltimore's Inner Harbor. (H. B. Settle.)

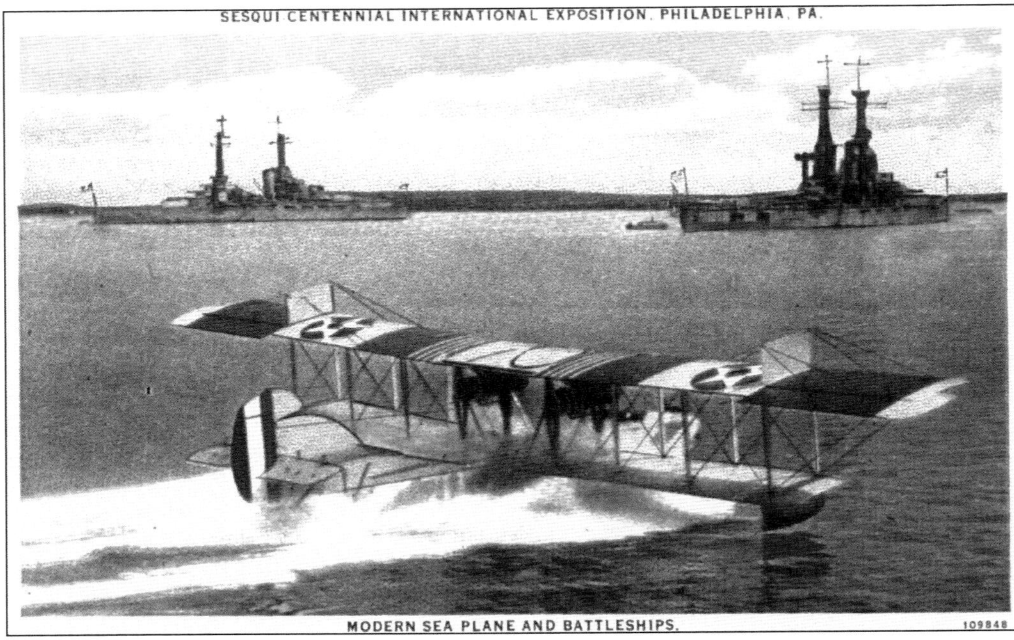

SEAPLANE AND BATTLESHIPS. In addition to naval vessels, the Philadelphia Naval Yard was also home to a seaplane factory and hangars dating back to World War I. These were located on the eastern side of the yard between Fourth and Sixth Streets. There was even a "turntable catapult" for seaplanes on pier No. 1. Here a seaplane is seen landing with two battleships in the distance. (John D. Cardinell.)

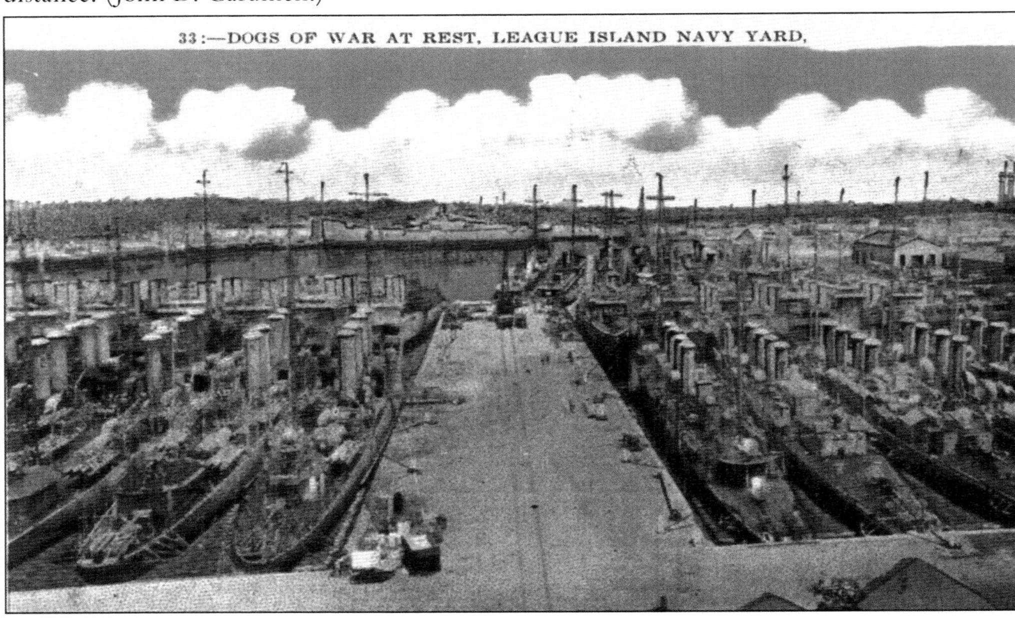

DOGS OF WAR AT REST. Another role for the navy yard was to play host to a large reserve fleet of ships. After World War I, the reserve basin on the western side of the yard was home to about 100 destroyers. Some of those mothballed vessels can be seen here tied up side by side and end to end. Here they were preserved for possible future use. (John D. Cardinell.)

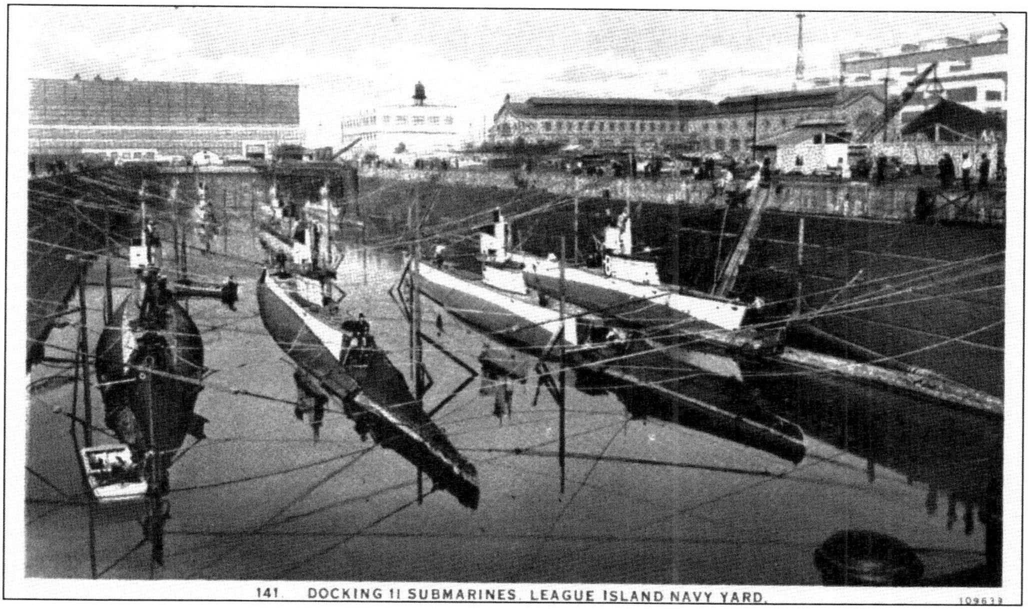

Docking Submarines. A submarine station was located between piers D and E on the south side of the reserve basin. After World War I, a fleet of 37 submarines of the K, L, N, and O classes were maintained here. In this postcard view, 11 of those vessels are pictured. (John D. Cardinell.)

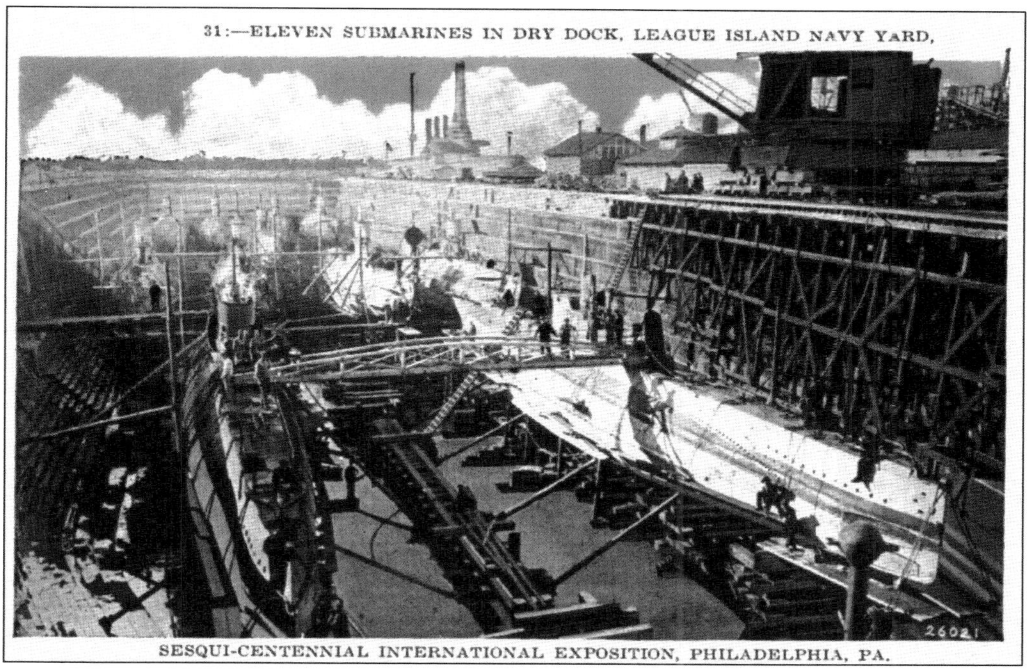

Submarines in Dry Dock. With five dry docks, the navy yard was well suited for doing repairs on all types of naval vessels. Here workers are engaged in doing repairs and modifications to a number of submarines at the same time. It was facilities such as these that enabled the yard to repair some 574 ships during World War II. (John D. Cardinell.)

ACROSS AMERICA, PEOPLE ARE DISCOVERING SOMETHING WONDERFUL. *THEIR HERITAGE.*

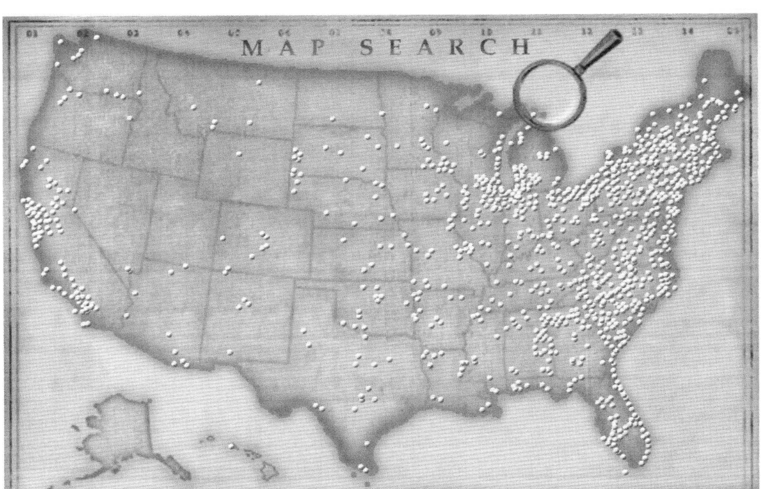